Convergences
Inventories of the Present

Edward W. Said, General Editor

The
Muslim
Jesus

. . . .

Sayings and Stories in Islamic Literature

. . . .

COLLECTED, EDITED, AND TRANSLATED BY

Tarif Khalidi

HARVARD UNIVERSITY PRESS

CAMBRIDGE, MASSACHUSETTS

LONDON, ENGLAND

First Harvard University Press paperback edition, 2003

Frontispiece: *Jesus and the Dead Dog.* One of forty-
one miniatures illustrating the book *Khamseh,* by the
Persian poet Nizami (British Library, MSAdd.6613).
Isfahan/Safavid, A.H. 1076–1077, A.D. 1665–1667.
Signed by the Turkoman artist Talib-Lala of the
Dhu'l-Kadar tribe. Jesus, riding a horse, admonishes
his disciples not to be repulsed by the stench of the
dead dog but instead to admire the whiteness of its
teeth; see Saying 127. Reproduced by permission of
the British Library.

Library of Congress Cataloging-in-Publication Data
Khalidi, Tarif, 1938–
The Muslim Jesus: sayings and stories in
Islamic literature / Tarif Khalidi.
p. cm.—(Convergences: inventories of the present)
Includes bibliographical references and index
ISBN 0-674-00477-9 (cloth)
ISBN 0-674-01115-5 (paper)
1. Jesus Christ—Islamic interpretations.
2. Jesus Christ in the Koran.   3. Islam—Relations—Christianity.
4. Christianity and other religions—Islam.
5. Islamic stories.   I. Title.   II. Convergences (Cambridge, Mass.)
BP172 .K495 2001
297.2'465—dc21   00-054155

For Hasib

Acknowledgments

. . . .

I have been very fortunate indeed in receiving the advice and help of many people in the somewhat lengthy career of this work. The idea for this book first occurred to me during a conversation in Beirut with my friend Samir Sayigh, an art critic and calligrapher. It was he who helped me to formulate the project of collecting and translating the sayings and stories of Jesus in Arabic Islamic literature. Years went by during which I did little more than keep half an eye open for any sayings by Jesus encountered in my readings in Arabic literature. These sayings were written down on scraps of paper and kept in a folder that gradually yellowed with age. To help focus my analysis, I gave several lectures on the subject in Beirut and elsewhere, and I am very grateful for the interest and acumen of many who heard me on the topic. But little progress was made. Another book intervened, and when that was finally dispatched the Jesus book again demanded attention.

My son Muhammad ʿAli, in a reversal of the familial norm, set about advancing the career of his father by volunteering many long hours to help me with the translation. Let me say at once that if these translations possess any grace at all, it is entirely the product of his elegant and precise English, to say nothing of his constant prodding to finish the work. A former student of mine at the American University of Beirut, Sulayman Murad, now embarked on his doctoral work, came to the rescue when successive versions of the sayings had become so entangled that I despaired of ever arranging them in proper order. Sulayman renumbered and reorganized the material with exemplary accuracy and in a very short time. I was delighted when he himself edited a collection of the sayings of Jesus from the great twelfth-century history of Damascus by Ibn ʿAsakir, and delighted also that this appeared in time for me to use it in preparing the present work.

I redid much of the spadework for this collection in Cambridge, first in 1992–1993 and then in 1996–1998. My colleague at King's, Keith Hopkins, read an early version of the work and made numerous and very pertinent observations for improving it. Another colleague and old friend, Basim Musallam, was, as usual, unfailingly selfless in finding the time to offer comments and advice. It was Edward Said who brought about its nativity. His acceptance of it in his series "Convergences" and his continued interest in its progress are gratefully and affectionately acknowledged. My thanks also to Lindsay Waters, Maria Ascher, and Kim Steere at Harvard University Press for their counsel, patience, and superb editing. A generous grant from the Diana Tamari Sabbagh Foundation enabled me to devote a whole year to Jesus. Two people in particular took a very deep interest in this work and eventually made it possible for me to write it: Basil Aql and Hasib Sabbagh. These two Palestinian patriots and philanthropists would much rather have remained anonymous. I almost exhausted their patience as they waited for it to appear. I cannot promise that the wait has been worth it. But to them I extend my affection and gratitude.

Contents

. . . .

Introduction

. . . .

Virgin Holding the Infant Jesus. From an album of thirty-one miniatures; Mughal, seventeenth century, with eighteenth-century additions (British Museum MS.Add.22470). According to Islamic lore, Jesus was born in the wilderness and beneath a palm tree, whose branches bent down so that the Virgin could pluck the fruit. The setting and the tree in this illustration may allude to that story. Copyright © The British Museum; reproduced by permission.

The Muslim Gospel

. . . .

The Arabic Islamic literary tradition of the premodern period contains several hundred sayings and stories ascribed to Jesus. What I have entitled The Muslim Jesus is a collection of these sayings and stories. As a whole, they form the largest body of texts relating to Jesus in any non-Christian literature. In referring to this body of literature, I shall henceforth use the phrase "Muslim gospel."

In bringing this collection together and presenting it to Western readers, my aim is primarily to introduce an image of Jesus little known outside Arabic Islamic culture. It is an image that might be of interest to those who wish to understand how Jesus was perceived by a religious tradition which greatly revered him but rejected his divinity. Hence, the Jesus presented here will in some ways be similar to the Jesus of the Christian Gospels, in others not. How and why this Muslim gospel arose is the subject of this Introduction.

The Muslim gospel is not found as a complete corpus in any one Arabic Islamic source. Rather, it is scattered in works of ethics and popular devotion, works of Adab (belles-lettres), works of Sufism or Muslim mysticism, anthologies of wisdom, and histories of prophets and saints. The sources range in time from the second/eighth century to the twelfth/eighteenth century.* As regards the sayings and stories, these vary in size from a single sentence to a story of several hundred words. They circulated in Arabic Islamic literature and lore all the way from Spain to China, and some of them remain familiar to educated Muslims today.[1]

* Throughout in such time expressions, the number preceding the slash indicates the Islamic date A.H., or *anno hegirae;* the one following the slash denotes the Christian date A.D., or *anno domini.*

Almost without exception, these sayings are very well crafted from the literary and linguistic points of view. Great care must doubtless have been taken by those who circulated them to fashion words and stories worthy of a figure known in the Qur'an and in the Muslim tradition as the "Spirit of God" and the "Word of God." A saying such as "Blessed is he who sees with his heart but whose heart is not in what he sees," or "Be at ease with people and ill at ease with yourself," could well have been spoken by the Jesus of the Gospels.

Where do these sayings and stories come from? The first and simple answer would be that they belong to the common age-old fund of wisdom found in the rich traditions of Near Eastern cultures. As will be shown below, and in greater detail in the commentaries, some of them are echoes of the Gospels, canonical and extracanonical, but many also seem to have their roots in what may broadly be called Hellenistic civilization. It is my intention to attempt to trace the origins of as many of them as possible. But given the diversity and richness of the materials in question, it would be a difficult task to accomplish in its totality. Other students of this gospel will no doubt be able to unearth parallels and thereby enrich our understanding of these sayings and stories.

Their exact number is unknown. Although commented upon by Western scholars since at least the eighteenth century, it was not until 1896 that the English orientalist David Margoliouth published a collection of seventy-seven of these sayings, translated mostly from one source. Twenty-three years later, in 1919, the Spanish orientalist Miguel Asin y Palacios collected and published 225 sayings, translating them into Latin and providing brief Latin commentaries. For his collection, Asin scoured fifty-six classical Arabic sources. The Asin collection has thus far remained the basic corpus of the Muslim gospel.[2]

When I began to collect these sayings some years ago, three considerations were uppermost. First, neither Margoliouth nor

Asin nor any other collector had been able to examine several sayings and stories in a number of early Islamic texts which have recently come to light. Prominent among these texts are several
works of piety, some of which date back as early as the second/
eighth century and contain the earliest sayings of the Muslim Jesus
so far known to us. This allows us to chart the origins and evolution of the Muslim gospel more thoroughly than before.[3]

Second, neither Margoliouth nor Asin nor any later scholar
has devoted much attention to the literary aspects of the Muslim
gospel, nor to its historical function and place in the evolution of
Muslim piety in general. What we have in this gospel are successive portraits of Jesus of intrinsic literary and theological interest—a Jesus resurrected in an environment where he becomes a
Muslim prophet, yet retains an identity not incongruent with what
we find in the canonical Gospels. In his new environment, Jesus
was to play a role of considerable importance in formulating or
fortifying certain Muslim definitions of piety, religious responsibility, and attitudes to government.

Third, and despite the vast modern literature on Christian-
Muslim relations and the images of Jesus in the Qur'an, the Hadith
(or Muslim "traditions"), and other religious texts of Islam, sur-
prisingly little attention has been paid to the overall impact of
these sayings and stories on Muslim perceptions of Christianity.[4]
For educated Muslims of the pre-modern period, at least, this gospel was (with the exception of the Qur'an and Hadith) where they
were most likely to encounter the figure of Jesus. Accordingly, no
account of the place which Jesus occupies in the Muslim literary
tradition as a whole can ignore the salience of the Muslim gospel.
If we ask about the significance of this gospel for the contemporary and ongoing dialogue between Christianity and Islam, we
might point to its relevance to historical and theological reconciliation and to the long-enduring search for a community of witness.
In its totality, this gospel is the story of a love affair between Islam

and Jesus and is thus a unique record of how one world religion chose to adopt the central figure of another, coming to recognize him as constitutive of its own identity.

This work is addressed to both specialist and nonspecialist readers. It is divided into two parts. The first, the Introduction, provides an overall historical and literary framework for these sayings and stories. The second consists of the gospel itself. The sayings are numbered and arranged in chronological order, and most are followed by bio-bibliographical references and commentary. Readers who are not particularly interested in the historical and theological context may wish to proceed straightway to the second part, where they can encounter the Muslim gospel directly and come to their own conclusions as to its literary or theological merits.

The Background

The Islamic image of Jesus first took shape in the Qur'an, and it is from here that the Muslim gospel emanates. Although the Jesus of the Muslim gospel takes on an identity quite different from the one found in the Qur'an, the Qur'anic Jesus remains an important basis of his later manifestations. Much has been written on Jesus as he appears in the Qur'an, and no startling originality is claimed for this section of the Introduction. However, we must anchor our subject in its own Islamic environment before we proceed to an examination of the corpus of the gospel itself.

It is now commonly recognized that Islam was born in a time and place where the figure of Jesus was widely known. From inscriptions, from Syriac, Ethiopic, and Byzantine sources, from modern analyses of pre-Islamic Arabian poetry, from newly discovered early Islamic materials, a picture is emerging of a pre-Islamic Arabia where diverse Christian communities, in Arabia itself or in its immediate vicinity, purveyed rich and diverse images of Jesus. It is well to remember that when Islam arrived on the scene of history, the Church of the Great Councils had not yet enforced its dogmas in the Near East. In other words, Islam was born amid many, often mutually hostile Christian communities and not in the bosom of a universal church.

In addition to a multifaceted Christianity, there was also an Arabian Judaic presence, of uncertain doctrinal orientation. But we should keep in mind here also that the Judaism projected in Arabia was a diffuse amalgam of scripture, lore, and myth. Arabia on the eve of Islam, a decentralized zone of the Hellenistic world, must be thought of as the home of a rich diversity of religious traditions, the Christian and the Jewish being merely the two most thoroughly examined by modern scholarship.

However, the starting point for the examination of these sayings and stories will be the Qur'an, and not pre-Islamic Arabia.[5] As a foundation text, the Qur'an inaugurated a new synthesis, a new deployment of religious language and beliefs. Where the Qur'anic Jesus is concerned, Western scholarship has generally sought to trace the filaments of influence underpinning that image. Less work has been done on the structure or formal analysis of the numerous references to Jesus in the Qur'anic text itself.

If we begin by reviewing the evolution of Western studies on the image of Jesus in the Qur'an, we note the persistence of a strand of analysis which seeks to situate the origins of that image in Christian apocryphal writings or among Christian or Jewish-Christian sects. In the early part of the twentieth century, this strand of analysis was generally embedded in polemic. Muhammad (very rarely the Qur'an) is said to have had a confused and/ or heretical notion of Christianity. The Qur'anic stories and sayings of Jesus which "he" narrated were fables and fantasies, or at best apocryphal material which, one is left to presume, circulated more easily in the marginal regions of the Byzantine world. Where these stories could not be securely traced back to an origin, they were sometimes said to be the product of a "fertile oriental imagination." Some scholars acknowledged that Jesus occupied a special place among the many prophets of the Qur'an. Others denied that Jesus was any more highlighted than, say, Abraham, Moses, Joseph, or David, who are also prominent Qur'anic prophets. On the plane of theology, some writers argue that the Christian concept of redemption is absent from the Jesus of the Qur'an and that therefore a genuine and total reconciliation between Islam and Christianity is at best problematic.[6]

Several factors, however, have acted to balance, if not entirely to change, these images and interpretations of the Qur'anic Jesus in Western scholarship. To begin with, the resurgence of scientific interest in folklore studies and a radical reassessment of the place and function of myth in systems of belief have led to a more tolerant, even sympathetic attitude to the "fables" of the Qur'an and of early Islamic literature in general. In some cases, it is recognized that such fables may in fact possess considerable importance—not so much in themselves but for their role in preserving Jewish or Christian materials that might otherwise have been lost.

Second, the discovery and subsequent publication of the Nag Hammadi "library," a collection of Gnostic and other early scriptures found in Egypt in 1945, has radically altered our understanding of the form and diffusion of early Christian texts and sectarian beliefs. In general, this means that we now know far more about Eastern Christianity, the immediate background of the Qur'anic Jesus, than was known half a century ago. A little before Nag Hammadi, the publication of religious texts of Syriac, Coptic, and Ethiopic Christianity had helped, though less dramatically than Nag Hammadi, to illumine the types of Christianity prevalent in regions in intimate contact with pre-Islamic Arabia.[7]

Third, and partly as a result of the first two factors, the New Testament Apocrypha have been assembled, translated, and analyzed with more accuracy and sympathy than ever before. Among other conclusions of this recent research is the emerging consensus that the apocryphal writings, considerable in volume, survived in active use among Eastern (and indeed Western) congregations well beyond their formal exclusion from the New Testament canon by the Church Councils of the fourth and fifth centuries.[8] For the Qur'anic images of Jesus and of the Christians, the implications are important. If these images were derived in part from the Apocrypha, the Qur'an was at least echoing a living—not an imaginary—Christianity.[9]

Last, the introduction of various tools of modern literary criticism into the analysis of the Qur'anic text has led to a shift in emphasis away from the delineation of "influence" and toward an attempt to understand the text on its own terms and territory.[10] The results of this endeavor are not uniformly convincing, but they do at least represent a new departure from the analysis of the Qur'anic images of Jesus in terms of influence or derivation, terms which are now recognized to be far more complex processes than was hitherto assumed.[11]

A Sketch of the Qur'anic Jesus

The Qur'an parades a large number of prophets in an admonitory narrative style quite unlike that of the Bible. This narrative style, in its rhythm and economy, is most often closer to poetry than it is to prose, and may well have had parallels with the oracular style of pre-Islamic diviners.[12] But the widely accepted modern view regarding the unique literary character of the Gospels seems to me to apply also to the Qur'an.[13] The Qur'an frequently proclaims its uniqueness in both content and form: there is nothing like it—its impact is that of a cataclysm.

> Were We to make this Qur'an descend upon a mountain
> You would see it utterly humbled,
> Split asunder from the awe of God. (Qur'an 59:21)

There is no essential difference in diction between the narrative and nonnarrative portions of the text. Throughout, the language is couched in a grammatical tense which might be called the eternal present. Past, present, and future are laid out in a continuum. The strictly narrative passages which concern prophets are often introduced with the phrase *wa idh* ("and when"), which carries the force of "Remember when . . ." or even "Do you not remember when . . ." One does not proceed far in Qur'anic narrative without the interjection of a phrase (or more) which asserts God's power over what is being narrated. He knew then, and He knows now, how the human story will end, since He is, as it were, the creator-narrator of history. It follows that what is being narrated is the "best" and the most "truthful" of all narratives: the final version. Where earlier religious communities had "tampered with" or otherwise distorted the revelations sent to them, the Qur'an announces its intention to set the record straight, to retell and rehabilitate all past encounters between prophets and God.

The interrelations among all the Qur'anic prophets are visible at the level of both narrative style and actual experience of prophethood. This is made more salient by the fact that the stories of various prophets are not found together but are scattered throughout the Qur'anic text. Prophetic narrative reinforces itself in a number of ways. Words spoken by a prophet or to him by God tend to find echoes, sometimes verbatim repetition, among other prophets. The same may be said for acts performed or experiences encountered. One may thus speak of a typology of Qur'anic prophets, a model of prophecy recognizable by the manner in which a particular prophet sets about his mission of warning a proud or sarcastic or ignorant community, the (often violent) rejection of his message, and ultimate vindication by God in the form of retribution. This typology is reinforced by the Qur'an itself, which proclaims that no distinction is, or should be, made among prophets and that true belief must include the belief in *all* prophets (Qur'an 4:150). It is in some such general typological framework of prophecy that the Jesus of the Qur'an should be placed, and often is not.[14]

However, granted the importance of locating Jesus in a particular prophetic milieu, the question is often posed: To what extent is Jesus singled out by the Qur'an for special esteem, and to what extent does he share in the general esteem shown to all Qur'anic prophets? In broad terms, the argument has tended to hinge largely upon the proper interpretation of two epithets applied to him in the Qur'an: he is said to be a "word" from God and a "spirit" from Him. Do these epithets denote a special place of honor on the prophetic rostrum, or are they simply rhetorical turns of phrase? And what is their origin?[15] A lengthy discussion of these questions would be irrelevant to the principal concerns of this work. But since the Qur'anic Jesus is central to all later Islamic elaborations of his image, a few words must be said regarding the issue of his singularity in the Qur'an.

In seeking an answer to this problem, some scholars have attempted to tabulate the number of references to prophets as an indicator of prominence.[16] But this method seems to me to be of limited use. It is particularly so in the case of Jesus. It may well be that prophets like Abraham, Moses, or Joseph have a presence which is quantitatively more dense. Nevertheless, such things as impact, resonance, effect, indirect allusion, and, above all, the quality and context of discourse are all matters that cannot be statistically measured. To approach this question, let us confine our attention to the prophetic figures of the Old and New Testaments. Here, one may argue that whereas, say, a devout Jew of the present day would find nothing theologically objectionable in the manner in which Moses, Joseph, and David are presented in the Qur'an, the same cannot be said for a devout Christian reading of the treatment of Jesus. Clearly, there is *something* about Jesus which makes his Qur'anic image so utterly different from the Jesus of the Gospels. The difference lies not so much in narrative tone (although here too the tone is wholly other), for the same may be said of the tone in which all stories of prophets are presented in the Qur'an. Rather, Jesus is a controversial prophet. He is the only prophet in the Qur'an who is deliberately made to distance himself from the doctrines that his community is said to hold of him. The term the Qur'an employs in this regard is "cleansing" (3:55): Jesus will be cleansed from the perverted beliefs of his followers, and furthermore he himself plays an active role in the cleansing process. In answer to God, Jesus explicitly denies any responsibility for advocating tritheism. God meanwhile denies the Crucifixion. With Jesus, as with no other prophetic figure, the problem is not only to retell his story accurately. There are major doctrinal difficulties with the Christian version of his life and teachings, to which the Qur'an repeatedly returns. In sum, the Qur'anic Jesus, unlike any other prophet, is embroiled in polemic.

There is first of all the question of his Crucifixion, which Saint Paul described as being "to the Jews an obstacle that they cannot get over, to the pagans madness" (1 Corinthians, 1:23). In denying the Crucifixion, did the Qur'an encounter the same difficulties? Did it simply adopt some Docetic form of Christianity? This would be an attractive solution, especially since Docetism (from Latin *doceo*, "to appear") is the exact equivalent of the Qur'anic *wa lakin shubbiha lahum* ("but so it was made to appear to them" [4:157]), the phrase with which the Qur'an denies the reality of the Crucifixion. Most scholars today would argue that while Docetic imagery is possible, the Jesus of the Qur'an is unlike the Docetic Jesus in all other respects: the Qur'anic Jesus is very much flesh and blood, while in Docetism he is a mere shadow.[17] In denying the Crucifixion, the Qur'an is in fact denying that the Jews killed him, and elevates him to God as part of his vindication as a prophet, thus reconciling him to the general typology of Qur'anic prophecy. It is the Ascension rather than the Crucifixion which marks the high point of his life in the Qur'an and in the Muslim tradition as a whole.

There is, secondly, the vigorous Qur'anic denunciation of the Trinity as tritheism. The most dramatic passage is cast in the form of an interrogation of Jesus by God:

> And when God said: Jesus, son of Mary,
> Did you tell mankind: Take me and my mother
> As two gods beside God?
> Jesus said: Glory be to You!
> It cannot be that I would say
> That which is not mine by right.
> Had I said it, You would have known it.
> You know what is in my soul,
> But I know not what is in Yours.
> Only You can truly know the unseen. (5:116)

This passage is merely the most confrontational. But it is no exaggeration to say that the Qur'an is obsessed with the specter of polytheism. Myriad passages, often in contexts that have nothing to do with Jesus, revert to the issue of God's having a son or consort.[18] One passage, in language of outrage, describes the reaction to such sacrilege:

> The heavens are well-nigh split asunder,
> The earth rent in chasms,
> The mountains prostrate, crushed. (19:90)

Accordingly, it may be argued that Jesus and his followers constitute one of the most theologically charged topics in the entire Qur'an.

The Qur'an does offer an explanation for this: the Christians are destined to sectarianism and mutual antagonism until the Day of Judgment (5:14). The Qur'an therefore outlines a creedal trajectory whose aim is to cut across the incessant quarrels and debates of the "People of the Book"—earlier religious communities possessing divine scriptures which they have perverted deliberately and for personal gain, or through misunderstanding, or in the pursuit of blind imitation. Thus, the stories of prophets in the Qur'an are not independent narratives but intertextual sermons of moral conduct which contrasts glaringly with the conduct and beliefs of their followers. The *true* followers of all these prophets have always been and will always be "Muslims."

With respect to form, the references to Jesus in the Qur'an can be divided into four groups: (1) birth and infancy stories, (2) miracles, (3) conversations between Jesus and God or between Jesus and the Israelites, and (4) divine pronouncements on his humanity, servanthood, and place in the prophetic line which stipulate that "fanatical" opinions about him must be abandoned. As regards the first two groups, there is little reason to question their close affinity with certain apocryphal gospels and with Syriac, Coptic, and Ethiopic literature.[19] His sinless birth—which in the Qur'an takes place under a palm tree—and the words he speaks as an infant in the cradle are all *ayat* ("signs"), manifestations of divine favor shown to him and his mother. His miracles are not narrated so much as listed as reminders of the power granted to him by God to cure the sick and raise the dead. Unlike the canonical Gospels, the Qur'an tilts backward to his miraculous birth rather than forward to his Passion. This is why he is often referred to as "the son of Mary" and why he and his mother frequently appear together. At his side, she confirms his miraculous pure birth. But his "death" is equally miraculous: he is lifted up to God, where according to later Islamic tradition he remained alive and waiting to fulfill his appointed role at the end of time, a role merely hinted at in the Qur'an (43:61).[20] He himself is described as an *aya*, a sign or miraculous proof of God's omnipotence; and although other prophets share this attribute—and share also, of course, the ability to effect miracles—Jesus is unique in his ability to inspire so much Qur'anic tension, the aim being to establish the ultimate truth about him.

His speech and the divine pronouncements concerning him seem to echo the prophetic career of Muhammad himself, or else seem designed to show that he is "merely" a servant of God—that is, a human being—who does not disdain that status. There is no Sermon on the Mount, no parables, no teachings on the law and the spirit, and of course no Passion. Instead, he has his faithful disciples who believe in him, he is humble and pious toward his mother, and he bears a message of God's unity which confirms earlier prophetic messages. But the clear bulk of references to Jesus come in the form of divine pronouncements which speak about him or on his behalf, passages that remind Jesus himself or mankind in general that God is the ultimate creator and master of the life and destiny of Jesus, as of all Creation. Here, then, is the true Jesus, "cleansed" of the "perversions" of his followers, a prophet totally obedient to his Maker and offered up as the true alternative to the Jesus of the Incarnation, Crucifixion, and Redemption.

But the Qur'anic tone is not by any means uniformly fierce. In point of fact, Jesus and the Christian communities are approached in a variety of moods: conciliatory, reassuring, and diplomatic, as well as menacing. The gates of God's mercy are left perpetually ajar. With every denunciation of Christians' unbelief, an exception is made for "the few" true believers, those being the wisest and most learned Christians (4:162). The legacy of Jesus is gentleness, compassion, and humility. The "peace" of Jesus is put in his own mouth as follows:

Peace be upon me the day of my birth,
The day of my death,
And the day I shall be raised up, alive. (19:33)

Christians are repeatedly invited to examine their scriptures for evidence of the coming of Muhammad, and Jesus is then given the distinction of explicitly announcing this coming, establishing a special affinity between the two prophets (61:6). The Qur'an pronounces Christians the closest of all religious communities to the Muslims, for among them are found priests and monks humbly devoting themselves to God, their eyes overflowing with tears as they listen to the Qur'an and come, presumably, to recognize its truth (5:82–85).[21]

In sum, it is difficult to arrive, from all these contrastive images, at a single vivid synthesis, a formula which captures the essence of the image of Jesus in the Qur'an. There are certain broad atmospheric continuities between the Qur'an on the one hand and certain books of the Old and New Testaments, canonical and apocryphal, on the other. A close reading of the Qur'an which paid special attention to its structure and diction would, I think, convey the impression of a text revealed in an environment of argument and counter-argument, of a text struggling to establish its authority amid the sneers and sarcasm of unbelievers or the babble of quarrelsome religious communities. The divine is ever-merciful, says the Qur'an, but much damage has also been done by religious ignorance and "exaggeration," and much harm by liars and hypocrites. "But most of all, man is contentious" (18:54), a verdict which the Qur'an helps to enforce by itself entering the endless human debate in order to settle certain issues, leave others to God, and teach the faithful what to say in answer to the taunts and challenges of their enemies. In the Qur'an, the followers of Jesus are an egregious example of man's tendency to distort or exaggerate the single message which God revealed to all prophets. The Qur'anic Jesus is in fact an argument addressed to his more wayward followers, intended to convince the sincere and frighten the unrepentant. As such, he has little in common with the Jesus of the Gospels, canonical or apocryphal. Rather, the Qur'anic image bears its own special and corrective message, pruning, rectifying, and rearranging an earlier revelation regarded as notorious for its divisive and contentious sects. The Qur'anic Jesus issues, no doubt, from the "orthodox" and canonical as well as the "unorthodox" and apocryphal Christian tradition. Thereafter, however, he assumes a life and function of his own, as often happens when one religious tradition emanates from another.

Writing about *The Shepherd of Hermas* and its affinities with earlier traditions, the noted biblical scholar Martin Dibelius uses words which, *mutatis mutandis*, could happily be applied to the Qur'anic Jesus and his spiritual affiliations: "There is no justification for explaining the strong connections of the book with Jewish tradition by postulating a Jewish-Christian origin for the author. Customary Semitisms based on Bible reading, Jewish cult-formulas, and Jewish paraenesis were taken over as their inheritance by second-century Christians in such measure that *we cannot interpret every trustee of the inheritance as a relative of the testator*" (emphasis added).[22] By the same token, the Jesus of the Qur'an is a trustee of an inheritance but not a relative of the testator.

Jesus in the Muslim Gospel

Early Islam—or "primitive Islam," as it is sometimes called—is currently the most controversial field in Islamic studies. The controversy centers on the traditional Islamic account of Islam's origins and of the development of its religious literature. From one side there have been attempts at form-critical analyses of the Qur'anic text, and conclusions have been arrived at which radically alter the traditional account of its composition, diffusion, and first appearance as a complete corpus. From another side, certain theories and techniques of literary criticism have been applied to the early strata of Muslim tradition and historiography, revealing the activity of later redactors who reworked and remolded the original materials, sometimes beyond recognition. Biblical form-criticism and literary critical theory have now invaded Islamic studies, but with disparate results.[23] The Jesus who emerges in the Muslim gospel appears to have originated during the first century and a half of Islamic history and thus has his roots in "primitive" Islam.

Early Islam was a porous environment. The conquests, carried out at speeds acknowledged to be dramatic by the standards of the ancient world, brought the early Muslims into contact with very diverse cultural traditions. Within two generations or so of the death of the Prophet Muhammad in 632 A.D., Muslim outposts and communities could be found all the way from Visigothic Spain to Buddhist Afghanistan, including the very diverse Christian and Jewish societies of North Africa and the Near East, to say nothing of important Samaritan, Sabian, and Zoroastrian groups in Syria, Iraq, and Iran. Did Islam spring fully developed from the womb of history, like the well-armed goddess Athena from the head of Zeus? Clearly not, even though some modern polemical Muslims write and speak as if it did—impressed, no doubt, by the epiphanic presence of the Qur'an almost *ab origine*. Yet neither the routine of government nor the body of religious law nor the elements of the cult were uniformly understood or practiced throughout this vast region of conquest.[24]

As for the Qur'an, although there is no compelling reason to deny that in Islam's first half-century it existed in a form largely similar to the text we possess today,[25] its status among believers in that early period was not necessarily comparable to what it later became. It seems at first not to have enjoyed a monopoly as a source of revelation but to have coexisted with an ever-expanding body of literature which we can loosely call Hadith, "traditions," some of which also claimed a privileged revelatory status. Thus, divine revelations to the prophets and pious figures of early Islam, moral maxims of indeterminate origin, stories of earlier prophets or saints—all these kinds of materials were highly relevant in the elaboration of Islamic piety, devotion, and social manners. Concurrently, the Muslims of this first century or so were generally quite receptive to the religious lore of Judaism, Christianity, and the other great religions of the new Muslim empire.[26] This receptivity, however, should not be thought of as a supine or unconstrained acceptance of non-Islamic cultural influence. Rather, early Islam already had in place certain basic structures of thought, certain modes of ordering and interpreting reality, which alone could make that receptivity and interaction possible.

But just as this porous Islamic environment should be kept in view, so too must we remember that Eastern Christianity of the seventh and eighth centuries A.D. was, in the phrase of one of its pioneer scholars, "literally inundated" with apocryphal works of all kinds, many of which were attributed to major early figures for the sake of authority.[27] In this early period, the agenda of interaction between Islam and Christianity was not set solely by the Qur'an but was also decided by the historical circumstances of social, spiritual, and indeed military encounter. What percolated from one community to the other was determined by what each saw as true or complementary or edifying in the traditions of the other, given the intimate spiritual affinities between them. For early Muslims, there was no prima facie reason not to accept a Christian story, tradition, maxim, or homily, provided it lay within the conceptual framework that Islam had already laid out for itself.

The Qur'an refers repeatedly to the "Torah," the "Evangel," and the "Psalms," and asks Jews and Christians to abide by what they find in them. How much of the Bible was accurately known to early Islam? And in what form? If one begins with the Qur'an, one finds that apart from its general conceptual and revelatory affinities with Jewish and Christian scriptures, traditions, and lore, verbatim quotations from the Old and New Testaments are very infrequent. Two passages stand out: the commandment stipulating an eye for an eye, and the Jesus saying in which a rich man entering paradise is likened to a camel passing through the eye of a needle. This suggests that the biblical materials from which the Qur'an reworked its own synthesis were diverse, and that while the Qur'an recognized the canonicity of the Torah and the Evangel, as evidenced by the admonition to Jews and Christians to turn to them for confirmation of the truth of Muhammadan prophecy, what exactly the Qur'an meant by these two scriptures remains uncertain. Concurrently, the Qur'an argues that these scriptures have been tampered with, and gives one example of such tampering (4:46), while condemning people who actually forge divine scriptures (2:79).[28] It is probable that the overall thrust of the Qur'anic teaching on revelation—that is to say, the invitation to the "People of the Book" to recognize and accept the finality of the Qur'an—overshadowed all other considerations. In other words, the Qur'an is the final criterion by which all earlier revelations are to be judged. In their pristine form, these earlier revelations must of necessity bear witness to the Qur'anic revelation. Where they do not, they must be judged corrupt.

But if we set aside the broader issue regarding the self-definition of the Qur'an and its relation to earlier scriptures, is there any evidence that such scriptures were available *in Arabic* in the early Muslim milieu? The starting point here too could be the Qur'an itself. In a passage remarkable for what it reveals of a connection between Muhammad and an unnamed source (most probably a Christian or a Jew), the Qur'an rebuts the charge that Muhammad is being taught what to say:

And We know that they say:
A mere human is teaching him.
The speech of him to whom they allude is foreign,
But this is clear Arabic speech. (16:103)

At issue here is not the *existence* of a particular person but the *language* in which he may have spoken to Muhammad or to anyone else. The Islamic tradition does preserve accounts, not inherently improbable, concerning several Meccan Arabs who possessed knowledge of Jewish and Christian scriptures, and these figures are generally accepted by Muslim opinion as having had close relations with Muhammad and even affected his spiritual development. What *is* denied by Islamic tradition as a whole is that such persons had any direct role in inspiring, let alone dictating, revelation. Nor can one conclude from this Christian or Jewish Meccan scholarly presence that any part of the Bible was or was not translated into Arabic. Linguistic evidence—that is to say, Arabic terms in the Qur'an with clear biblical antecedents—are equally inconclusive as evidence for or against the existence of an Arabic Bible. It is more likely that in coopting the biblical tradition, the Qur'an adapted into its Arabic vocabulary such terms as would be familiar to its audience, rather than incorporating these terms from an already existing Arabic biblical text or fragments.

During the first two centuries of Islam, there is no evidence of any substantial change in this picture, and current research would date the appearance of the earliest Arabic lectionary or Bible to about the middle of the third/ninth century. Under what guise, then, did the Bible appear to the Muslims of the first two centuries? Research in this field is still hesitant, not least because the early Arabic Islamic tradition is one in which important early texts continue to come to light every year in great profusion, either in editions or in discoveries of manuscripts. Many Islamic texts prior to the ninth century A.D., texts of piety or asceticism in particular, refer often to the "Torah" or to "Wisdom" *(Hikmah)* in such terms as "It is said in the Torah or Hikmah" *(ja'a fi'l Tawrat; ja'a fi'l Hikmah)*, followed by a moral maxim. Early Western scholarly attempts to locate the origins of these maxims concluded that very few of them were in fact traceable to the Bible. Later scholarship was likewise hesitant, but very recent scholarship is at last beginning to suggest general sources, though the specific originals cannot always be located.[29]

This ongoing research is of direct relevance to the Muslim gospel, because these same pietistic or ascetic texts which refer vaguely to the "Torah" and "Wisdom" refer also to specific sayings by prophets, prominent among them being the corpus of sayings ascribed to Jesus. In the commentaries to each saying, I have indicated, where I was able to do so, some possible sources or parallels. But before we move to a broad examination of the gospel itself, something must be said of the context in which the Islamic Jesus makes his first appearance and of the scholars who purveyed his image.

The Early Context

As we have seen, early Islamic piety cast its net wide in order to supplement the ethical teachings of the Qur'an. There were compelling historical reasons for such openness, reasons that had to do with the course of Islamic history itself, quite apart from the spiritual continuities with Judaism and Christianity. The early Islamic empire witnessed a series of dramatically victorious conquests. But there was also a dramatic succession of very divisive civil wars, pitting Muslim against Muslim, region against region, tribe against tribe, and even, in certain urban centers, class against class. With conquests came sudden and vast wealth, on a scale hardly imaginable to the conquerors, many of whom had been raised in a frugal, often subsistence-level Arabian environment. The early patriarchal caliphate, a system of government that may have worked reasonably well at the beginning of Muslim imperial expansion, was no longer adequate to bear the economic and administrative strains of a realm which had come to rival the empires of Alexander and Rome. Profound changes began to occur. The political center of

gravity of the empire shifted from Arabia to Syria, and then gradually to Iraq and regions further east. A crisis developed over the
function and definition of government. Greater centralization and
uniformity of rule became necessary to hold the empire together.
The patriarchal caliph was gradually replaced by an autocrat,
modeled to some extent on earlier Byzantine and Persian autocra-
cies.[30] A repressive state came into being, with its regular army, tax
collection procedures, bureaucracy, and (what concerns us most
directly here) religious scholars who would act as its defenders.
Early Islamic piety was therefore faced with the spectacle of deep
and rapid political transformations, and with a wide range of
moral options by way of response.

The earliest product of Islamic scholarship took the form of
Hadith. The word itself has a fairly wide range of meanings: a report, an account, a tale, a tradition related from someone, a discourse. It could be either written or oral. It was normally transmitted as a self-contained unit, generally accompanied by a list of its
transmitters (*isnad*). Early Hadiths were generally short, perhaps
no more than two or three lines in length, rarely much longer. In
content, the corpus of early Hadiths may be compared to a ball of
many-colored threads. Some were ethical maxims, some had legal implications, some were straightforward narratives of events,
some were eschatological descriptions of paradise or hell, some
were cultic in nature, some purported to be from ancient scripture,
and so forth. In the first two Islamic centuries, we must assume an
ever-increasing body of Hadiths, growing perhaps as a result of
the law of supply and demand. The early community demanded
guidance on a wide gamut of topics of private and public concern,
and Hadith supplied this demand. As the primary building blocks
of Muslim scholarship, Hadiths are the focus of a great deal of
modern Western scholarly controversy which need not occupy us
here. It is important to remember, however, that Hadith quickly

became a storehouse of the various spiritual moods of early Islam and the medium through which legal opinions, sects, and doctrines were crystallized.

Who were the "authors" of the early Hadiths? So far as can be determined, Hadiths were first put into circulation by groups who came to be known as *'ulama'* or *fuqaha'*, religious scholars acting in their individual capacities as respected men of learning or as members of loosely linked, like-minded groups who thought of themselves as guardians of particular traditions associated with particular regions, cities, or political "parties." Who did they narrate from? Their narratives stemmed from the Prophet, from a pious Companion *(Sahabi)* of the Prophet, from some highly regarded spiritual figure of the early days of Islamic history considered to be a spiritual Successor *(Tabi'i)* of the Companions, and from ancient revealed scriptures or religious lore of the Judaic and Christian traditions.

Speaking in very broad terms of early spiritual moods, we might single out two dominant and conflicting strands. The first could be described as a mood of anxious expectation, one that was most of all impressed by the drama of events around it—the high hopes raised by victory, followed quickly by the mortification of civil strife. This was a spectacle rich in moral lessons, an invitation to examine conscience and history. Often accompanying this mood was an ascetic outlook which turned away from the luxury of the elite, blaming it for the moral degradation of the community and contrasting it with the simple and frugal life of Muhammad and his generation. The other mood was more "realist," recognizing the need for a strong authority which alone could unite the community, impose uniformity of belief and practice, and avert the turmoil of civil war. In general, the first strand was politically quietist, preferring the cultivation of inner moral life, whereas the second was largely supportive of government, in the belief that any government was better than none. The purveyors of the first mood tended to be preachers *(qussas)*, Qur'an reciters *(qurra')*, and ascetics *(zuhhad)*; the purveyors of the second were more likely to be jurists *(fuqaha')* and religious scholars *('ulama')*. But this division should not be taken too literally, since public preaching was an activity indulged in by all parties. What is particularly salient for our purposes here is a political distinction that can be drawn between progovernment scholars on the one hand and oppositional or quietist groups on the other. The kinds of Hadith that these groups circulated tended to reinforce their overall attitudes to such issues as the unity of the community, the integrity of the ruler, the freedom of the will, the eternal decree of God, the fate of the sinner, and similar politico-theological issues dominating the horizons of Islam in its first two centuries.[31]

The Hadith categories which concern us most directly here are the two categories which could be called apocalyptic and "biblical." Jesus was to emerge in both as a major figure. Where the first category is concerned, Jesus soon became a central figure in the broadly accepted Muslim "scenario" relating to the end of the world. The eschatological role of Jesus, the Second Coming, though not very detailed in the Gospels, seems to have captured the imagination of the Eastern churches, whence it may well have filtered into mainstream Muslim dogma.[32] But it must also be emphasized that the Qur'anic Jesus (as, for instance, in 43:61, referred to above) was a principal inspiration for the eschatological. In broad terms, two central actors made their appearance in Muslim eschatology: the Muslim Mahdi (or Messiah) and Jesus. Muslim tradition assigned to each a series of tasks, at the end of which the world would come to an end. When the Hadith texts came to be edited and standardized in authoritative and carefully arranged and divided collections, such as those of Bukhari and Muslim in the mid-third/ninth century, the Jesus of the eschaton survived, but not the Jesus of the "biblical" materials. (that is, the Muslim gospel). Hadith had by then become specialized and centered chiefly

on Muhammadan Hadith, to the exclusion of other materials—
which of course continued to circulate but in other forms of literature, other genres.

Here, then, we see a parting of the ways. The Jesus of the
eschaton was enshrined in authoritative Hadith collections, becoming a somewhat distant figure of no immediate or pragmatic moral
relevance to Muslim piety. But another Jesus continued to pros-
per—the Jesus encountered in works of piety and asceticism and
in a genre of religious literature called "Tales of the Prophets"
(Qisas al-Anbiya'), where he was not only a living moral force but
also a figure who played a role in intra-Muslim polemics.[33] It is this
other Jesus, the Jesus of popular piety and devotion whose sayings
and stories, called here the Muslim gospel, continued to appear in
Arabic Islamic literature throughout the premodern period—that
is, right up to the eighteenth century.

It must first be stressed that Jesus does not appear alone in
ascetic-pietistic literature. He is accompanied by other Qur'anic
prophets, to whom sayings and stories were also ascribed. Prominent among these prophets are Moses, David, Solomon, Job,
Luqman, and John the Baptist. In addition, this early type of literature included ascetic and pietistic Hadiths from Muhammad, his
Companions, and celebrated "saints" of the early Muslim community, the whole constituting a sort of anthology often divided under chapter headings, such as the merits of worship, sadness and
weeping, worldly and otherworldly knowledge, awe and fear of
God, humility, the virtues of silence and honesty, the remembrance of death, the merits of poverty, repentance, and so forth.
These and similar headings may be taken as broadly representative
of the topics with which the early ascetic tradition was concerned.

In the "Tales of Prophets" genre, each prophet was given a
separate section, and a wider group of prophets is represented.
The stories and sayings of Adam, Noah, Abraham, al-Khidr, Jonah, Isaiah, and Ezra are among the most prominent.[34] It is likely

that the ascetic-pietistic literature preceded the "Tales" genre, but as these genres developed, they frequently duplicated sayings and stories between them. There is no compelling reason not to date both types of material to the late first or early second century A.H. (late seventh or early eighth century A.D.), provided we remember that successive transmission tended to increase the literary polish and presentation of this corpus. Where Jesus and the other prophets are concerned, it can be seen that just as he had a peculiar and salient status and configuration in the Qur'an, this is likewise true regarding his sayings and stories in the Muslim gospel. To illustrate, let us briefly examine the broad literary character and evolution of the sayings ascribed to the other prophets, by way of contrast.

The first impression we obtain from the early collections of these prophetic sayings and stories is that each prophet represents a somewhat narrow moral type. David represents repentance, Job represents divine comfort after travail, Noah represents gratitude, Adam represents weeping for sin, Luqman represents ancient, perhaps Persian wisdom, and so forth.[15] These stories and sayings depend closely upon the Qur'an by way of illustration or expansion. In several instances, it is God who speaks to the prophets in warning, encouragement, or edification. The atmosphere, language, rituals, ethos, and so forth are all totally Islamic. From time to time, contemporary knowledge of geography is brought in to identify certain places in a prophetic story. Many stories are interspersed with Muslim Hadiths, either from Muhammad or from some pious figure of early Islam. Accordingly, these are not stories of prophets left alone to speak for themselves but are heavily annotated, "updated," linguistically glossed, provided with numbers, ages, and dates, fortified by constant reference to the Qur'an, and designed to look forward to the coming of Muhammad. In many cases, attempts are made to dress up these stories so that they appear to be in conformity with increasingly rigorous Hadith standards of transmission and are thus provided with respectable chains of transmission (isnad).[36]

As this tradition of prophetic tales developed, other intellectual climates—in addition to that of Hadith—came to influence it. Thus, in the well-known collection of prophetic tales by al-Kisaʾi (date unknown; perhaps tenth to eleventh centuries A.D.), the spirit of Adab, or belles-lettres, is noteworthy.[37] The sayings and stories tend to gain in literary merit and polish, and in some cases to approach wisdom literature; this is particularly evident in the case of Luqman. Certain well-established genres of Adab become visible—for example, the genre called awaʾil, or "firsts," where the "first person" to have done or said something is recorded. Of significance, too, is the introduction of verse, which is put in the mouth of prophets or their contemporaries to enhance the action. The mission of many prophets begins at age forty, a convention aimed at emphasizing Muhammad's conformity with the prophetic type. Certain features of one prophet's life are repeated in another's, the end result being the establishment of particular "signs" of prophecy which only the foolish or obdurate will fail to recognize. Satan plays the primary role of seducer, simulator, and sorcerer and dramatizes the action throughout. The principal formula of witness is "There is no god but God, and Abraham [or Salih or Hud or whoever] is the Prophet of God." This helps to entrench uniformity of confession and discourse in the tradition, and bring it into line with Qurʾanic usage and views of prophetic continuity.

The best-known collection of prophets' tales in the classical literature is the one compiled by Thaʿlabi (d. fifth/eleventh century). Adab and Sufism (Muslim mysticism) combine to render these tales refined in style, as well as reflective of a particular moral code associated with Sufism. They are structured in the form of majalis al-dhikr, or Sufi devotional sessions. The Sufi mood permeates the whole: the collection emphasizes the wretchedness of earthly life, the infinite mercy of God, the Muhammadan reason for the world's existence, the many Sufi figures who narrate these stories, the ascetic sayings characteristic of all prophets. The tales here are even more heavily annotated by venerable commentators, who are thought of as the founding fathers of the Sufi tradition. A process of redaction is visible, as is the attempt to bring the tales into line with a particular Muslim ideology. In point of fact, these tales frequently seem more like Sufi homilies than prophetic narratives. With Tha'labi, the tradition of prophets' tales reaches a particular point of development beyond which it does not advance very far in the premodern period.[38]

Emergence and Development

Amid this literature as a whole, Jesus stands out for the quantity and above all the quality of his sayings and stories. Whereas the sayings and tales of other prophets tend to conform to specific and narrowly defined moral types, the range and continuous growth of the Jesus corpus has no parallels among other prophets in the Muslim tradition. Two historical factors should be considered by way of explanation.

First, the Qur'an, as argued earlier, was primarily concerned with rectifying a certain doctrinal image of Jesus and had little to say on his ministry, teachings, and passion. The Muslim gospel probably arose from a felt need to complement and expand the Qur'anic account of his life. In this limited respect, the process of formation of the Muslim gospel can be compared to the formation of the apocryphal and other extracanonical materials in the Christian tradition, and probably for the same reasons.[39]

Second, the overall process by which the Muslim gospel came into being must be thought of not as a birth but more as an emanation, a seepage of one religious tradition into another by means textual and nontextual alike. The overwhelming Christian presence in central Islamic regions such as Syria, Iraq, and Egypt in the first three centuries of Islam meant intimate encounters with a living Christianity suffused with rich and diverse images of Jesus. Doubtless the slow but steady increase in the number of converts from Christianity played an important intermediary role, as witnessed in the *isnad* of some sayings and stories as well as in the putative Christian origin of several transmitters, which is revealed in their personal names. But the Qur'anic fascination with Jesus must also have been a powerful stimulus in the assembly and diffusion of the gospel in the Muslim environment.

The recent publication of several texts of Muslim piety and asceticism from the second and third Islamic centuries (eighth–ninth centuries A.D.) has brought us nearer than ever before to the period of origin of the Islamic Jesus. While the published collections of the sayings and stories by Western scholars like Margoliouth and Asin derive the bulk of these sayings from later Islamic authors in which *isnad* is scanty or nonexistent, the early texts now being published often preserve the original *isnad* of the Jesus corpus, enabling us to form a more accurate idea of its early Islamic habitat and diffusion. I have elsewhere attempted an analysis of the early chains of transmission related to this corpus, and readers familiar with the literature who might wish to pursue this topic can do so there.[40] Here I shall make only general observations about the earliest transmitters of the gospel and their geographic origins.

From an examination of the biographies of the transmitters of the earliest Jesus sayings, it seems that the working lives of the majority of them fell somewhere between the mid-first and the mid-second century of the Muslim era (roughly 700–800 A.D.). According to traditional generational Islamic practice, they would be classified as "Successors" *(Tabiʿun)* or "Successors of Successors" *(Tabiʿu al-Tabiʿin)*. In many cases, they narrate the sayings and stories on their own authority and without ascription to an earlier Companion *(Sahabi)* of Muhammad from whom Muhammadan Hadith would normally have been derived. Their *isnad*-less form may also indicate their archaic character. In other words, the

Jesus sayings were allowed to circulate in the Islamic environment in relative freedom and without the increasingly rigorous standards which Muhammadan Hadiths were expected to satisfy.

Iraq—more particularly, the city of Kufa—was in all likelihood the original home of the Muslim gospel. The founding fathers of the tradition were all Kufan, although other cities and regions such as Basra, Mecca, Medinah, Syria, and Egypt were also represented by venerable transmitters. That Kufa was the original home of the Muslim Jesus should come as no surprise to students of early Islam, who have long recognized the seminal importance of this city in the genesis of systematic Muslim scholarship. Whether in strictly religious subjects like Hadith, Qur'anic exegesis, theology, and jurisprudence, or in "secular" subjects like grammar, historiography, genealogy, and belles-lettres, Kufan scholars are regularly found in attendance at their birth. Kufa was also the home of the earliest traditions and interpretations which eventually led to the rise of Islam's two great wings: Sunnism and Shi'ism.[41]

Many of these Kufan founding fathers are described in the biographical sources as ascetics (*zuhhad*) or devout worshipers (*'ubbad*), and many are described as preachers and Qur'an readers who belonged to the ranks of "popular" rather than "official" scholars. Many of them are also authors of short moral epigrams or sermons, and many relate on their own authority a category of Hadith called *hadith qudsi* (sacred Hadith, in which God is the speaker), a mark of the prestige they enjoyed in scholarly circles. These preachers and ascetics were a mobile group, traveling from place to place, admonishing rulers or else turning away from politics, shocked at the luxury and moral degeneracy of the ruling classes, and preaching a more personal type of piety. Many were repelled by the way in which the newly crystallizing class of *'ulama'* (religious scholars) were making their peace with the state and putting their knowledge of religious law to political use in support of unjust rulers or policies, thus enhancing their own power and prestige. In the earliest strata of the Muslim gospel, much is heard of scholars who pervert religious knowledge or who fail to practice what they preach. Somewhat like the ascetic desert fathers of early Christian Egypt, who lived in tension with the official church and often refused appointment as bishops, many of these early Muslim ascetics refused to serve the state as judges or legal experts. For these ascetics, the conflict between Jesus and the Pharisees was a natural moral paradigm. No prophet was better suited to illustrate the struggle between the letter and the spirit, between the man created for the Sabbath and the Sabbath created for man, between earthly kingdoms and the Kingdom of God.

The later collectors and transmitters of the Muslim gospel cannot be as easily characterized as its founding fathers. The sayings and stories seem to have kept pace with the changing spiritual and conceptual moods of Muslim civilization. Hence, no generalizations are possible regarding the agendas and motivations of later transmitters, although the bio-bibliographical commentaries in this volume provide some indications.

The Earliest Sayings: Character and Function

The earliest sayings and stories, eighty-five or so in number, mostly belong to two major collections of ascetic literature: *Kitab al-Zuhd wa'l Raqa'iq* (The Book of Asceticism and Tender Mercies), by Ibn al-Mubarak (d. 181/797), and *Kitab al-Zuhd* (The Book of Asceticism), by Ibn Hanbal (d. 241/855). In general, these sayings fall into four basic groups:

1. Sayings with an eschatological import;
2. Quasi-Gospel sayings;
3. Ascetic sayings and stories;
4. Sayings which appear to echo intra-Muslim polemics.

1. The first group may be said to reflect and expand the role of Jesus at the end of time, a role already hinted at in the Qur'an.

Several sayings, however, stress the fact that Jesus is no better informed than any mortal about when the "Hour" shall come. Rather, the coming of the "Hour" is still, for him, cause for dread and renewed prayer: "Whenever the Hour was mentioned in the presence of Jesus, he would cry out and say: 'It is not fitting that the son of Mary should remain silent when the Hour is mentioned in his presence.'" On the Day of Judgment he will act as a rallying point for those believers who "flee the world with their faith intact," a patron saint of all who renounce earthly ambitions for fear of moral contamination. His messianic role in the last days is enshrined in such Hadiths about him as "Jesus will sit on the pulpits of Jerusalem as a fair judge for twenty years."[42]

2. The second group consists of sayings and stories that have a Gospel core but that have expanded or changed in such a way as to acquire a distinctly Islamic stamp. On the face of it, these Gospel sayings would appear to have belonged originally to a corpus of Jesus sayings, perhaps to a lectionary, or else to a common stock of Gospel materials widely known in Muslim circles of piety. This core includes such sayings as "You are the salt of the earth" (Matthew 5:13); "Look at the birds in the sky" (Matthew 6:26); "When you fast, put oil on your head" (Matthew 6:17); "Your left hand must not know what your right hand is doing" (Matthew 6:3); "Store up treasures for yourselves in heaven" (Matthew 6:19); "Happy the womb that bore you" (Luke 11:27–28); "Learn from me, for I am gentle and humble in heart" (Matthew 12:29). The impression one obtains from this Gospel core is that much of it comes from the Sermon on the Mount in Matthew.[43]

This Gospel core was then Islamized in various ways. Thus, whereas the Jesus of Matthew, in answer to the woman who blesses him, says, "Happier those who hear the word of God and keep it," the Jesus of the Muslim gospel is more specific: "Blessed is he who reads the Qur'an and does what is in it."[44] Again, and in order to establish authenticity, we find comments inserted on the speaking style of Jesus, as in the following: "Jesus said to his disciples, 'In truth I say to you'—and he often used to say 'In truth I say to you.'"[45] But let us consider the following: "Jesus was asked: 'Prophet of God, why do you not get yourself an ass to ride upon for your needs'? Jesus answered, 'I am more honorable in God's sight than that He should provide me with something which may distract me from Him.'"[46] We have difficulty determining whether such a saying, apart from its obvious ascetic slant, is or is not connected with the entry into Jerusalem and the Muslim denial of the whole Passion narrative, of which there is hardly any trace in the Muslim gospel.

3. The third and largest group of sayings and stories may be thought of as establishing the outlines of Jesus as a patron saint of Muslim asceticism. Here, renunciation of the world is total and uncompromising. Identification with the poor is crucial to his mission. Poverty, humility, silence, and patience are, as it were, the four cardinal virtues. The world is a "ruin" and all worldly goods must be shunned. The believer must keep the afterlife perpetually before his eyes; he is a sorrowing traveler, "stranger," or "guest" in this world. From the viewpoint of style, these sayings lack parables, one of the most characteristic modes of speech of the Jesus of the Gospels. Instead, there are stories in which Jesus encounters certain people or situations, and these stories act out the moral rather than narrate it in parable form. The absence of parables in the Muslim gospel may be connected with the scarcity of the parable as a literary form in the Qur'an itself—a connection that would provide another instance of the Qur'anic imprint on the Muslim Jesus. As regards origin and diffusion, several sayings in this group are also ascribed to Muhammad, 'Ali, or other venerable figures of early Islam.[47]

4. Underpinning all three groups of these earliest sayings is a doctrinal content that is of relevance to several major early intra-

Muslim controversies. The Muslim Jesus of our sayings was no mere or distant model of ethics but a figure who seems at times to lend his support to certain factions and against others in internal Muslim polemics, and to take sides on such stormy issues as the role of scholars in society and their attitude to government, the dispute over free will versus predestination *(qadar)*, the question of faith and sin, and the status of the sinful believer or ruler. These were deeply divisive conflicts, many of them being important triggers of the civil wars that wracked the first century and a half of Islamic history. Is it possible to attempt—with all due caution—to draw a polemical profile of the early Muslim Jesus?

I have detailed elsewhere the evidence for the views set forth below, but some qualifications are still in order.[48] The Muslim gospel as an entire corpus, and somewhat like Muhammadan Hadith, was not the exclusive preserve of any one single mood, party, or sect. The founding fathers who transmitted or circulated the earliest Jesus sayings, often on their own authority, presumably exercised subtlety in ascribing certain views to Jesus. Thus, it is difficult in many cases to pinpoint the original doctrine or polemical intent of the Muslim transmitter. In his Muslim habitat, however, Jesus was not simply a figure who was credited with bits and pieces of polemic or wisdom, haphazardly and without purpose. He was chosen to represent a particular mood of piety and polemic because he was already enshrined in the common stock as a single moral force, a living figure with well-defined contours. Bearing these qualifications in mind, we can fairly describe the overall mood of the early Islamic Jesus as consistent with a number of Muslim doctrinal positions.

First, this mood was consistent with *irja'*, a term of broad significance denoting an early Muslim movement which generally avoided becoming involved in civil wars and refrained from branding any Muslim an unbeliever because of doctrinal differences, provided faith in the one God was not abandoned. The

Murji'a, or party of *irja'*, was not a fully homogeneous group, but it tended in its early days to support the existing government, irrespective of the private morality of the ruler.[49] On the whole, the group was politically quietist, and ready to make peace with the ruling dynasty—even to serve it. A number of sayings in the Muslim gospel are consonant with this mood: for example, "Just as kings have left wisdom to you, so you should leave the world to them," or "As for kings, if you do not contend against them, they will not contend against you in your religious belief." On the question of leaving the fate of the sinner up to God's judgment, a position implicit in the very term *irja'*, the earliest attested saying of Jesus appears to lend its support: "Jesus saw a person committing theft. Jesus asked, 'Did you commit theft?' The man answered, 'Never! I swear by Him than whom there is none worthier of worship. Jesus said, 'I believe God and falsify my eye.'" This seeming assertion of the primacy of faith as against the condemnation of sin, even when committed *in flagrante*, is reinforced in such sayings as, "Do you not see how God refuses to deny men mercy because of their sins?"[50] It may be that asceticism also tended to predispose these transmitters to renounce worldly affairs and leave the final computation of human sins to God, accepting a kind of division of labor whereby kings are allowed to rule while the pious are left with divine wisdom. One could argue that this was in fact a Muslim reworking of the "render unto Caesar" commandment, taken by these ascetic transmitters to mean the need to draw a line between the private and public spheres of rights and responsibilities.

Second, and in line with this delineation of moral spheres, a number of early sayings display, as we have seen, a great deal of anger against scholars who crossed over to align themselves with government, thus betraying their mission to the community in favor of self-advancement. Here, numerous sayings may be cited: "Do not make your living from the Book of God"; or "Jesus was asked: 'Spirit and Word of God, who is the most seditious of men?' He replied, 'An erring scholar. If a scholar errs, a host of people will fall into error because of him.'"[51] The possession of religious scholarship implied an awesome moral responsibility, an exclusive vocation. One needs to emphasize that these images of the ideal scholar of religion (*alim*) are among the very earliest in the Islamic tradition as a whole. Thus, for example, in a saying like, "Jesus said to his disciples, 'Do not take wages from those whom you teach, except such wages as you gave me," the notion is introduced that religious knowledge must be dispensed freely—an ideal that generated a dispute which was to have a long history in Islamic piety.

Third, the sayings which seem to echo Muslim polemics may possibly have been embedded in sermons or else in texts suitable for homiletic use. Predestination (*qadar*) was one salient issue in this politico-theological debate. The free-will party, the Qadarites, were seen by some members of the first ruling dynasty of Islam, the Umayyads (661–750 A.D.), as a potentially dangerous opposition movement capable of holding rulers accountable for political misdeeds. Here the Islamic Jesus appears to throw his authority behind the anti-Qadarites, in favor of a distinctly individual rather than public or political accountability. The most explicit of Jesus' sayings on the topic of *qadar* is the following: "Jesus said, '*Qadar* is a mystery [*sirr*] of God.' Therefore, do not ask about the mystery of God."[52] On the question of sins (*ma'asi*), closely associated with predestination in the early polemics, the Islamic Jesus is again emphatic in counseling that God's mercy is infinite—that while sins are hateful and reprovable, the remedy lies not in rebellion but in private devotion. Above all, one must not set oneself up as a moral judge: "Jesus said, 'Do not examine the sins of people as though you were lords [*arbab*] but examine them, rather, as though you were servants ['*abid*].'"[53] Here we might detect a veiled critique of the Kharijite movement, one powerful wing of which was responsible for a hundred-year war against imperial authority in the name of the moral integrity of the ruler. If we were to argue that there was a distinct early divide in Islam between those who emphasized the legitimacy and integrity of leadership as the most urgent political and moral necessity, and those who emphasized the unity of the community as being the most urgent, the early sayings of Jesus can be seen as tending to support the latter side.

The Later Sayings and Stories

The initial core of sayings and stories examined above was repeatedly augmented and was transmitted from one generation to the next. Some sayings were expanded or glossed; others were shortened. In later centuries, other intellectual moods were to affect this corpus, as will be seen below. But the crafting of these sayings was always of a high order. This becomes clear when the climate of Adab, or belles-lettres, began to influence the Muslim gospel. The largest collection of the sayings in an early Adab work is found in the literary anthology entitled ʿUyun al-Akhbar, by Ibn Qutayba (d. 276/889). Curiously enough, Ibn Qutayba transmits a number of sayings accurately translated from the Gospels, as well as sayings which belong to the Muslim gospel, yet he does not comment on their juxtaposition.[54] The ascetic component is still present; but in this anthology, one of the earliest and best-known works of Adab in Arabic literature, we find for the first time such sayings as, "The Messiah (may peace be with him) said, 'The world is a bridge. Cross this bridge but do not build upon it'"; and "Be in the middle but walk to the side."[55] Such sayings seem to be moving the gospel from a generally ascetic to a more broadly ethical and Adabi perspective. This move coincided with the maturity in the third/ninth century of a genre of wisdom literature which one might call gnomological, and which had its origins in the preceding century in the works of figures like Ibn al-Muqaffaʿ (d. circa

139/756). To his celebrated translations from Persian wisdom were now added sayings and stories of the Greek sages and philosophers. Many of these were, like the Jesus sayings, Islamized—that is, brought into line with Muslim piety and ethics.[56] Thus, Jesus becomes, in addition to the patron saint of ascetics, something of a model of conduct and good manners, as in the following: "Christ passed by a group of people who hurled insults at him, and he responded with blessings. He passed by another group who insulted him, and he responded likewise. One of his disciples asked, 'Why is it that the more they insult you, the more you bless them? It is as if you were inviting this upon yourself.' Christ replied, 'A person can bring forth only what is within him.'"[57]

Also in the third/ninth century the Muslim gospel was influenced by what might be called the Shi'i mood. Several Shi'i works are represented in our collection, and they display some peculiar features in the image of Jesus. To comprehend these Shi'ite images, we must first remember that Kufa, the probable birthplace of the Muslim gospel, was also of fundamental importance in the genesis of Shi'ism. In several currents of early Shi'i thought, comparisons with Jesus were drawn in order to sustain theological argumentation. Some second/eighth-century Shi'ite groups, for instance, argued that just as Jesus in the Qur'an was made to ascend to God, so also their imams were not dead but invisible. Other groups would defend the perfect knowledge of an infant imam by comparing this to the Qur'anic infant Jesus' speaking in his cradle. The martyrdom of Muhammad's grandson Husayn—a central event in Shi'i sensibility—produced, in later Shi'i thought, a number of traditions which compared Husayn with Jesus in such things as their miraculous births and the similarity of their prophetic and spiritual genealogies, which they both inherited through their mothers. Replete with cosmogenic speculation, Shi'i thought gave prominence to various strands of illuminationist hierarchies and lines of descent, and certain Shi'i sects (for example, the

Isma'ilis) were said by other Shi'is to come close to embracing Christian concepts like the Trinity.[58] On the whole, however, the Shi'i sayings of Jesus do not differ in spirit from the Sunni sayings, although the Shi'i sayings display certain peculiar features (which will be pointed out in the commentaries).

Reflecting the influence of these diverse moods, the Muslim gospel begins to show an increase in the story form. Jesus is now seen acting out his ministry through encounters with humans, animals, and nature. Sometimes a metaphor or parable from the canonical Gospels is dramatized—that is to say, it becomes a narrative involving Jesus.[59] More often, we meet stories of uncertain origin but perhaps with roots in Near Eastern Christian lore, stories which depict Jesus as a lord of nature, an interlocutor of animals and of natural objects like mountains, stones, or skulls. From them, Jesus draws a powerful, almost poignant response, as if he were literally uncovering the secrets of God's created world—an interpreter of and witness to the divine wisdom and compassion proclaimed by nature: "Jesus passed by a cow which was calving in great distress. 'O Word of God,' the cow said, 'Pray that God may deliver me.' Jesus prayed, 'O Creator of the soul from the soul, You who bring forth the soul from the soul, deliver her.' The cow dropped its young." In several stories, he prescribes cures for maladies: "Jesus passed by a town in which a man and his wife were shouting at each other. 'What is the matter with you?' he asked. 'O prophet of God,' the man said, 'This is my wife. She is a good enough and virtuous woman, but I want to separate from her.' 'But tell me, in any case, what is the matter with her,' said Jesus. 'Her face is worn out, although she is not old,' the man said. Jesus turned to the woman and said, 'Woman, do you wish to restore smoothness to your face?' 'Yes,' she replied. 'When you eat,' said Jesus, 'Beware of gluttony, for when food piles up in the stomach and becomes excessive, the face loses its smoothness.' She did so, and her face regained its smoothness."[60] But as Jesus turns to nature, an ideal of social service and commitment enters the stories to balance the excessive asceticism and withdrawal he exemplified earlier: "Jesus met a man and asked him, 'What are you doing?' 'I am devoting myself to God,' the man replied. 'And who is taking care of you?' asked Jesus. 'My brother,' the man replied. Jesus said, 'Your brother is more devoted to God than you are.'"[61]

First we have the ascetic saint; then comes the lord of nature, the miracle worker, the healer, the social and ethical model. The corpus keeps expanding, and as it does so it gathers into itself successive images and moods. Not long after the age of Ibn Qutayba, the Sufi mood—which inherited, among other things, the ascetic tradition of Islam's first two centuries—began to treat Jesus as a figure of central spiritual relevance and affinity.[62] Clearly, the mystical and often metanomian branch of any tree of religion is the one that most closely intertwines with the similar branch on a neighboring tree. This is why, in the Judeo-Christian-Muslim context, the religious identity of a mystical passage selected at random is often untraceable. The Jesus of Islamic Sufism became a figure not easily distinguished from the Jesus of the Gospels, and one reason must undoubtedly have been the growing familiarity with the Gospels among Muslim scholars.[63] Yet the Jesus of the Gospel sermons fitted comfortably into the role of the Sufi preacher *(waʿiẓ)*, as is evident in the following: "Jesus preached to the Israelites. They wept and began to tear their clothes. Jesus said, 'What sins have your clothes committed? Turn instead to your hearts and reprove them'"; "Every man slain shall be avenged on the Day of Judgment except a man slain by the world, which shall avenge itself upon him."[64] If some modern Western Christian scholars warn us against attaching overdue importance to the Qurʾanic epithets of Jesus as the "Word" and "Spirit" of God, in the Sufi texts these two epithets are absolutely central to the structure of his image. Indeed, the great Sufi master Ibn ʿArabi (d. 638/1240) invents a new honorific for him: "The Seal of Saints" *(Khatam al-Awliya').*[65]

The sayings of Jesus thus acquire a new visibility in such classic Sufi texts as *Qut al-Qulub,* by Abu Talib al-Makki (d. 386/996), and *Hilyat al-Awliya',* by Abu Nuʿaym al-Isbahani (d. 430/1039). By the time of Ghazali (d. 505/1111), whose majestic *Ihya' ʿUlum al-Din* (The Revival of Religious Sciences) contains the largest number of sayings ascribed to Jesus in any Arabic Islamic text, Jesus was enshrined in Sufi sensibility as the prophet of the heart par excellence. In the strictly ethical sections of the *Ihya',* Ghazali argues that a full understanding of the mysteries of the heart and its innermost nature is beyond the reach of human intellect. Hence the need for metaphors and parables *(amthal)* to express these mysteries; and hence the prominence of the sayings of Jesus in the *Ihya'* as being among the most intuitive accounts of the human heart. Jesus, of course, is not the only central figure on the Sufi stage. To begin with, there is Muhammad, the first begetter of the Sufi spirit. Next there is ʿAli, depicted by Ghazali as the most profound interpreter of Muhammad.[66] And there are also the great Sufi saints: al-Junayd, Sahl al-Tustari, Ibrahim ibn Adham, and others. But Jesus' sayings are dense and rhythmic, constantly reappearing at the high points of Ghazali's moral argument as it ties together a vast array of Hadiths.

For a sharper delineation of this particular image of the Muslim Jesus, one might briefly consider the chapters devoted to the human soul in Ghazali's *Ihya'.* The Ghazalian soul is essentially Platonic in structure and Aristotelian in its activity. But the Platonic-Aristotelian elements are merely the outline, the building blocks. Intention *(niyya)* on the one hand and divine omniscience on the other are essential features of the field in which the soul moves. Equally essential is the soul's never-ending struggle with Satan. At one point, Ghazali compares the soul to a target pierced with arrows from all sides; at another, to a fortress to which Satan is laying siege. The great temptation for the soul is not simply vice but diversion. The whisperings of Satan never cease, even for the holiest; and they assume subtle shapes like sarcasm, the invitation to one-time indulgence, the seduction of the easy option, and the kindling of anger. The remedy lies in a heart turned perpetually toward God, constantly on guard against the temptation of haste and heedlessness (al-'ajala wa'l khiffa).

For reasons such as these, Jesus was, of all the prophets, particularly suitable as a moral model. The struggle of Jesus with Satan, for example, prominently displayed in the Gospels, may well have been decisive in the formation of early Christian sensibility, whence it may, as a mood, have percolated into Islamic Sufism.[67] Ghazali finds it appropriate not only to cite the sayings and stories of Jesus in great number but also to comment on them—for example: "It is related that Jesus once laid his head to rest upon a stone. Satan passed by and said, 'So, then, Jesus, I see you have found something to desire in this world after all!' Jesus picked up the stone from under his head and flinging it at him said: 'Take this, and the world with it!'" Ghazali now comments: "In point of fact, he who owns even a stone to use as a pillow for sleeping already owns of the world something which Satan can use to advantage against him. Thus, a person who spends the night in prayer and finds a stone nearby on which he can lay his head may be constantly tempted to sleep and to lay his head upon it. Were it not for the stone, the matter would not have occurred to him. And all this has to do with a stone! Can you imagine the case of someone who owns sumptuous pillows and beds and beautiful gardens? When would such a person ever feel the urge to worship God?"[68]

Conclusion

In this introduction I have tried to provide readers with a broad cultural and historical context for the Muslim gospel. There remain a few points of clarification.

The first has to do with the Islamic elements in this gospel. Jesus is always identified as a Muslim prophet—and this must be constantly borne in mind, for he is, after all, a figure molded in an Islamic environment. As if to emphasize the fact, several stories depict him reciting the Qur'an and explaining it, praying in the Muslim manner, and going on pilgrimage to Mecca. Several sayings underline not only his human nature but his helplessness as well. Yet there remain certain sayings and stories which are not entirely consonant with average Muslim sensitivities—for instance, the story of Jesus and the pig: "A pig passed by Jesus. Jesus said, 'Pass in peace.' He was asked, 'Spirit of God, how can you say this to a pig?' Jesus replied, 'I hate to accustom my tongue to evil.'" There is even a story which reproduces his last prayer *on the Cross,* and another where Jesus affirms to a man in a dream that he was indeed crucified. It is as if, even though he is a Muslim creation, the Islamic Jesus, once created, maintains some distance from the strict orthodoxy of his creators. Traditions from the time of Muhammad stress the special closeness with Jesus, for it is said that no prophet was sent in the interval between them. A well-known incident in the life of Muhammad relates how, when Muhammad entered Mecca in triumph and ordered the destruction of all idols and images, he came upon a picture of the Virgin and Child inside the Ka'ba. Covering them with his cloak, he ordered all other images to be wiped out except that one, an act which the sources describe as one of special reverence.[69]

The second point has to do with the relevance of the Muslim gospel for the study of comparative religion. The Islamic Jesus is, after all, a compound image, filtered and transmitted in a particular environment. But even if we think of him as an artificial creation, he seems to be an unusual instance of the way in which one religion reaches out to borrow the spiritual heroes of another religion in order to reinforce its own piety. For a historian of religions or ideas, this phenomenon is curious and worthy of investigation.

Quite apart from what it may reveal of contacts between Islam and Christianity on the plane of history, it may well have something to teach us today about how religious cultures in general interact, enrich themselves, and learn to coexist.

Coexistence brings me to my final point. This process of interaction appears to mask a deeper religious or theological reality—namely, the need that Christianity and Islam have for complementarity. The Islamic Jesus of the Muslim gospel may be a fabrication. We may even come to discover who fabricated him and why, as the preceding pages have attempted to do. Nevertheless, he remains a towering religious figure in his own right—one who easily, almost naturally, rises above two religious environments, the one that nurtured him and the other that adopted him. Amid the current tensions between Christianity and Islam in certain regions of the Middle East and in Europe, it is salutary to remind ourselves of an age and a tradition when Christianity and Islam were more open to each other, more aware of and reliant on each other's witness.

In order to "remind" (a term very dear to the Qur'an), the Muslim gospel assembled here has the advantage of a certain impact and novelty. Here is a Jesus who on the one hand is shorn of Christology, but who on the other is endowed with attributes which render him meta-historical and even, so to speak, meta-religious. In his Muslim habitat, Jesus becomes an object of intense devotion, reverence, and love. He bears the stamp of Qur'anic *nubuwwah,* or prophecy, but as he advances inside the Islamic tradition he ceases to be an argument and becomes a living and vital moral voice, demanding to be heard by all who seek a unity of profession and witness.

The Sayings and Stories

· · · · · · ·

Jesus and the Pharisees. On of the seventy-two miniatures illustrating the book *Kulliyat,* by the Persian poet Saʾdi (British Library MS.Add.24944). Shiraz/ Safavid, A.H. 974, A.D. 1566. Jesus is seated in the center, haloed in flames, while a Pharisee is seen flinging himself at a plate of food. The sayings and stories contain many condemnations of the gluttony and greed that allegedly typify scholars of the law. Reproduced by permission of the British Library.

A WORD ON THE COMMENTARIES

In general, I have selected the earliest version of each saying or story, but I have also appended references to citations in later sources, in approximate chronological order. In addition, I provide references to three major collections of these sayings:

> Miguel Asin y Palacios, "Logia et agrapha domini Jesu apud moslemicos scriptores, asceticos praesertim, usitata," *Patrologia Orientalis*, 13 (1919), 335–431; and 19 (1926), 531–624.

> Hanna Mansur, "Aqwal al-Sayyid al-Masih ʿind al-kuttab al-muslimin al-aqdamin" [The Sayings of Christ in Ancient Muslim Writers], *Al-Masarra* (1976), 45–51, 115–122, 231–239, 356–364; ibid. (1977), 107–113; ibid. (1978), 45–53, 119–123, 221–225, 343–346, 427–432, 525–528, 608–611.

> James Robson, *Christ in Islam* (London: Allen and Unwin, 1929).

The abbreviation *EI* 2 refers to the *Encyclopaedia of Islam*, new edition, ed. H. A. R. Gibb et al. (Leiden: Brill, 1960–).

Where editions or texts are defective, I have tried to indicate this in the references or commentaries.

In formulations of dates—e.g., "131/748" or "first/seventh century"—the number preceding the slash refers to the Islamic calendar (*anno hegirae*, or A.H.), while the number following the slash refers to the Christian calendar (*anno domini*, or A.D.).

I have kept the commentaries as brief as possible, attempting first of all to place the sayings in their Islamic context and to ask how their Muslim audience might have received them. But I have also tried where possible to suggest parallels to them in the Gospels, the Apocrypha, and other literatures of the Near East and beyond. In a few cases, I appended no comments at all where I judged none were needed. Where my readers recognize an origin for any of these sayings, I would hope that this might enhance their interest in the corpus as a whole.

The commentaries that Asin appended to his collection are in Latin and therefore of limited access. This is regrettable because many of his comments are still of great value; I have referred the reader to them in several places.

There are five sayings whose Arabic originals I have not been able to trace. I have given the references to them as cited by Asin.

1 Jesus saw a person committing theft. Jesus asked, "Did you commit theft?" The man answered, "Never! I swear by Him than whom there is none worthier of worship." Jesus said, "I believe God and falsify my eye."

Hammam ibn Munabbih (d. 131/748), *Sahifat Hammam ibn Munabbih,* p. 34 (no. 41). Cf. Muslim, *Sahih,* 7:97; al-Turtushi, *Siraj al-Muluk,* p. 434; Ibn al-Salah, *Fatawa wa Masa'il ibn al-Salah,* 1:181–182; Majlisi, *Bihar al-Anwar,* 14:702 (variant); (Asin, p. 579, no. 184; Mansur, no. 208; Robson, p. 59).

Hammam ibn Munabbih was the brother of Wahb, the celebrated and semi-legendary authority on pre-Islamic antiquities. The Hadith collection from which this story of Jesus was taken is claimed by its modern editor to be the oldest surviving collection of Hadith; see the introduction to the collection, cited in the Bibliography. If the editor's views are accepted, this would mean that stories about Jesus circulated in Muslim circles as early as the first/seventh century.

The story seems to suggest the primacy of faith, which overrides any sin, even those committed *in flagrante.* It may also suggest abstention from judgment, in order perhaps to preserve social peace, thus giving the sinner the benefit of the doubt. The story may well have political implications: rulers should be left to God's judgment even if they are manifest sinners.

2 Jesus said, "Blessed is he who guards his tongue, whose house is sufficient for his needs, and who weeps for his sins."

'Abdallah ibn al-Mubarak (d. 181/797), *Kitab al-Zuhd wa al-Raqa'iq,* pp. 40–41 (no. 124). Cf. Ibn Abi al-Dunya, *Kitab al-Samt wa Adab al-Lisan,* pp. 189–190 (no. 15); Ibn Hanbal, *Kitab al-Zuhd,* p. 229 (no. 850) ('Abdallah b. 'Umar instead of Jesus); al-Qushayri, *al-Risala,* p. 68 (the Prophet Muhammad instead of Jesus); Ibn 'Asakir, *Sirat,* p. 151, no. 158; and al-Zabidi, *Ithaf al-Sada al-Muttaqin,*

7:456 (slight rearrangement of order) (Asin, p. 597, no. 217; Mansur, no. 254; Robson, p. 61).

ʿAbdallah ibn al-Mubarak was a well-known Hadith scholar who took a special interest in ascetic traditions. On his life and works, including the manuscript problems of the work from which these Jesus sayings are taken, see the modern editor's introduction to Ibn al-Mubarak's *Kitab al-Zuhd,* in the Bibliography.

The saying echoes the tone of the Sermon on the Mount. The phrase "Blessed is" (Arabic *tuba*) is meant to be a faithful reproduction of Jesus' style of speaking and occurs in several other sayings.

3 Jesus said to his people, "Do not talk much without the mention of God, lest your hearts grow hard; for the hard heart is far from God, but you do not know. Do not examine the sins of people as though you were lords, but examine them, rather, as though you were servants. Men are of two kinds: the sick and the healthy. Be merciful to the sick and give thanks to God for health."

ʿAbdallah ibn al-Mubarak (d. 181/797), *al-Zuhd,* p. 44 (no. 135). Cf. Abu Rifaʿa, *Kitab Badʾ al-Khalq,* p. 196; Ibn ʿAbd Rabbihi, *al-ʿIqd al-Farid,* 3:143 (Asin, p. 541, no. 112; Mansur, no. 10; Robson, pp. 51–52, partial); see also al-Samarqandi, *Tanbih al-Ghafilin,* p. 139 (Asin, p. 558, no. 142; Mansur, no. 42; Robson, pp. 55–56); Abu Nuʿaym, *Hilyat al-Awliyaʾ,* 6:58; Ibn ʿAsakir, *Sirat,* p. 162, nos. 178ff.

Several commandments are conflated here: "Do not babble"; but also, quite clearly, "Do not argue." This is Qurʾanic in sentiment. The hard-hearted are supposedly made so by argument and counter-argument. This breeds stubbornness and, eventually, heresy. "But you do not know" (Arabic *walakin la taʿlamun*) is also

Qur'anic in phrasing. The next commandment, about lords and servants, warns against moral judgment, and may allude to early and puritanical Muslim sects like the Khawarij, who adopted an uncompromising attitude to major sinners, pronouncing them unbelievers.

4 Jesus said, "If it is a day of fasting for one of you, let him anoint his head and beard and wipe his lips so that people will not know that he is fasting. If he gives with the right hand, let him hide this from his left hand. If he prays, let him pull down the door curtain, for God apportions praise as He apportions livelihood."

'Abdallah ibn al-Mubarak (d. 181/797), *al-Zuhd*, pp. 48–49 (no. 150). Cf. al-Ghazali, *Ihya' 'Ulum al-Din*, 3:287; Ibn 'Asakir, *Sirat*, p. 175, no. 201 (Asin, p. 389, no. 55; Mansur, no. 137; Robson, p. 46).

The core of this saying comes from the Gospels, where the reference is to the Pharisees. Here, however, all hypocrites are targeted. This is one way in which specific Gospel allusions are excised in the process of Islamizing the sayings. The very last phrase, "for God apportions praise as He apportions livelihood" appears to be unconnected with what came before, but may also be part of the same process of Islamization.

5 Gabriel met Jesus and said to him, "Peace be upon you, Spirit of God." "And upon you peace, Spirit of God," said Jesus. Then Jesus asked, "O Gabriel, when will the Hour come?" Gabriel's wings fluttered and he replied, "The questioned knows no more about this than the questioner. It has grown heavy in the heavens and the earth; it will only come upon you suddenly." Or else he said, "Only God will reveal it when it is time."

'Abdallah ibn al-Mubarak (d. 181/797), *al-Zuhd*, p. 77 (no. 228). Cf. *Qu'ran* 7:187; (Asin, p. 585, no. 198; Mansur, no. 244; Robson, p. 92).

The story appears to be a recasting of Qur'an 7:187, where the person questioned about the Hour is Muhammad. The two phrases "it has grown . . . suddenly" and "Only God . . . time" are direct quotations from that Qur'anic verse. The saying clearly demonstrates that Jesus has no special or superhuman powers or knowledge. There are parallels to this story in Hadith, where a person asks Muhammad about the Hour and is answered with the phrase, "the questioned knows no more about this than the questioner." This helps to reinforce the Qur'anic view that Jesus, although a revered prophet, was a mere human.

6 Whenever the Hour was mentioned in the presence of Jesus, he would cry out and say, "It is not fitting that the son of Mary should remain silent when the Hour is mentioned in his presence."

'Abdallah ibn al-Mubarak (d. 181/797), *al-Zuhd*, pp. 77–78 (no. 229). Cf. Ibn 'Asakir, *Sirat*, p. 121, no. 100.

This story is closely connected with the previous one, driving home the moral. It also emphasizes the helplessness of Jesus where the Hour is concerned. In other words, he not only does not know when it is to come, but is himself subject to its terrors, like any other human being.

7 Jesus said to his disciples, "Do not take wages from those whom you teach, except such wages as you gave me. Salt of the earth, do not become corrupt. Everything when it becomes corrupt can be treated with salt, but if salt is corrupted it has no remedy. Know that you possess two traits of ignorance: laughter without [cause for] wonder, and morning nap without wakefulness."

ʿAbdallah ibn al-Mubarak (d. 181/797), *al-Zuhd*, p. 96 (no. 283). Cf. Ibn Hanbal, *al-Zuhd*, p. 144 (no. 478), p. 147 (no. 491); al-Samarqandi, *Tanbih*, p. 70 (rearrangement of order) (Asin, p. 553, no. 132; Mansur, no. 32; Robson, pp. 54–55); Ibn ʿAbd al-Barr, *Jamiʿ Bayan al-ʿIlm*, 1:185 (not Jesus); Ibn ʿAsakir, *Sirat*, p. 190, no. 231.

The idea that a truly genuine teacher teaches for free is at least as old as Socrates. It is also to be found in the Jewish tradition, in the Gospels, and in Islamic ethics. The phrase "I ask you no wages for this [revelation]" occurs five times in Sura 26 of the Qurʾan. The "salt of the earth" is of course from the Gospels, but its moral is here more fully drawn. Indeed, many sayings in the Muslim gospel make explicit or else interpret what is left hanging as allegory in the Gospels. The last sentence, "Know that . . . wakefulness," here too appears unconnected with what preceded, belonging to the general category of polite manners (Adab). The commandment about wakefulness is probably intended to encourage the faithful to pass the night in prayer. It is possible that Ibn al-Mubarak simply conflated three separate sayings into one. For a similar condemnation of morning sleep, see the Mishnaic tractate *Pirkey Aboth*, in J. H. Hertz, *Sayings of the Fathers* (London: East and West Library, 1952), p. 45, no. 14.

8 Jesus said to his disciples, "Just as kings have left wisdom to you, so you should leave the world to them."

ʿAbdallah ibn al-Mubarak (d. 181/797), *al-Zuhd*, p. 96 (no. 284). Cf. Ibn Hanbal, *al-Zuhd*, p. 144 (no. 475); al-Samarqandi, *Tanbih*, p. 190 (fuller version); Ibn ʿAsakir, *Sirat*, p. 135, no. 123 (Asin, p. 563, no. 147; Mansur, no. 48; Robson, p. 90).

An early and important political saying, perhaps an echo of the "render unto Caesar" commandment in the Gospels. The saying points to what was to become a very important scenario of Islamic history: kings versus *ʿulamaʾ*. The saying suggests that there should be a sort of division of labor between kings and religious scholars. Leaving the world to kings is of course politically quietist in tone, but the general historical context is the struggle brewing between the early *ʿulamaʾ* and the early caliphs as exemplified in the archetypal career of a celebrated scholar-ascetic such as al-Hasan al-Basri (d. 110/728); see *EI* 2 for more information. Several Jesus sayings are also attributed to al-Hasan, as will be indicated in the appropriate places below.

9 Jesus said, "Son of Adam, if you do a good deed, try to forget it, for it abides with Him who will not forget it." He then recited the following [Quranic] verse: "'We do not neglect the reward of him who does a good deed.' If you commit an evil deed, let it remain right before your eyes." Ibn al-Warraq said, "Near your eyes."

ʿAbdallah ibn al-Mubarak (d. 181/797), *al-Zuhd*, p. 101 (no. 301). Cf. Ibn ʿAsakir, *Sirat*, p. 168, no.190.

The first sentence is close in sentiment to the Gospel commandment about the anonymity of charity. That Jesus should recite a Qurʾanic verse would not be at all unnatural in a Muslim context; the Qurʾan, after all, is *the* Book and all prophets in the Qurʾan are Muslims. The comment by Ibn al-Warraq is a later gloss. The two sayings which follow this one also contain editorial glosses.

For more information on Ibn al-Warraq (d. 378/988), see p. 21 of the editor's introduction to Ibn al-Mubarak's *Kitab al-Zuhd*.

10   Jesus said, "O disciples, seek the love of God by your hatred of sinners; seek to be near Him by [doing] that which distances you from them; and seek His favor by being angry with them." He [Malik] said, "I do not know which [commandment] he began with." They said, "Spirit of God, whose company then shall we keep?" He replied, "Keep the company of him whose sight reminds you of God, whose speech increases your knowledge, whose deeds make the afterlife desirable."

'Abdallah ibn al-Mubarak (d. 181/797), *al-Zuhd*, p. 121 (no. 355). Cf. Al-Jahiz, *al-Bayan wa al-Tabyin*, 1:399 and 3:175; Ibn Abi'l Dunya, *Kitab al-Awliya'* in *Mawsu'at Rasa'il*, 4:17, no. 25 (partial; attributed to Muhammad); Ibn 'Abd Rabbihi, *al-'Iqd*, 3:143 (the last part only) (Mansur, no. 7); Ibn 'Abd al-Barr, *Jami'*, 1:126; al-Ghazali, *Ihya'*, 2:157; Ibn 'Asakir, *Sirat*, p. 179, nos. 208ff. (Asin, p. 358, no. 15, Mansur, no. 100; Robson, pp. 43–44).

The Jesus of the Gospels, who consorts with sinners, is not often encountered in the Muslim gospel, where Jesus is distinctly and consistently a more fierce and ascetic figure. See, however, Saying 81, below.

"Malik" is Malik ibn Mighwal (d. 159/775–776), an early Kufan traditionist who transmitted many sayings of Jesus. Part of this saying also occurs in a Muhammadan Hadith; see Ibn Abi'l Dunya, cited above. In Arabic wisdom literature, similar sayings are attributed to Luqman, a pre-Islamic sage who gave his name to Sura 31 of the Qur'an. Luqman is best known for his lengthy admonitions to his son, two of which resemble our saying here; see al-Mubashshir ibn Fatik, *Mukhtar al-Hikam*, pp. 271, 275.

11 Jesus used to tell his followers, "Take mosques to be your homes, houses to be stopping places. Eat from the plants of the wilderness and escape from this world in peace." Sharik said, "I mentioned this to Sulayman, who added, 'and drink pure water.'"

'Abdallah ibn al-Mubarak (d. 181/797), *al-Zuhd*, p. 198 (no. 563). Cf. Ibn 'Abd Rabbihi, *al-'Iqd*, 3:143; Ibn 'Asakir, *Sirat*, p. 138, no. 128 (Asin, p. 541, no. 111; Mansur, no. 9; Robson, p. 73).

This saying is an early image of Jesus as a wandering ascetic who owns nothing, travels from place to place, and lives off the land. It will be refined in later sayings and was to become the dominant portrait of Jesus' way of life in Muslim literature. The idea that the believer is a pilgrim on this earth is of course in the Gospels, but escaping from the world "in peace" (or perhaps "with faith intact") is a prominent feature of the Islamic Jesus. "Drink pure water" is probably to be understood metaphorically to mean something like "Keep yourselves clean." The reference to mosques (Arabic *masajid*) indicates that they are, in a Muslim context, the primordial places of worship.

Sharik (d.177/794) was a famous judge and traditionist. Sulayman ibn al-Mughira (d.165/781–782) was a Basran traditionist.

12 Jesus said, "For the patient man, misfortune soon results in ease; for the sinner, ease soon results in misfortune."

'Abdallah ibn al-Mubarak (d. 181/797), *al-Zuhd*, p. 222 (no. 627). Cf. Ibn 'Asakir, *Sirat*, p. 198, no. 241.

Patience is of course a trait of asceticism in many religious traditions. The sentiment here belongs to a font of wisdom of Near

Eastern origin difficult to identify with any one single cultural tradition. One could even detect a certain Stoic element in this saying.

The Arabic displays a well-crafted inversion of word order, a chiasmus.

13 Jesus said, "There are four [qualities] which are not found in one person without causing wonder: silence, which is the beginning of worship; humility before God; an ascetic attitude toward the world; and poverty."

'Abdallah ibn al-Mubarak (d. 181/797), *al-Zuhd*, p. 222 (no. 629). Cf. Ibn Abi al-Dunya, *al-Samt*, pp. 573–574 (n. 647); al-Samarqandi, *Tanbih*, p. 77 (slight variation); Ibn 'Asakir, *Sirat*, p. 142, no. 139 (Asin, p. 554, no. 135; Mansur, no. 35; Robson, p. 55).

The listing of qualities in this manner is typical of the style of Adab (belles-lettres); it is a mnemonic pedagogical device. This saying is also attributed to Muhammad.

14 Jesus passed by ruins and said, "Ruin of ruins!" or else he said, "O ruin that has been ruined, where are your people?" Something from the ruins answered him, "Spirit of God, they perished, so exert yourself for God," or else the voice said, "The decree of God was in earnest, so you too must seek Him in earnest."

'Abdallah ibn al-Mubarak (d. 181/797), *al-Zuhd*, p. 225 (no. 640). Cf. Ibn Hanbal, *al-Zuhd*, p. 282 (no. 1057) ('Abdallah b. 'Umar instead of Jesus); Ibn 'Asakir, *Sirat*, p. 183, no. 215.

There are several stories in the Muslim gospel where Jesus addresses ruins, acting as an interrogator of nature. This is another peculiar trait of the Islamic Jesus and evokes the images of ruined habitations in the Qur'an, as well as similar encounters with ruins by Muhammad in the Hadith. The connection with asceticism is of course quite clear, but the intention may also be to bring Jesus more closely into line with Muhammad's prophetic experiences, given Muhammad's oft-cited Hadith that Jesus is the closest of prophets to him; see, e.g., Ibn ʿAsakir, *Sirat*, p. 54–55, no. 43.

15 Jesus said, "Strive for the sake of God and not for the sake of your bellies. Look at the birds coming and going! They neither reap nor plough, and God provides for them. If you say, 'Our bellies are larger than the bellies of birds,' then look at these cattle, wild or tame, as they come and go, neither reaping nor plowing, and God provides for them too. Beware the excesses of the world, for the excesses of the world are an abomination in God's eyes."

ʿAbdallah ibn al-Mubarak (d. 181/797), *al-Zuhd*, p. 291 (no. 848). Cf. Ibn Abi al-Dunya, *Kitab al-Qanaʿa* in *Mawsuʿat Rasaʾil*, 1:71, excerpt no. 173; al-Samarqandi, *Tanbih*, p. 168 (variant) (Asin, p. 563, no. 146; Mansur, no. 47; Robson, pp. 72–73); Abu Hayyan, *al-Imtaʿ wa al-Muʾanasa*, 2:127; al-Ghazali, *Ihyaʾ*, 4:260 (slight variation) (Mansur, no. 163); Ibn ʿAsakir, *Sirat*, p. 166, no. 187.

The core of this saying comes from the Gospels, with the moral made explicit; compare Saying 7, above. The Islamic version brackets the saying with a sentence at the beginning ("Strive for the sake of God . . .") and another at the end ("Beware the excesses of the world . . .").

16 Jesus addressed his followers the night he was raised to heaven, saying: "Do not make your living from [teaching] the Book of God. If you refrain from doing so, God will seat you upon pulpits a single stone of which is better than the world and all that is therein." ʿAbd al-Jabbar said, "These are the seats mentioned by God in the Qurʾan: 'Upon a seat of truth with a mighty king.'" Jesus was then raised to heaven.

ʿAbdallah ibn al-Mubarak (d. 181/797), *al-Zuhd*, p. 507 (no. 1447).

Cf. no. 7, above. For the gloss inserted at the end of the saying, see Qurʾan 54:55. The pulpits referred to are of course in paradise. ʿAbd al-Jabbar ibn ʿUbayd ibn Salman (d. 112/730) was a Hadith scholar, reputedly of Christian origin.

17 Jesus was asked, "Spirit and Word of God, who is the most seditious of men?" He replied, "The scholar who is in error. If a scholar errs, a host of people will fall into error because of him."

ʿAbdallah ibn al-Mubarak (d. 181/797), *al-Zuhd*, p. 520 (no. 1474). Cf. al-ʿAmiri, *al-Saʿada wa al-Isʿad*, p. 169; al-Makki, *Qut al-Qulub*, 1:174 (Asin, p. 545, no. 122; Mansur, no. 24; Robson, p. 52); al-Mawardi, *Adab al-Dunya wa al-Din*, p. 30; Ibn ʿAsakir, *Sirat*, p. 190, no. 232 (slightly variant).

Jesus is addressed by his Qurʾanic sobriquets, as he will be so often in later sayings. This saying about scholars has important political and theological connotations: scholars have an immense public responsibility. During the early Abbasid period, in which this saying circulated, scholars emerged as a distinct class in society. The new Abbasid caliphs actively courted scholars in their attempts to establish bases of support for the dynasty. Among scholars, attitudes varied widely as regards the new state and its claims for legitimacy. The saying clearly enjoins great caution, and may even be a veiled criticism of scholars who volunteered to serve the new state by putting their religious knowledge and social prestige too eagerly at its disposal.

In Arabic wisdom literature, a saying similar to this is ascribed to Hermes, identified with the Qur'anic prophet Idris; see Al-Mubashshir ibn Fatik, *Mukhtar al-Hikam*, p. 25 ("The error of a scholar wrecks a ship, which then sinks and causes a host of people to drown"). See also, e.g., the Mishnaic tractate *Pirkey Aboth*, in Hertz, *Sayings of the Fathers*, p. 60, no. 16.

18 John son of Zachariah met Jesus and said, "Tell me what it is that draws one near to God's favor and distances one from God's wrath." Jesus said, "Avoid feeling anger." John asked, "What arouses anger and what makes it recur?" Jesus replied, "Pride, fanaticism, haughtiness, and magnificence." John said, "Let me ask you another." "Ask what you will," replied Jesus. "Adultery—what creates it and what makes it recur?" "A glance," said Jesus, "which implants in the heart something that makes it veer excessively toward amusement and self-indulgence, thus increasing heedlessness and sin. Do not stare at what does not belong to you, for what you have not seen will not make you wiser and what you do not hear will not trouble you."

'Abdallah ibn al-Mubarak (d. 181/797), *al-Zuhd*, appendix p. 12 (no. 44). Cf. al-Turtushi, *Siraj*, p. 252; and al-Ghazali, *Ihya*', 3:168 (shorter version) (Asin, p. 366, no. 31; Mansur, no. 116; Robson, p. 45).

There are a number of Jesus and John stories in the Muslim gospel; see also Sayings 39, 53, 54, 124, 236, 239, and 287 in this volume. The question-and-answer form is quite common in Adab works. In broader terms, the motif of the two wise men exchanging bits of wisdom is found in stories of the philosophers in Greek literature. One Jesus-John encounter recalls a Greek encounter; see Saying 124, below. According to Islamic tradition, Jesus and John were maternal cousins. In the Qur'an, heedlessness (Arabic *ghafla*) is often the prelude to sin.

19　There was drought in the time of Jesus. A cloud passed by. Jesus looked up and saw an angel driving it on. He called out to him, "Where to?" "To the land owned by So-and-So," replied the angel. Jesus went out until he came to the man indicated and found him repairing ditches with a shovel. Jesus asked him, "Did you want more?"—that is to say, more rain. "No," said the man. "Did you want less?" "No," said the man. "What have you done with your harvest this year?" "What harvest?" said the man, "A pest is devastating it." "What did you do last year?" asked Jesus. "I divided my land into three parts: a third for land, cattle, and family; a third for the poor, the indigent, and travelers; and a third for my own use." Jesus said, "I know not which of these three brings greater reward."

'Abdallah ibn al-Mubarak (d. 181/797), *al-Zuhd*, appendix p. 32 (no. 126). The text is defective in several places. Cf. Ibn Abi al-Dunya, *Kitab Islah al-Mal*, in *Mawsuʿat Rasaʾil*, 2:96, excerpt no. 322 (variant).

This is the first full-length story, with Jesus encountering a pious and patient farmer. The manner in which the farmer distributes his wealth exceeds the legal Muslim requirements of alms giving, thus meriting angelic reward as well as the approval of Jesus. In form, the story itself may have begun life as a parable. But instead of being narrated by Jesus, as would be expected in the Gospels, it is transformed into a narrative where Jesus is a participant whose role is to activate, to "wrap up," or to draw out the moral of the story. This is typical of several such stories in the Muslim gospel.

There is a story about a pious Christian Egyptian shepherd which has elements closely resembling our story here. See Benedicta Ward, trans., *The Sayings of the Desert Fathers* (London: Mowbray, 1984), p. 60.

20   The disciples asked Jesus, "Tell us, which man is the most devoted to God?" "He who labors for the sake of God without seeking the praise of mankind," replied Jesus. "Which man offers sincere counsel for the sake of God?" they asked. "He who begins by fulfilling his duties toward God before his duty to men [and prefers] the duties of God to the duties of men. When faced with two choices, worldly matters and matters of the afterlife, he begins with what concerns the afterlife and then turns his attention to this world."

'Abdallah ibn al-Mubarak (d. 181/797), *al-Zuhd*, appendix p. 34 (no. 134). (The text has been slightly reconstructed in one place.) Cf. Ibn 'Asakir, *Sirat*, p. 171, no. 195.

Here too, the question-and-answer technique owes much to the methodology of Adab.

21   As Christ [went out] with a crowd of disciples between a running river and a rotting serpent, there came a beautifully colored bird, shining like gold, and alighted nearby. Shaking itself, it shed its feathers, revealing the ugliest of sights—a little bald red thing. The bird came to a pool, wallowed in the slime, and emerged black and ugly. It then faced the flowing waters, washed itself, returned to its shed feathers, reassumed them, and recovered its beauty. So also does the sinner, when he forsakes his religion and plunges into sin; and so too does repentance resemble the washing away of filth in the shallow stream. The sinner then recovers his religion when he reassumes his shed skin and feathers. And these are parables.

'Abdallah ibn al-Mubarak (d. 181/797), *al-Zuhd,* appendix pp. 44–45 (no. 171). The text is defective in several places but can be reconstructed from Ibn 'Asakir, *Sirat,* p. 201, no. 247.

This is a curious story, and the fact that the text is defective in several places makes reconstruction and understanding difficult. What is clear, however, is that it narrates an encounter with nature, where the various elements of the story exemplify various ethical qualities and states of existence: the river of life, the serpent of sin, and the bird-man in between—ugly when sinful, beautifully clean and plumed when pious. As in Saying 19, above, Jesus is a participant-observer in the allegory. It is as if the Islamic Jesus needs to reinterpret the Jesus of the Gospels, partly perhaps in order to "cleanse" him from the misinterpretation of his wayward followers, as the Qur'an attempts to do. Among other things, this means that the parables cannot be left to stand as is, but must be fully explicated, turned inside out, made into Akhbar—that is, quasi-historical narratives. This is probably the intention behind the very last phrase, "And these are parables," meaning "This is how parables must be understood."

22 Jesus used to say, "Love of paradise and fear of hell beget patience in adversity and draw the servant [of God] away from worldly comfort."

'Abdallah ibn al-Mubarak (d. 181/797), *al-Zuhd,* appendix p. 46 (no. 175). Cf. al-Ghazali, *Ihya',* 4:180 (fuller version); Ibn 'Asakir, *Sirat,* p. 136, no. 125 (Mansur, no. 152).

"From worldly comfort": "from feeling secure in this world" is an alternative reading.

23 The disciples came to Jesus and said, "Spirit and Word of God, show us our forefather Sam son of Noah, so that God may increase us in certainty [of faith]." So he set out with them to the tomb of Sam and said, "Answer, by God's leave, O Sam son of Noah!" Sam arose with the aid of God, standing like a towering palm tree. Jesus said to him, "How long did you live, O Sam?" He answered, "I lived for four thousand years. For two thousand I was a prophet, and I lived two thousand more." Jesus asked him, "How was the world in your sight?" Sam answered, "It was like a house with two doors. I entered through one and left through the other."

'Abd al-Malik ibn Hisham (d. 218/833), *Kitab al-Tijan,* p. 27. Cf. Waqidi, *Maghazi,* 1:121; Ibn Abi al-Dunya, *Kitab Dhamm al-Dunya,* in *Mawsu'at Rasa'il,* 2:110–111, excerpt no. 229.

Ibn Hisham was the author-editor of the earliest surviving biography of Muhammad. The work from which this story is taken is devoted to the antiquities of Arabia, and the work's attribution and authenticity are in some doubt. For the life and works of Ibn

Hisham, see *EI* 2. For another Sam resurrection story, see the bibliographical citations to Saying 59, below.

There are several sites in the Middle East today which purport to be tombs of biblical figures like Noah. Some of these tombs are fifty yards or more in length. In another version of the Sam story, the disciples seek to test the ability of Jesus to resurrect not just the recently dead but the dead of old. Sam in the Islamic tradition was the longest-lived of the prophets; see the work by Ibn Abi al-Dunya, cited above. In any case, the world as described by Sam serves to reinforce the preachings of Jesus regarding its insignificance.

24 It was revealed to Jesus: "A land is cursed if its rulers are young boys."

Muhammad ibn Sa'd (d. 230/845), *al-Tabaqat al-Kubra*, 6:29.

Muhammad Ibn Sa'd was a Hadith scholar and author of the earliest biographical dictionary in Islamic literature; see *EI* 2. This revelation ("through the tongue of Jesus" in the original Arabic) is patently political. If one were to speculate about its context, one might recall that the earliest crisis involving the succession of a minor in Islamic history was Mu'awiya II, grandson of the first Mu'awiya. He was a sickly teenager and died soon after his accession, to be succeeded by Marwan I, an old man. That crisis was the immediate prelude to the Second Civil War (682–695 A.D.) in Islamic history, a deeply divisive conflict which was also fertile in Hadiths, many of an apocalyptic nature. This saying is also found in Ecclesiastes 10:16—"Woe to thee, O land, when thy king is a child!" I owe this reference to Dr. Maria Ascher.

25 God revealed to Jesus: "O Jesus, admonish yourself. Once admonished, admonish people. Otherwise, be modest in my sight."

Ahmad ibn Hanbal (d. 241/855), *Kitab al-Zuhd*, p. 93 (no. 300). Cf. al-Qushayri, *al-Risala*, p. 117; al-Ghazali, *Ihya'*, 1:68; and idem, *Ayyuha al-Walad*, p. 140 (Asin, p. 352, no. 7; Mansur, no. 190; Robson, p. 78).

Ahmad ibn Hanbal was a towering figure of early Islamic history: Hadith scholar, jurist, and prominent political figure of his age and eponymous founder of the Hanbali school of law, one of the four major schools of Sunni Islam. For more on his life, see *EI* 2. The textual condition of many of his surviving works is unsatisfactory. The two sources used here, *Kitab al-Zuhd* and *Kitab al-Wara'*, are both uncritical reproductions of earlier Egyptian editions and are rife with typographical errors. Every effort has been made to remedy the often defective state of the texts.

In technical Islamic terminology, Saying 25 is a *hadith qudsi*, a sacred or divine Hadith, because the speaker is God himself; see William A. Graham, *Divine Word and Prophetic Word in Early Islam* (The Hague: Mouton, 1977). Many *hadith qudsi* were revealed to Muhammad but many also to other prophets. Implied in this saying is the divine admonition to Jesus to practice what he preaches, with the further implication that Jesus is human and not above being admonished, or even rebuked by God, if necessary. All this tallies closely with the substance and tone of the words addressed to Jesus by God in the Qur'an.

26 Jesus was standing near a grave with his disciples—or, he said, with a few of his followers—as a dead man was being lowered into the grave. They mentioned the darkness, loneliness, and narrowness of the grave. Jesus said, "You were once in a place narrower than this, in your mothers' wombs. If God wishes to expand [His mercy], He does so."

Ahmad ibn Hanbal (d. 241/855), *al-Zuhd*, p. 93 (no. 301). Cf. Ibn 'Asakir, *Sirat*, p. 203, no. 250.

The motif of words of wisdom spoken by a graveside is common in Greek literature, and possibly in ancient Persian as well. The most famous example of this genre is the tale of the seven wise men standing by the deathbed of Alexander the Great, a story found in several classical Arabic literary anthologies. The words of comfort that Jesus addresses to his disciples bear some stylistic resemblance to verses in the Qur'an where the Muslims are comforted by God—for example, 3:103, 139; 7:86; 22:5.

27 Christ said, "Make frequent mention of God the Exalted, also of His praise and glorification, and obey Him. It suffices for one of you when praying, and if God is truly pleased with him, to say: 'O God, forgive my sins, reform my way of life, and keep me safe from hateful things, O my God.' "

Ahmad ibn Hanbal (d. 241/855), *al-Zuhd*, p. 93 (no. 302).

This is one of several prayers ascribed to Jesus.

28 Jesus said, "Blessed is the believer, and then again blessed, for God watches over his progeny after his death."

Ahmad ibn Hanbal (d. 241/855), *al-Zuhd*, p. 93 (no. 304). Cf. al-Zabidi, *Ithaf*, 8:440 (Mansur, no. 256).

29 Jesus used to say, "If any of you gives alms with the right hand, let him hide this from the left. If he prays, let him draw down the curtain of his door, for God apportions His favor as He does His sustenance."

Ahmad ibn Hanbal (d. 241/855), *al-Zuhd*, p. 94 (no. 307).

See the commentary on Saying 4, above.

30 Jesus was asked, "Prophet of God, why do you not get yourself an ass to ride upon for your needs?" Jesus answered: "I am more honorable in God's sight than that He should provide me with something which may distract me from Him."

Ahmad ibn Hanbal (d. 241/855), *al-Zuhd*, p. 94 (no. 309). Cf. Ibn Abi al-Dunya, *Kitab Dhamm al-Dunya*, in *Mawsuʿat Rasaʾil*, 2:69, excerpt no. 130; al-Ghazali, *Ihyaʾ*, 4:320 (Asin, p. 414, no. 86; Mansur, no. 168; Robson, p. 73); Ibn ʿAsakir, *Sirat*, p. 130, nos. 114, 115; Ibn al-Jawzi, *Dhamm al-Hawa*, p. 64; and al-Damiri, *Hayat al-Hayawan al-Kubra*, 1:229.

If the question addressed to Jesus in this saying is an allusion to his entry into Jerusalem on Palm Sunday, the answer that Jesus gives has no bearing on that event but is the answer of an ascetic totally preoccupied with God.

31 Jesus said to the disciples, "Truly I say to you, you desire neither this world nor the next." They said, "Prophet of God, explain this matter to us, for we used to think that we desired one of them." He said, "Had you desired this world, you would have obeyed the Lord of the world, who holds the keys of its treasures in His hands. Had you desired the other world, you would have obeyed the Lord who owns it, and He would have given it to you. But you want neither the one nor the other."

Ahmad ibn Hanbal (d. 241/855), *al-Zuhd,* pp. 94–95 (no. 310).

The phrase "Truly I say to you" is a conscious imitation of the speaking style of Jesus, lending authority to the saying. The reference to man's desiring neither this world nor the next is an echo of the Qur'anic view of man as essentially fickle, unstable, oscillating between diverse choices and unable to make up his mind; see, e.g., Qur'an 3:152; 4:137; 17:11; 30:7.

32 Jesus said, "Why do I not observe in you the best of worship?" They said, "What is the best of worship, Spirit of God?" He said, "Humility before God."

Ahmad ibn Hanbal (d. 241/855), *al-Zuhd,* p. 95 (no. 312).

Humility before God is the most essential aspect of worship, as opposed to *kibr,* or pride, a prominent Qur'anic sin. In the Qur'an, some Christians are commended for their humility and for their lack of *kibr;* see Qur'an 5:82.

33 Jesus said, "Place your treasures in heaven, for the heart of man is where his treasure is."

Ahmad ibn Hanbal (d. 241/855), *al-Zuhd,* p. 95 (no. 313). Cf. Ibn Abi al-Dunya, *Kitab Dhamm al-Dunya,* in *Mawsu'at Rasa'il,* 2:25, excerpt no. 31; Ibn 'Asakir, *Sirat,* p. 184, no. 218; Ibn 'Arabi, *al-Futuhat al-Makkiyya,* 2:812 (Asin, p. 583, no. 192; Mansur, no. 223; Robson, p. 60).

Although this is a verbatim translation of a Gospel saying, it is included here because of its historical interest, being an early example of Muslim access either to a Gospel translated into Arabic or to a lectionary. For further details, see the sources listed in Note 29 to the Introduction.

34 Satan said to Jesus when he placed him in Jerusalem, "You claim to raise the dead. If you can truly do so, ask God to turn this mountain to bread." Jesus said, "Do all people live from bread?" Satan said, "If you are what you claim to be, jump from this place, for the angels will receive you." Jesus said, "God ordered me not to put myself to the test, for I do not know whether He will save me or not."

Ahmad ibn Hanbal (d. 241/855), *al-Zuhd,* pp. 95–96 (no. 314). Cf. Ibn al-Jawzi, *Kitab al-Adhkiya*, p. 37 (variant) (Mansur, no. 212).

In the Arabic original, this story is narrated by "a monk," conceivably to lend it authenticity. It is yet another instance of a story with a Gospel core—the tale of the temptation in the desert—but with an Islamic "twist" in the very last phrase, "for I do not know whether he will save me or not." This appears to be the work of the Muslim editor, who once again intervenes to underline the human helplessness of Jesus.

35 The disciples failed to find their prophet, so they went out to seek him and found him walking upon water. One of them said to him, "Prophet of God, shall we walk toward you?" "Yes," he replied. As the disciple put one foot forward and then the next, he sank. Jesus said, "Stretch forth your hand, you man of little faith. If the son of Adam had a grain or atom's weight of faith, he would walk upon water."

Ahmad ibn Hanbal (d. 241/855), *al-Zuhd*, p. 96 (no. 315). Cf. Ibn Abi al-Dunya, *Kitab al-Yaqin*, in *Mawsu'at Rasa'il*, 1:22–23, excerpt no. 11; Ibn 'Asakir, *Sirat*, p. 116, no. 94; (Cf. Asin, p. 568, no. 160; Mansur, no. 58; Robson, pp. 90–91 [variant]).

A Gospel miracle. It is devoid of personal or place names, as is the norm in the Muslim gospel. The reasons for this anonymity are not entirely clear but may perhaps be related to the equally impersonal narratives of Jesus found in the Qur'an.

36 Jesus used to say, "Charity does not mean doing good to him who does good to you, for this is to return good for good. Charity means that you should do good to him who does you harm."

Ahmad ibn Hanbal (d. 241/855), *al-Zuhd*, p. 96 (no. 317) and p. 142 (no. 469). Cf. Ibn 'Asakir, *Sirat*, p. 155, no. 166.

A recasting of Matthew 5:46.

37 God revealed to Jesus: "O Jesus, I have granted you the love of the poor and mercy toward them. You love them, and they love you and accept you as their spiritual guide and leader, and you accept them as companions and followers. These are two traits of character. Know that whoever meets me on Judgment Day with these two character traits has met me with the purest of works and the ones most beloved by me."

Ahmad ibn Hanbal (d. 241/855), *al-Zuhd*, p. 97 (no. 320).

This is another divine Hadith; see commentary on Saying 25, above. The description of Jesus as "spiritual guide" (Arabic *imam*) of the poor is a purely Islamic sobriquet and serves to single him out from other prophets in the Islamic tradition. The word "poor" (Arabic *masakin*) was also applied to early groups of Muslim ascetics and Sufis, and may indicate an early instance of the link which was later to become very strong between the Sufis and Jesus. The Sufis adopted Jesus as one of their major spiritual heroes. The "two traits of character" are love of the poor and mercy toward them.

Very similar words are addressed by Muhammad to ʿAli; see Ibn Abiʾl Hadid, *Sharh Nahj al-Balagha,* 11:232.

38

38 Whenever the Hour was mentioned, Jesus used to cry out in anguish like a woman.

Ahmad ibn Hanbal (d. 241/855), *al-Zuhd,* p. 97 (no. 321).

See Saying 6, above. Jesus wailing like a woman underlines his helplessness, distancing him further from divinity. In the Qurʾan, the Hour is known only to God; see Qurʾan 7:187.

39

39 Jesus met John and said to him, "Admonish me." He said, "Avoid feeling anger." He said, "This I cannot do." He said, "Do not own any wealth." He said, "As for this—it is possible."

Ahmad ibn Hanbal (d. 241/855), *al-Zuhd,* p. 97 (no. 322). Cf. al-Ghazali, *Ihyaʾ,* 3:161 (slight variation) (Asin, p. 366, no. 30; Mansur, no. 115; Robson, p. 64).

See Saying 18, above. This exchange further emphasizes the human failings of Jesus. He is incapable of restraining his anger, although willing not to own any wealth.

40 Jesus passed by, calling out in obedience to God: "Here I am, your slave, son of your slave woman, daughter of your slave." Before him passed seventy prophets, riding camels with halters made of fibers, until they prayed in the mosque of Khayf.

Ahmad ibn Hanbal (d. 241/855), *al-Zuhd,* pp. 97–98 (no. 324).

This is a curious story but it should be recalled that Jesus, like all prophets before him, was of course a Muslim and thus performed the pilgrimage among other Muslim rites, these last being primordial; see, for example, Ibn Qutayba, *'Uyun,* 2:290. On Moses performing the pilgrimage to the same mosque, see Ibn Babuya, *'Ilal,* 2:104. The mosque of Khayf is in Mina, outside Mecca. Halters made of palm-tree fibers were used by delegations paying homage to Muhammad; see Ibn Hisham, *Sira,* 4:244. This may suggest that earlier prophets were, so to speak, paying homage to the last and greatest of their line. The number seventy is frequently met with in both biblical and Islamic contexts—e.g., the seventy disciples of Jesus in Luke 10:1, as well as the seventy sects into which Islam will be divided in Hadith.

41 Jesus said, "O Disciples, which of you can build a house upon the waves of the sea?" They said, "Spirit of God, who can do that?" He said, "Beware the world and do not make it your abode."

Ahmad ibn Hanbal (d. 241/855), *al-Zuhd,* p. 98 (no. 325). Cf. Ibn Abi al-Dunya, *Kitab Dhamm al-Dunya,* in *Mawsu'at Rasa'il,* 2:156, excerpt no. 370; al-Ghazali, *Ihya',* 3:201 (Asin, p. 373, no. 40; Mansur, no. 124; Robson, p. 67).

An echo of Matthew 7:24–27, but here the parable is once again transformed into a direct rhetorical question. The moral is thus made explicit.

42 Jesus used to say, "Truly I say to you, to eat wheat bread, to drink pure water, and to sleep upon dunghills with the dogs more than suffices him who wishes to inherit paradise."

Ahmad ibn Hanbal (d. 241/855), *al-Zuhd*, p. 98 (no. 326). Cf. Ibn Qutayba, *'Uyun al-Akhbar*, 2:363; Ibn Abi al-Dunya, *Kitab Dhamm al-Dunya*, in *Mawsu'at Rasa'il*, 2:75, excerpt no. 138; Ikhwan al-Safa', *Rasa'il Ikhwan al-Safa'*, 3:34; and al-Ghazali, *Ihya'*, 4:180 (Asin, p. 400, no. 70; Mansur, no. 152; Robson, p. 70 [shorter version]).

Among modern educated Muslims, this is perhaps Jesus' best-known saying. Cf. the two later versions of it, Sayings 67 and 113, below. This is the ascetic ideal at its most austere. The world as a dunghill is also an image employed by Muhammad; see Ibn Abi al-Dunya, *Kitab Dhamm al-Dunya*, 2:21, excerpt no. 19.

43 Jesus said, "It is of no use to you to come to know what you did not know, so long as you do not act in accordance with what you already know. Too much knowledge only increases pride if you do not act in accordance with it."

Ahmad ibn Hanbal (d. 241/855), *al-Zuhd*, p. 98 (no. 327). Cf. al-Ghazali, *Ihya'*, 1:69–70 (shorter version) (Asin, p. 353, no. 9; Robson, p. 43).

Knowledge *('ilm)* and Act *('amal)* are frequently coupled in early works of Adab, asceticism, and so forth. For a Gospel parallel, see Matthew 5:19. Some early Hadith scholars also adopted the view that amassing knowledge (e.g., of Hadith) is useless or even dangerous unless accompanied by good works *(a'mal);* see, e.g., Ibn 'Abd al-Barr, *Jami' Bayan al-'Ilm*, 2:4ff. Other sayings by Jesus make the same point. Many similar sayings are also attributed to

Muhammad, 'Ali, and other Muslim figures. See also, for example, *Pirkey Aboth*, in Hertz, *Sayings of the Fathers*, p. 51, no. 22.

44 Jesus said, "Time revolves around three days: a yesterday which has passed away and during which you have been admonished, a today which supplies your needs, and a tomorrow in which you do not know what is in store for you. All matters revolve around three things: a thing whose rightness has become apparent to you and which you must follow, a thing whose evil has become apparent to you and which you must shun, and a thing which appears uncertain to you and which you must defer to God."

Ahmad ibn Hanbal (d. 241/855), *al-Zuhd*, p. 98 (no. 328). Cf. al-Jahiz, *al-Bayan*, 2:35; al-Mawardi, *Adab*, p. 127; al-Ghazali, *Ihya'*, 4:389; Ibn 'Asakir, *Sirat*, p. 158, no. 171 (Asin, p. 420, no. 96; Mansur, no. 178; Robson, p. 49 [the second part]).

The theme of time divided into days is found in Islamic works of Adab, asceticism, and *wasaya* (testaments), where it is sometimes ascribed to pre-Islamic sages. See, e.g., Ahmad Zaki Safwat, *Jamharat Khutab al-'Arab* (Beirut, 1985), pp. 119–120, 122.

45 Jesus said, "Console me, for my heart is soft and I hold myself in low esteem."

Ahmad ibn Hanbal (d. 241/855), *al-Zuhd*, p. 98 (no. 329). Cf. Ibn 'Asakir, *Sirat*, p. 71, no. 60.

An echo, perhaps, of Matthew 11:29. The human weaknesses of Jesus are, once again, to the fore.

46 Christ said, "Whoever has learned, acted, and imparted knowledge—he is the one who is called great in the kingdom of heaven."

Ahmad ibn Hanbal (d. 241/855), *al-Zuhd*, pp. 98–99 (no. 330). Cf. Ibn ʿAbd al-Barr, *Jamiʿ*, 1:124, al-Ghazali, *Ihyaʾ*, 1:17 (Asin, p. 349, no. 1; Mansur, no. 89; Robson, p. 42); Ibn ʿAsakir, *Sirat*, p. 186, nos. 221ff.; al-Abshihi, *al-Mustatraf*, 1:19.

See Saying 43, above. The expression "great in the kingdom of heaven" is of course derived from the Gospels. See, e.g., the dispute over who is the greatest, in Luke 22:24; and in Matthew 5:19, 18:1–4. For "imparted knowledge" I read ʿ*allama*, although ʿ*alima*, "acquired knowledge," is also possible.

47 Jesus was asked, "How can you walk on water?" He replied, "Through certainty of faith." He was told, "We too have certain faith." Jesus asked, "Do you believe that stones, mud, and gold are all equal in your sight?" "No," they replied. He said (or I think he said), "They are all the same in my sight."

Ahmad ibn Hanbal (d. 241/855), *al-Zuhd*, p. 99 (no. 331). Cf. al-Makki, *Qut*, 1:263 (fuller version) (Mansur, no. 29); Asin, p. 378, no. 49; Mansur, no. 58, Robson, p. 69 (variant and shorter version). See also Ibn Abi al-Dunya, *Kitab al-Yaqin*, in *Mawsuʿat Rasaʾil*, 1:37, excerpt no. 40; al-Qushayri, *al-Risala*, p. 118 (partial; attributed to Muhammad).

See Saying 35, above. The story of Jesus walking on the waters in Matthew 14:22ff., is recast here into a question-and-answer form in order to make explicit the practical meaning of faith, with its corollary: despising the world.

48 A man came to Jesus and said, "Teacher of goodness, teach me something that you know and I do not, that benefits me and does you no harm." Jesus asked, "What would that be?" The man said, "How can a servant be truly pious before God?" Jesus replied, "The matter is easy. You must truly love God in your heart and work in His service, exerting all your effort and strength, and be merciful toward the people of your race as you show mercy to yourself." He said, "Teacher of goodness, who are the people of my race?" Jesus replied, "All the children of Adam. And that which you do not wish done to you, do not do to others. In this way you will be truly pious before God."

Ahmad ibn Hanbal (d. 241/855), *al-Zuhd*, p. 99 (no. 332).

This is essentially a paraphrase of Matthew 22:34–40.

49 Jesus used to prepare food for his followers, then call them to eat and wait upon them, saying: "This is what you must do for the poor."

Ahmad ibn Hanbal (d. 241/855), *al-Zuhd*, p. 99 (no. 333).

For Jesus as a patron of the poor, see Saying 37, above. It is possible that this is a Muslim retelling of the Last Supper in Matthew 26:18ff., but without the sacrament of the Eucharist.

50 When Jesus sent out his messengers to resurrect the dead, he would say to them: "Say this and that, and if you find a trembling and a tear, then at that point pray."

Ahmad ibn Hanbal (d. 241/855), *al-Zuhd*, p. 99 (no. 334).

The instructions to the disciples are in Matthew 10:5ff. Shivers and tears are frequently the mark of Sufis and ascetics in early Islam; hence, here, a sign of recognition of true believers.

51 Jesus said to his disciples, "In truth I say to you"—and he often used to say, "In truth I say to you"—"those among you who sorrow most in misfortune are the most attached to this world."

Ahmad ibn Hanbal (d. 241/855), *al-Zuhd*, p. 100 (no. 338). Cf. Abu Nuʿaym, *Hilyat*, 4:67 (Mansur, no. 67).

The imitation of the speaking style of Jesus is again made explicit. It is difficult to pin down any specific origins for this saying, which appears to reflect a moral stance common to many religious and ascetic traditions. It could even have Stoic parallels. In any case, the saying reinforces a Muslim image of Jesus already more fiercely ascetic than the Jesus of the Gospels.

52 The disciples said, "O Jesus, who are 'the friends of God Almighty upon whom no fear shall come nor shall they grieve?'" Jesus replied, "They are the ones who look into the heart of this world while the rest of mankind looks at its surface, who look forward to the end of the world while the rest of mankind looks at the fleeting present. They kill of the world what they fear might kill them and abandon what they know will abandon them. Hence, what once they considered of much worldly account they now consider negligible. When they make mention of it, this is only in passing, and their joy at what they gain from it is sadness. They reject every chance of worldly gain and disdain every chance of worldly glory without just cause. For them, the world is grown old and tattered but they do not renew it. It has fallen into ruin around them, but they do not rebuild it. It has died in their hearts but they do not resurrect it. They destroy it in order to rebuild their afterlife with it. They sell it in exchange for that which lasts. They reject it and are thus the truly happy in it. They look at its people, fallen dead and disfigured upon the earth, and renew the mention of death and kill the mention of life. They love God and the mention of God, seeking His light and shining through His light. Wonders are related of them and they relate wondrous things. The Book of God is known through them and they act in accordance with it. The Book of God makes mention of them and they make mention of the Book. Knowledge of the Book comes through them and through it they themselves acquire knowledge. They expect no gain greater than what they have gained, no peace other than what they hope for, no fear other than what they shun."

Ahmad ibn Hanbal (d. 241/855), al-Zuhd, pp. 100–101 (no. 339). Cf. al-Jahiz, al-Bayan, 3:140; Ibn ʿAbd Rabbihi, al-ʿIqd, 3:144 (Mansur, no. 13); Abu Nuʿaym, Hilyat, 1:10 (Mansur, no. 63); al-Mawardi, Adab, p. 112; Ibn ʿAsakir, Sirat, p. 199, no. 245.

The term "friends of God" (Arabic *awliya' Allah*) was a technical term for early ascetics and Sufis. The phrase "the friends . . . grieve" is from Qur'an 10:62. Jesus is thus made to comment on this verse of the Qur'an; see, e.g., Saying 9, above. In the Arabic, the balanced phrases, the contrasts, the parallelisms all indicate a great deal of care in the literary crafting of this saying, in order to make the eloquence worthy of a prophet who is, in the Qur'an, a Word from God. Among his other attributes, Jesus is an eloquent prophet. The "ruin" theme, the "killing of desire" theme, and the "appearance and reality" theme are all well represented in the Muslim gospel.

53

John and Jesus met and John said, "Ask God's forgiveness for me, for you are better than me." Jesus replied: "You are better than me. I pronounced peace upon myself, whereas God pronounced peace upon you." God recognized the merit of them both.

Ahmad ibn Hanbal (d. 241/855), *al-Zuhd*, p. 122 (no. 392).

Another Jesus-and-John story, set this time in a Qur'anic context. The phrase "I pronounced peace upon myself" is a reference to Qur'an 19:33, whereas it is God who pronounces peace upon John, as in Qur'an 19:15. The saying ends with divine reconciliation and peace upon them both because of their humility.

54

A man who had committed adultery was brought to Jesus, who ordered them to stone him. Jesus said, "But no one should stone him who has committed what he has committed." They let the stones fall from their hands, all except John son of Zachariah.

Ahmad ibn Hanbal (d. 241/855), *al-Zuhd*, p. 122 (no. 394).

This is a version of the Gospel story describing the stoning of an adulterous woman, transformed here into a man. The gender transformation is not entirely clear, nor is the ending, unless the object is to emphasize the sinlessness of prophets, in this case John, who is also honored in the previous story.

55 Jesus said, "What God loves most are the strangers." He was asked, "Who are the strangers?" He replied, "Those who flee [the world] with their faith [intact]. They shall be gathered together with Jesus on the Day of Judgment."

Ahmad ibn Hanbal (d. 241/855), *al-Zuhd*, p. 124 (no. 402). Cf. al-Ghazali, *Ihya'*, 3:271; and al-Suhrawardi, *'Awarif al-Ma'arif*, 1:265 (in both, Muhammad instead of Jesus).

On the phrase "Those who flee . . . intact," see the commentary to Saying 11, above. The man of faith as an alien is a frequent image in Near Eastern Christian literature. It underlies the anchorite way of life. Jesus is now their patron, although the Jesus of the Gospels is in no sense an anchorite. The Islamic intertext, so to speak, is a well-known Hadith of Muhammad in which he says that Islam began its life as an "alien" *(gharib)* and will end it as an "alien." Because the saying is also ascribed to a famous early Muslim figure, the saintly 'Abdallah ibn 'Umar (d. 73/693), there may also be a hidden political message here—namely, the attitude of the believer in times of civil discord. The true believer should escape such discord "with his faith intact."

56 Jesus said, "Slaves of this world, instead of dispensing alms, be merciful to those whom you treat unjustly."

Ahmad ibn Hanbal (d. 241/855), *al-Zuhd*, p. 141 (no. 466).

This saying may echo the teaching of Jesus on almsgiving, in Matthew 6:1ff.

57 Jesus said, "Leave people alone. Be at ease with people and ill at ease with yourself. Do not seek to earn their praises or merit their rebuke. Perform what you have been commanded to do."

Ahmad ibn Hanbal (d. 241/855), *al-Zuhd*, p. 142 (no. 467). Cf. Ibn Abi al-Dunya, *al-Samt*, pp. 615–616 (no. 743); and Miskawayh, *al-Hikma al-Khalida*, p. 180.

Being at ease with other people and ill at ease with oneself is an ethical sentiment found in the pre-Socratics.

58 God revealed to Jesus: "Make me your sole concern. Make me as your treasure for your afterlife. Trust in me and I shall suffice you. Do not take anyone else to be your lord, or I shall abandon you."

Ahmad ibn Hanbal (d. 241/855), *al-Zuhd*, p. 142 (no. 468).

This is another divine revelation (*hadith qudsi*). It sounds like a prayer, couched in a terse Adab style.

59 Jesus set out to visit a brother of his. He was met by a man who said to him, "Your brother has died." So Jesus turned back. When the daughters of his brother heard that Jesus had turned back, they came to him and said, "Prophet of God, your turning back from us is harder to bear than the death of our father." He said, "Go forth and show me his grave." They went forth until they showed Jesus his grave. He called out to him in a loud voice, and the dead man appeared, his hair having turned gray. Jesus asked, "Are you not So-and-So?" "Yes," the man replied. "Then what is it that I see has happened to you?" "I heard your voice and imagined it to be the Great Scream [of Judgment Day]," the man replied. All the while, the man's wife saw and heard what Jesus had done. She said, "Blessed is the belly that carried you and the breasts from which you fed." Jesus said, "Blessed is he whom God has taught His Book and who dies without having become haughty."

Ahmad ibn Hanbal (d. 241/855), *al-Zuhd*, pp. 142–143 (no. 470). Cf. idem, pp. 96–97 (no. 318) and p. 97 (no. 319); Ibn Abi al-Dunya, *Kitab man ʿAsha baʿda al-Mawt*, in *Mawsuʿat Rasaʾil*, 3:53, no. 59 (the dead man is Sam son of Noah); al-Samarqandi, *Tanbih*, p. 10 (slightly variant); Ibn ʿAsakir, *Sirat*, p. 90, no. 80, and p. 152, nos. 160, 161 (variant) (Asin, p. 552, no. 131; Mansur, no. 31; Robson, p. 109); and al-Ghazali, *Ihyaʾ*, 3:328 (partial) (Asin, p. 390, no. 56; Mansur, no. 138; Robson, p. 46).

The Gospel context might be Luke 7:1–17 and 11:27, or John 11. The Islamic elements here are the *Sayhu*, or Great Scream, which Qurʾan 11:67 says will bring the world to its end, during which period Jesus will play a major eschatological role. To the blessings of the woman, Jesus responds by referring to the Book of God, the heavenly prototype of revelation, referred to in Qurʾan 85:22 as the "Well-Protected Tablet" *(al-Lawh al-Mahfuz)*, from which all divine revelations descend.

60 Jesus said, "I toppled the world upon its face and sat upon its back. I have no child that might die, no house that might fall into ruin." They said to him, "Will you not take a house for yourself?" He replied, "Build me a house in the path of the flood." They said, "Such will not last." They also asked Jesus, "Will you not take a wife?" He replied, "What do I do with a wife that might die?"

Ahmad ibn Hanbal (d. 241/855), *al-Zuhd*, p. 143 (no. 471). Cf. Ibn Abi al-Dunya, *Kitab Dhamm al-Dunya*, in *Mawsuʿat Rasaʾil*, 2:26–27, excerpt nos. 32, 33, 34; Ibn ʿAbd Rabbihi, *al-ʿIqd*, 3:173 (partial); Ibn ʿAsakir, *Sirat*, p. 141, no. 136 (variant) (Asin, p. 543, no. 118; Mansur, no. 17; Robson, pp. 73–74).

The anti-marriage sentiment, though incongruent with early Islamic ethics, is nevertheless not uncommon in certain Sufi writers—e.g., in Abu Talib al-Makki (d. 386/996).

For the question about a house, see also Sayings 110 and 302, below. In Arabic wisdom literature, a similar question is put to the Greek philosopher Diogenes; see al-Mubashshir ibn Fatik, *Mukhtar al-Hikam*, p. 75: "He was asked, 'Why do you not acquire a house where you can be at ease?' He answered, 'A house is needed because one can feel at ease in it, but I am at ease because I do not have a house.'"

61 Jesus said, "The greatest sin is love of the world. Women are the ropes of Satan. Wine is the key to every evil."

Ahmad ibn Hanbal (d. 241/855), *al-Zuhd*, p. 143 (no. 472). Cf. Ibn Abi al-Dunya, *Kitab Dhamm al-Dunya*, in *Mawsu'at Rasa'il*, 2:170, excerpt no. 416 (Malik ibn Dinar instead of Jesus).

As a "Muslim" prophet, Jesus could be expected to pronounce wine-drinking reprehensible. The same saying is also attributed to Malik ibn Dinar, a Basran ascetic (d. circa 130/748).

62 Jesus used to say, "Love of the world is the root of all sin. Worldly wealth is a great sickness." They asked, "What is that sickness?" He said, "Its owner cannot avoid pride and self-esteem." They asked, "Suppose he avoided this?" Jesus replied, "The cultivation of wealth distracts man from the mention of God."

Ahmad ibn Hanbal (d. 241/855), *al-Zuhd*, p. 143 (no. 473). Cf. al-Jahiz, *al-Bayan*, 3:191; al-Makki, *Qut*, 1:263; al-Raghib al-Isfahani, *Muhadarat al-Udaba'*, 1:512; Ibn 'Asakir, *Sirat*, p. 145, no. 146.

This question-and-answer saying deploring wealth, as well as the following saying, have clear Gospel echoes.

63 Jesus said, "In truth I say to you, the folds of heaven are empty of the rich. It is easier for a camel to pass through the eye of a needle than for a rich man to enter paradise."

Ahmad ibn Hanbal (d. 241/855), *al-Zuhd*, p. 143 (no. 474).

The analogy of the camel and the eye of the needle is also found in Qur'an 7:40, one of a small number of such Gospel images reproduced verbatim in the Qur'an.

64 Jesus said to the disciples, "O disciples, do not cast pearls before swine, for the swine can do nothing with them. Do not impart wisdom to one who does not desire it, for wisdom is more precious than pearls and whoever rejects wisdom is worse than a swine."

Ahmad ibn Hanbal (d. 241/855), *al-Zuhd*, p. 144 (no. 477). Cf. al-Ghazali, *Ihya'*, 1:63 (slight variation) (Asin, p. 350, no. 4; Mansur, no. 92; Robson, pp. 42–43).

Here, too, the original Gospel saying is made explicit, its implications fully drawn out.

65 Christ said, "If you desire to devote yourselves entirely to God and to be the light of the children of Adam, forgive those who have done you evil, visit the sick who do not visit you, be kind to those who are unkind to you, and lend to those who do not repay you."

Ahmad ibn Hanbal (d. 241/855), *al-Zuhd*, pp. 144–145 (no. 480). Cf. Abu Nu'aym, *Hilyat*, 5:238–239 (Mansur, no. 73).

Various Gospel commandments are conflated here. See Matthew 5:16, 42.

66 Jesus was walking by the Pass of Afiq with one of his disciples. A man crossed their path and prevented them from proceeding, saying, "I will not let you pass until I have struck each of you a blow." They tried to dissuade him but he refused. Jesus said, "Here is my cheek. Slap it." The man slapped it and let him pass. He then said to the disciple, "I will not let you pass until I have slapped you too." The disciple refused. When Jesus saw this, he offered him his other cheek. He slapped it and allowed both to go. Jesus then said, "O God, if this is pleasing to You, your pleasure has reached me. If it does not please You, You are more worthy of righteous anger."

Ahmad ibn Hanbal (d. 241/855), *al-Zuhd*, p. 145 (no. 481).

A curious reworking of the Gospel commandment to turn the other cheek. The Pass of Afiq is said by classical Arab geographers to be a mountain pass leading down into the Ghawr Depression of the Jordan. In some Muslim traditions, Afiq is also the place where Jesus will kill the Anti-Christ at the end of time; see Ibn ʿAsakir, *Sirat*, p. 266, no. 344. The words that Jesus finally addresses to God justify his self-restraint.

67 Jesus said to the disciples, "I would have you eat barley bread and escape from the world in safety and peace. Truly I say to you, the sweetness of this world is the bitterness of the world beyond, and the bitterness of this world is the sweetness of the world beyond. The true worshipers of God are not those who live in comfort. Truly I say to you, the most evil among you in act is a scholar who loves this world and prefers it to right conduct. Could he do so, he would have all people act the way he does."

Ahmad ibn Hanbal (d. 241/855), *al-Zuhd*, p. 145 (no. 482). Cf. Ibn Abi al-Dunya, *Kitab Dhamm al-Dunya*, in *Mawsuʿat Rasaʾil*, 2:153, excerpt no. 361; al-Makki, *Qut*, 1:256 (partial); Ibn ʿAsakir, *Sirat*, p. 165, no. 184.

Barley bread was the food of the poor. The injunction about eating barley bread occurs in several other sayings; see 113, 136, and 146, below. A similar advice is ascribed to the Greek philosopher Democritus; see G. S. Kirk, J. E. Raven, and M. Schofield, *The Presocratic Philosophers,* 2nd ed. (Cambridge: Cambridge University Press, 1995), p. 433, note 1. The attack on worldly scholars is resumed in this saying and made even more vehement.

68 Jesus used to say, "I preach to you so that you may learn. I do not preach to you so that you may grow conceited."

Ahmad ibn Hanbal (d. 241/855), *al-Zuhd,* p. 145 (no. 483). Cf. Ibn ʿAbd al-Barr, *Mukhtasar Jamiʿ Bayan al-ʿIlm,* p. 100 (fuller version) (Asin, p. 567, no. 156; Mansur, no. 87; Robson, p. 57).

The conceit of scholars is a frequent target in the Muslim gospel.

69 Christ said, "Not as I will but as You will. Not as I desire but as You desire."

Ahmad ibn Hanbal (d. 241/855), *al-Zuhd,* pp. 145–146 (no. 484).

These words may be a paraphrase of Matthew 26:39.

70 No word spoken to Jesus was dearer to him than "that poor man."

Ahmad ibn Hanbal (d. 241/855), *al-Zuhd,* p. 146 (no. 485). Cf. al-Makki, *Qut,* 1:263; and al-Ghazali, *Ihya',* 4:191–192 (fuller version) (Asin, p. 402, no. 73; Mansur, no. 155; Robson, p. 71).

See Sayings 37 and 49, above.

71 The disciples said, "Christ of God, look at the house of God—how beautiful it is!" He replied, "Amen, Amen. Truly I say to you, God will not leave one stone of this mosque upon another but will destroy it utterly because of the sins of its people. God does nothing with gold, silver, or these stones. More dear to God than all these are the pure in heart. Through them, God builds up the earth, or else destroys it if these hearts are other than pure."

Ahmad ibn Hanbal (d. 241/855), *al-Zuhd*, p. 146 (no. 486). Cf. al-Ghazali, *Ihya'*, 3:396 (Asin, p. 392, no. 62; Mansur, no. 144; Robson, p. 47).

The "temple" of the Gospel saying in Matthew 24:1 here becomes a "mosque." See Saying 11, above.

72 Jesus said, "Satan accompanies the world. His deceit accompanies wealth. His seductiveness accompanies caprice. His ultimate power accompanies the appetites."

Ahmad ibn Hanbal (d. 241/855), *al-Zuhd*, p. 146 (no. 487). Cf. Abu Nu'aym, *Hilyat*, 5:252; Ibn 'Asakir, *Sirat*, p. 148, no. 151 (Mansur, no. 75).

73 Jesus used to say, "O disciples, do not seek the world by destroying yourselves; seek your salvation by abandoning what is in the world. Naked you came into the world and naked you shall depart. Do not seek what sustenance tomorrow may bring, but let each day's sustenance suffice and tomorrow will bring its own concerns. Pray God to bring you sustenance day by day."

Ahmad ibn Hanbal (d. 241/855), *al-Zuhd*, p. 146 (no. 488). Cf. Ibn Abi al-Dunya, *Kitab Dhamm al-Dunya*, in *Mawsuʿat Rasaʾil*, 2:68, excerpt no. 128.

The nakedness saying is from Job 1:21. The rest is a recasting of Matthew 6:34.

74 Jesus used to say, "My God, I can no longer rid myself of that which I hate, nor can I attain the benefit of what I desire. The matter is now in another's hand, and I have become accountable for my work. There is no poor man poorer than me. Do not let my enemy gloat over me. Do not let my friend turn against me. Do not let my faith be my ruin, and do not set over me one who is unmerciful toward me."

Ahmad ibn Hanbal (d. 241/855), *al-Zuhd*, p. 147 (no. 490). Cf. ibid., pp. 146–147 (no. 489); Miskawayh, *al-Hikma*, p. 131; al-Ghazali, *Ihyaʾ*, 1:324 (Asin, p. 355, no. 11; Mansur, no. 98; Robson, p. 81); Ibn ʿAsakir, *Sirat*, p. 122, no. 103.

The helplessness of Jesus is emphasized. There are echoes here of the complaints to be found in, e.g., Job or Micah. A very similar saying is attributed to the eighth-century scholar-ascetic Bakr al-Muzani in Ibn Saʿd, *Tabaqat*, 7:210–211.

75 The Israelites chided Jesus for his poverty. He said to them, "Wretched people, you have been led astray by riches. Have you ever seen anyone who disobeyed God in seeking poverty?"

Ahmad ibn Hanbal (d. 241/855), *Kitab al-Wara'*, no. 228. Cf. al-Jahiz, *al-Bayan*, 3: 155.

The admonition about the lure of riches may echo Matthew 13:22.

76 As Jesus was on his wanderings, the heavens suddenly opened and the rain poured down, so he took refuge in a cave. There he found a shepherd, so he moved away from him and took refuge in a thicket. There he found a lion crouching. Jesus raised his head and said, "My Lord, you have given everyone a refuge except me." God revealed to Jesus: "O Jesus, your refuge is with me, under the shadow of my throne and in the abode of my mercy. I shall marry you to a thousand comely maidens and feed people for a thousand years at your wedding. On the Day of Judgment, a crier shall announce: 'Come and attend the wedding of the ascetic friend of God.'"

Ahmad ibn Hanbal (d. 241/855), *al-Wara'*, no. 318. Cf. Ibn 'Asakir, *Sirat*, p. 134, no. 121; al-Antaki, *Tazyin al-Aswaq*, 1:71; and al-Zabidi, *Ithaf*, 8:87 (variant) (Asin, p. 370, no. 37; Robson, p. 66).

For possible origins of this story, see the comments by Asin, who, however, mistranslates the saying in two places, reading 'arsh (throne) for 'urs (wedding ceremony).

Are we meant to think a little about why a shepherd and why a lion? Are they simply denizens of the wilderness, companions of Jesus on his travels? God's words to Jesus, on the other hand, mean that his asceticism in this world will be amply rewarded in the next. The reward of asceticism is perfect accord with God's heavenly abode, which includes a divinely arranged wedding. Jesus will not be a bachelor forever. This is conceivably related to the preference for celibacy expressed by certain early ascetic-Sufi figures within a society that encouraged marriage and was afraid of the dangers of heresy implicit in extreme asceticism.

77 The day that Jesus was raised to heaven, he left behind nothing but a woolen garment, a slingshot, and two sandals.

Hannad ibn al-Sariyy (d. 243/857), *Kitab al-Zuhd*, no. 553. Cf. Ibn ʿAsakir, *Sirat*, p. 134, no. 122 (variant).

Hannad was an important and early collector of ascetic traditions. For information on his life and works, see the introduction to his edited writings, cited in the Bibliography.

This description of what Jesus left behind may echo Mark 6:7–9. This is an early account of the personal appearance and possessions of Jesus. The *midraʿa* was a woolen garment much favored by ascetics and Sufis. For a similar account of the worldly belongings of Egyptian desert Christian ascetics, see Ward, *The Sayings of the Desert Fathers*, pp. 18–19, no. 42.

78 Jesus used to eat the leaves of the trees, dress in hair shirts, and sleep wherever night found him. He had no child who might die, no house which might fall into ruin; nor did he save his lunch for his dinner or his dinner for lunch. He used to say, "Each day brings with it its own sustenance."

Hannad ibn al-Sariyy (d. 243/857), *al-Zuhd*, no. 559. Cf. Kalabadhi, *al-Taʿarruf li-Madhhab Ahl al-Tasawwuf*, p. 7; al-Ghazali, *Ihyaʾ*, 4:220 (partial); al-Suhrawardi, *ʿAwarif*, 2:249; (Asin, p. 405, no. 77; Mansur, no. 158; Robson, p. 71); Ibn ʿAsakir, *Sirat*, p. 124, nos. 108ff.

See Sayings 60 and 73, above. We have further details here of Jesus' daily life and habits. The theme of living from day to day echoes Matthew 6:25–34.

79 Christ came upon a group of people who were crying. He asked, "Why are these people crying?" He was told, "They are afraid of their sins." He said, "Abandon them and you will be forgiven."

Abu 'Uthman al-Jahiz (d. 255/868), *al-Bayan wa al-Tabyin*, 1:399 and 3:167. Cf. Ibn 'Abd Rabbihi, *al-'Iqd*, 2:268 (Mansur, no. 3); ibid., 3:181 (Asin, p. 543, no. 119; Mansur, no. 18; Robson, p. 52); and Miskawayh, *al-Hikma*, p. 153.

Jahiz is a towering literary figure of classical Arabic Islamic culture, with very wide interests in practically all the arts and sciences of his age. For information on his life and works, see *EI* 2.

Thus far, the sayings of Jesus have come mostly from two sources, Ibn al-Mubarak and Ibn Hanbal. The tone of these sayings and stories has been predominantly ascetic. This is not surprising, given the nature and interests of these sources. But the fierce asceticism—the almost antisocial character—of many of them will henceforth slowly be invaded by the spirit of Adab. Thus, more will be heard about ethical behavior, good manners, and social intercourse. A subtle change comes over the language of Jesus, which grows more flowery, metaphorical, epigrammatical. The ascetic dimension is not abandoned, but is now overlaid with a veneer of gentlemanly, civil deportment. Jesus becomes more like a Muslim Adib (a gentleman scholar, a sage), and loses some of his fierce asceticism.

In this story, Jesus rebukes groups that one might call penitents. In Islamic history, the Penitents *(al-Tawwabun)* were an early Shi'ite group who mourned their abandonment of 'Ali and his family. 'Ali, cousin and son-in-law of the Prophet, and the fourth caliph of Islam, was the focal point of loyalty and affection of the Shi'ites. There could be an indirect allusion to such groups here, since Jahiz was generally hostile to religious excesses, especially among the Shi'ites. There is also a certain irony in the words of Jesus—typical perhaps of a wit or satirist, or else of the apt answer of an Adib.

80

Christ passed by a group of Israelites who insulted him. Every time they spoke a word of evil, Christ answered with good. Simon the pure said to him, "Will you answer them with good each time they speak evil?" Christ said, "Each person spends of what he owns."

Abu 'Uthman al-Jahiz (d. 255/868), *al-Bayan*, 2:177. Cf. Ibn Qutayba, *'Uyun*, 2:370; Ibn 'Asakir, *Sirat*, p. 156, no. 169.

The context here is clearly one of good manners and courtesy. There may be echoes also of Matthew 5:22. The story ends with a *bon mot;* one can almost imagine Jesus smiling as he delivers it. Also noteworthy is that, around this time, more of the stories and sayings begin to include the names of other actors—e.g., Simon—perhaps to lend vividness to the narrative. The Arabic has *al-safi* ("the pure"), but this is most likely a mistake for *al-safa* ("the rock"), meaning Peter.

It may be worth noting that the Egyptian desert fathers commended the virtue of suffering insults as a means of humbling the soul. See Ward, *The Sayings of the Desert Fathers*, p. 69, no. 1.

81

Jesus was seen leaving the house of a prostitute. Someone said to him, "Spirit of God, what are you doing in the house of this woman?" "It is the sick that a physician visits," he replied.

Abu 'Uthman al-Jahiz (d. 255/868), *al-Bayan*, 3:140 (Asin, p. 537, no. 104; Mansur, no. 237; Robson, p. 50). Cf. Ibn Qutayba, *'Uyun*, 2:370.

See Matthew 9:12 and 21:31.

82 Jesus said, "The world is Satan's farm, and its people are his plowmen."

Abu 'Uthman al-Jahiz (d. 255/868), *al-Bayan*, 3:140–141. Cf. Ibn 'Abd Rabbihi, *al-'Iqd*, 3:143 (Asin, p. 543, no. 117; Mansur, no. 8, Robson, pp. 84–85).

The world as Satan's farm is an unusual image, although it may echo some of the Jesus parables.

83 Jesus said, "Woe unto you, slaves of this world! How your practices contradict your principles, and your whims your reason! Your words are a remedy which cures disease, but your actions are a disease which defies cure. You are not like the vine, which has fine leaves, tasty fruit, and is easy to reach, but are in truth like the acacia tree, which has few leaves, many thorns, and is difficult to reach! Woe unto you, slaves of this world! You have placed good works beneath your feet, [thinking] that they can be attained by whoever so wishes, and have placed this world far above your heads, [thinking] that it cannot be reached. You are neither pious slaves nor worthy freemen. Woe unto you, wage-earners of sin! You take your wages and spoil the work. You shall meet with what you most fear, for the Taskmaster will soon see the work you have spoilt and the wages you

have taken. Woe to you, debtors of evil! You begin with gifts before discharging your debt, you volunteer to perform what is superfluous but do not perform what you have been commanded to do. The owner of the debt will not accept gifts until his debt has been discharged."

Abu 'Uthman al-Jahiz (d. 255/868), *al-Bayan*, 3:157. Cf. Ibn 'Abd Rabbihi, *al-'Iqd*, 3:173 (Asin, p. 540, no. 110; Mansur, no. 15; Robson, p. 73).

The rebukes here are reminiscent of the rebukes addressed by Jesus to the Pharisees in Matthew 23:13ff. They are carefully constructed with rhyming and parallelisms. The Islamic elements are detected in technical terms like *nawafil* (superfluous acts, or acts of supererogation). The Pharisees of the Gospels become "slaves of the world."

84 Jesus said, "You work for this world, where you are provided for without working; whereas you do not work for the afterlife, where you will not be provided for except by working."

Abu 'Uthman al-Jahiz (d. 255/868), *al-Bayan*, 3:166. Cf. Ibn Abi al-Dunya, *Kitab Dhamm al-Dunya*, in *Mawsu'at Rasa'il*, 2:165, excerpt no. 401 (fuller version); Ibn 'Abd Rabbihi, *al-'Iqd*, 3:143 (Asin, p. 541, no. 113; Mansur, no. 11; Robson, p. 73); ibid., 3:209; al-Mawardi, *Adab*, p. 101; Ibn 'Asakir, *Sirat*, p. 195, no. 237.

This and the following are well-crafted sayings, typical of the Adab spirit and displaying elegant inversions of word order.

85 Christ said, "It is a sign of how trivial the world is to God that only in the world is He disobeyed, and only by forsaking the world can His bounty be attained."

Abu 'Uthman al-Jahiz (d. 255/868), *al-Bayan*, 3:166.

86 Jesus said to the disciples, "Man is created into this world in four stages, in three of which he feels secure and in the fourth of which he is ill-disposed and fears that God will forsake him. In the first stage, he is born in three darknesses: the darkness of the belly, the darkness of the womb, and the darkness of the placenta. God provides for him in the darkness of the cavity of the belly. When he is brought out from the darkness of the belly, he falls upon milk which he does not advance toward on foot or leg, or obtain with his hand or move strongly toward, but he is forced to it and rewarded with it until flesh and blood grows upon him. Weaned from milk, he falls upon the third stage: food provided by his parents, who earn it either lawfully or unlawfully. When his parents die, people take pity on him, one person feeding him, another giving him drink, another sheltering him, and another clothing him. When he falls upon the fourth stage and has grown strong and erect and has become a man, he fears that he will not be provided for, so he attacks people, betrays their trust, robs their belongings, and carries away their wealth, fearing that God Almighty might forsake him."

Abu 'Uthman al-Jahiz (d. 255/868), *al-Mahasin wa al-Addad*, pp. 82–83. Cf. Abu Hayyan, *al-Imta' wa al-Mu'anasa*, 2:127; and al-Bayhaqi, *al-Mahasin wa al-Masawi'*, p. 309. (Asin, p. 537, no. 105; Mansur, no. 236; Robson, pp. 50–51). Cf.

Ibn Abi al-Dunya, *Kitab al-Qana'a wa'l Ta'affuf*, in *Mawsu'at Rasa'il*, 1:57, excerpt no. 126; Ibn 'Asakir, *Sirat*, p. 170, no. 193.

An elaborate disquisition on the stages of man's life and the making of a criminal. The theme of life as stages is universal. Crime is
the product of despair at God's bounty.

87 God said to Jesus, "I shall send after you a religious community who, when I am generous to them,
give thanks and praise, and, when I withhold, are patient
and content, without their having any forbearance or
knowledge." Jesus asked, "But how can they do this, O
God, without forbearance or knowledge?" God replied,
"I grant them some of my own forbearance and knowledge."

(Asin, p. 601, no. 224; Mansur, no. 238.)

God addresses Jesus, and the community referred to is obviously
Islam. There is a passage in Matthew (23:34) in which Muslims
may have found a convenient reference to the coming of Muhammad—indeed, even to his Hegira, his emigration from Mecca to
Medinah. God privileges the Islamic community, with Jesus acting
as witness. The question that Jesus addresses to God may refer to
the pre-Islamic Arabian era, where virtues like forbearance *(hilm)*
and knowledge *('ilm)* were supposedly lacking. Hence the Islamic
epithet for that era: *Jahili*—that is, violent and blind.

88 Jesus was asked, "Which of your deeds is the
best?" He answered, "Leaving alone that which does not
concern me."

Abu 'Uthman al-Jahiz (d. 255/868), *Kitab Kitman al-Sirr*, 1:162. Cf. Abu Nu'aym, *Hilyat*, 1:227 (Mansur, no. 64).

89 God inspired Jesus to send out missionaries to the kings of the earth. He sent out his disciples. Those sent to nearby regions agreed to go, but those sent afar were loath to go, saying, "I do not speak the tongue of those to whom you have sent me." Jesus said, "O God, I ordered my disciples to do what You ordered me and they have disobeyed me." God revealed to him, saying, "I shall spare you this trouble." So God caused each disciple to speak the tongue of those to whom he was sent.

Ibn 'Abd al-Hakam (d. 257/870), *Kitab Futuh Misr*, p. 45.

Ibn 'Abd al-Hakam, historian of early Islamic Egypt, was a member of a distinguished family of Egyptian Hadith scholars and historians.

This story is a recasting of the mission of the Twelve (Matthew 10), with possible references to Pentecost (Acts 2:1–13). Here, however, the helplessness of Jesus is the cause for divine intervention.

90 Christ said to his followers: "If people appoint you as their heads, be like tails."

'Abdallah ibn Qutayba (d. 271/884), *'Uyun al-Akhbar*, 1:266.

Ibn Qutayba, a younger contemporary of Jahiz, was a renowned literary figure, anthologist, critic, and Hadith scholar, with very wide interests in history and in non-Muslim religions. His Jesus sayings and stories are important in the corpus as a whole. Thus, he appears to have been the earliest Muslim writer who actually quoted genuine Gospel sayings, but alongside non-Gospel materials, which are translated here.

There is no exact equivalent in the Gospels to this saying, although sentiments similar to it may be detected in (for example) Matthew 23:11–12 and 20:27. It is quite possible that a political message is being passed on, a reminder to Muslim rulers to behave with humility, as did the early caliphs. In point of fact, the image of the early Islamic period as a golden age was being formulated by the lawyers and historians of Ibn Qutayba's period, and Jesus is perhaps invoked to buttress this formulation.

91 Jesus met a man and asked him, "What are you doing?" "I am devoting myself to God," the man replied. Jesus asked, "Who is caring for you?" "My brother," replied the man. Jesus said, "Your brother is more devoted to God than you are."

ʿAbdallah ibn Qutayba (d. 271/884), ʿUyun, 1:327. Cf. Ibn ʿAbd Rabbihi, al-ʿIqd, 2:371 (Asin, p. 539, no. 109; Mansur, no. 5; Robson, p. 51); al-Ghazali, Ihyaʾ, 2:64; Ibn ʿAsakir, Sirat, p. 202, no. 249.

In this saying, the ethics of social solidarity and compassion transcend individual, solitary worship. Jesus is no longer the lone ascetic but a caring attendant upon those in need; no longer the patron saint of those who escape with their faith intact but a more socially committed figure, lauding the virtues of communal responsibility.

92 Christ said, "Till when do you describe the road to travelers by night while you yourselves remain behind with the perplexed? Only a little religious knowledge suffices, but many should be your deeds."

'Abdallah ibn Qutayba (d. 271/884), *'Uyun*, 2:127. Cf. Ibn 'Asakir, *Sirat*, p. 185, no. 219.

See Saying 43, above, on the contrast between religious knowledge *('ilm)* and good deeds *('amal)*. The first part of this saying may be an echo of Jesus' rebuke of the Pharisees in Matthew 15:14 and 23:16ff.

93 Christ said, "The most hateful of scholars to God is one who is fond of backbiting, who likes to occupy a seat of honor in an assembly, to be invited to feasts, and to have sacks of food emptied for him. Truly I say to you, such men have obtained their wages in this world, and God shall multiply their punishment on the Day of Judgment."

'Abdallah ibn Qutayba (d. 271/884), *'Uyun*, 2:127. Cf. Miskawayh, *al-Hikma*, p. 125.

In Matthew 23:5–6, it is the Scribes and Pharisees who like to take seats of honor at banquets. Here, as elsewhere, the religious scholars *('ulama')* replace the Scribes and Pharisees as the targets of rebuke.

94 "At the end of time, there will be religious scholars who preach abstinence but do not themselves abstain, who encourage yearning for the afterlife but do not themselves yearn, who forbid visits to rulers but do not themselves desist, who draw near to the rich and distance themselves from the poor, who recoil from the lowly and fawn upon the mighty. They are the tyrants and the enemies of the Merciful God."

'Abdallah ibn Qutayba (d. 271/884), *'Uyun*, 2:129–130. Cf. Ibn 'Abd Rabbihi, *al-'Iqd*, 2:227 (Asin, p. 539, no. 108; Mansur, no. 2; Robson, p. 84). In Ibn Qutayba the saying is ascribed, vaguely, to "an ancestor" *(qala ba'd al-salaf);* in Ibn 'Abd Rabbihi it is ascribed to Jesus.

There are many Muhammadan Hadiths about the end of the world and the "signs" thereof. Many of these depict situations at the end of time, when normal customs or habits will be totally reversed. Here, the *'ulama'* are once more the target. Their behavior echoes the behavior of the Pharisees rebuked by Jesus in Matthew, and merits a more direct censure of Muslim scholars who sell their integrity in order to gain favor with rulers, a reversal of the true vocation of scholars.

95 Jesus said, "He who speaks without mentioning God is merely babbling. He who reflects without self-admonition is merely heedless. He who is silent without reflecting is merely wasting time."

'Abdallah ibn Qutayba (d. 271/884), *'Uyun*, 2:178. Cf. al-Samarqandi, *Tanbih*, p. 78 (fuller version) (Asin, p. 554, no. 136; Mansur, no. 36; Robson, p. 55).

This is a typical Adab piece of wisdom, owing much to early ascetics like al-Hasan al-Basri on the one hand and to rationalist intellectuals like Ibn al-Muqaffa' (d. circa 139/756) on the other. It is in rhyming prose *(saj')*, a style associated with, and worthy of, the wise or prophetic figures of the past, Islamic and non-Islamic.

96 "In truth I say to you: he who utters words of wisdom and he who hears them are partners, and the one more worthy of being called wise is he who practices wisdom. In truth I say to you, if you were to find a lamp lit with tar on a dark night, you would make use of its light, notwithstanding the evil-smelling tar. So also should you take wisdom from whoever you find possessing it."

'Abdallah ibn Qutayba (d. 271/884), *'Uyun*, 2:268. Cf. Ibn 'Abd al-Barr, *Mukhtasar Jami' Bayan al-'Ilm*, p. 96 (partial) (Asin, p. 567, no. 155; Mansur, no. 86; Robson, pp. 56–57).

A recasting, in part, of Matthew 5:14–16 and, perhaps, 7:24–26. The new element is the evil-smelling naphtha contrasted with the light of wisdom *(hikmah)*, and the substitution of *hikmah* for the metaphorical "light" in Matthew. The imitation of the speaking style of Jesus lends it "authenticity"; see Saying 51, above. There are several Muhammadan Hadiths about acquiring wisdom from all quarters. In the Qur'an, *hikmah* is what a human being needs to accept religious faith. It later acquires a more strictly rational and scientific meaning and is used as a contrast to *'ilm*, reserved for religious knowledge. Jesus here is as much a patron of intellectuals as he is a patron of those whose good deeds shine in the darkness.

97 Jesus said to his companions, "If you are truly my brothers and friends, accustom yourselves to the enmity and hatred of men. For you shall not obtain what you seek except by abandoning what you desire. You shall not possess what you love except by tolerating what you hate."

'Abdallah ibn Qutayba (d. 271/884), *'Uyun*, 2:268. Cf. Ibn Abi al-Dunya, *Kitab Dhamm al-Dunya*, in *Mawsu'at Rasa'il*, 2:104, excerpt no. 214 (fuller version); Ibn 'Asakir, *Sirat*, p. 178, no. 207.

The two halves of this saying do not seem well matched. The first half may echo Matthew 10:34–39. The second half appears to belong to an ascetic or Stoic sentiment teaching contempt of desires.

98 "Blessed is he who sees with his heart but whose heart is not in what he sees."

'Abdallah ibn Qutayba (d. 271/884), *'Uyun*, 2:268.

An elegant saying, with no exact parallels in the Gospels but nevertheless Jesus-like in its terse profundity.

99 Christ said, "The world is a bridge. Cross this bridge but do not build upon it."

'Abdallah ibn Qutayba (d. 271/884), *'Uyun*, 2:328. Cf. al-Mubarrad, *al-Kamil*, 1:98; Ibn 'Abd Rabbihi, *al-'Iqd*, 3:173 (slight variation) (Mansur, no. 16); al-Makki, *Qut*, 1:256; al-Ghazali, *Ihya'*, 4:218 (Asin, p. 376, no. 46; Mansur, no. 128; Robson, p. 68); and al-Zabidi, *Ithaf*, 9:332 (fuller version) (Mansur, no. 156).

For more on this famous and well-traveled saying, see Note 55 to the Introduction. The saying is ascribed to al-Hasan al-Basri by al-Mubarrad (d. 285/898), a contemporary of Ibn Qutayba.

100 Christ passed by a group of people who hurled insults at him, and he responded with blessings. He passed by another group who insulted him, and he responded likewise. One of his disciples asked, "Why is it that the more they insult you, the more you bless them, as if inviting this upon yourself?" Christ said, "A person can bring forth only what is within him."

'Abdallah ibn Qutayba (d. 271/884), *Uyun*, 2:370. Cf. Ibn 'Abd Rabbihi, *al-'Iqd*, 2:276 (Mansur, no. 4); al-Turtushi, *Siraj*, p. 257; and al-Ghazali, *Ihya'*, 3:175 (Asin, p. 367, no. 32; Mansur, no. 117; Robson, pp. 45–46).

See Saying 80, above.

101 Christ said, "Be in the middle but walk to the side."

'Abdallah ibn Qutayba (d. 271/884), *Uyun*, 3:21. Cf. al-Jahiz, *al-Bayan*, 1:256 ('Ali b. Abi Talib instead of Jesus); al-Mubarrad, *al-Kamil*, 1:210)(variant); Ibn 'Asakir, *Sirat*, p. 149, no. 152 (Robson, p. 62).

The meaning of this cryptic pronouncement is not entirely clear. It may be that one is enjoined to be *in* this world but not *of* it, an interpretation I owe to a former student of mine, J. M. Laing. A "community of the center" is how the Qur'an describes the Muslims; see Qur'an 2:143.

102 Christ said, "You will not commit adultery as long as you avert your eyes."

'Abdallah ibn Qutayba (d. 271/884), *Uyun*, 4:84. Cf. Warram, *Majmu'a*, 1:62 (variant).

A recasting of Matthew 5:26–29. The phraseology, however, is Qur'anic: see, e.g., Qur'an 24:30–31.

103 Jesus passed by a cow which was calving in great distress. "O Word of God," the cow said, "Pray that God may deliver me." Jesus prayed, "O Creator of the soul from the soul, begetter of the soul from the soul, deliver her." The cow dropped its young.

ʿAbdallah ibn Qutayba (d. 271/884), *ʿUyun*, 4:123.

For Jesus conversing with a serpent, see Sayings 145 and 286, below. There are no references to cows and few to cattle in the New Testament. In the Apocryphal New Testament, there are several stories, mostly involving the Apostles, in which various animals speak, see, e.g., M. Rhodes James, *The Apocryphal New Testament* (Oxford: Clarendon Press, 1924), Index of Subjects, s.v. "animals."

104 Jesus said, "I reflected upon creation and found that he who has not been created is, in my view, happier than him who has."

Abu Bakr ibn Abi al-Dunya (d. 281/894), *Kitab al-Ashraf*, p. 228; Cf. Ibn ʿAsakir, *Sirat*, p. 123, nos. 104, 105.

Abu Bakr ibn Abiʾl Dunya was a well-known Hadith scholar and collector of ascetic traditions from Muhammad and other Islamic and non-Islamic figures. His collection of Jesus stories and sayings is very large and accompanied by full chains of transmission *(isnad)*. For any detailed investigation of the origins of these stories, his collection is of primary importance. His Jesus sayings and stories were extensively used by al-Ghazali and others, as indicated. For information on his life and works, see *EI* 2.

This is a curious saying, not akin to anything in the Gospels, except perhaps Matthew 26:24, which concerns the treachery of

Judas. There are possible parallels with two Apocryphal Gospels, the Gospel of Thomas and the Gospel of Philip; see Bentley Layton, *The Gnostic Scriptures* (New York: Doubleday, 1987), p. 383, excerpt 19 (Thomas) and p. 339, excerpt 49 (Philip).

105 Jesus said, "As God is my witness, the world has not dwelt in the heart of a servant without his heart attaching itself to three things in it: labor, whose burden is never alleviated; poverty, which cannot be surmounted; and hope, which cannot be fulfilled. The world is both a pursuer and a thing pursued. It pursues him who seeks the afterlife until his term of life comes to an end, whereas the afterlife pursues him who seeks this world until death comes and seizes him by the neck."

Abu Bakr ibn Abi al-Dunya (d. 281/894), *Kitab al-Qana'a wa al-Ta'affuf* in *Mawsu'at Rasa'il*, 1:68, excerpt no. 162. Cf. Ibn 'Asakir, *Sirat*, p. 146, no. 147; al-Zabidi, *Ithaf*, 9:332 (Asin, p. 598, no. 221; Mansur, no. 258; Robson, p. 77).

The dominant sentiment here seems to be of a world where no goals are ever achieved or achievable. The world as pursuer and pursued is a frequent motif in the Jesus sayings.

106 It is reported that the world was revealed to Jesus and that he saw it in the form of a toothless hag covered with every adornment. "How many men have you married?" Jesus asked her. "I cannot count them," the hag replied. "Did they all die before you, or did they all divorce you?" Jesus asked. "Neither, for I killed them all," she replied. Jesus said, "What wretches they are, your husbands that remain! For they do not learn from your former husbands how you killed them one after the other, nor are they on their guard against you."

Abu Bakr ibn Abi al-Dunya (d. 281/894), *Kitab Dhamm al-Dunya*, in *Mawsu'at Rasa'il*, 2:24, excerpt no. 27 (cf. excerpt nos. 28, 29, 30, ascribed to various Muslim ascetics). Cf. al-Ghazali, *Ihya'*, 3:210 (Asin, p. 375, no. 45; Mansur, no. 127, Robson, p. 68). See also Ibn Hanbal, *al-Zuhd*, 363 (no. 1433, variant; not a Jesus story).

This is a well-known story, as attested by its currency in Muslim ascetic literature and its attribution to various ascetic figures. Asin suggests John 4:7ff. as a parallel, although the image of the woman adorned is found in both the Old Testament (e.g., Ezekiel 13:17ff.) and the Qur'an, which condemns excessive female adornment (e.g., 24:60 and 33:33). See also Revelation 17:1–18.

107 Jesus said, "The heart of a believer cannot really support the love of both this world and the next, just as a single vessel cannot really support both water and fire."

Abu Bakr ibn Abi al-Dunya (d. 281/894), *Kitab Dhamm al-Dunya*, in *Mawsu'at Rasa'il*, 2:44, excerpt no. 76. Cf. al-Ghazali, *Ihya'*, 3:200 (Asin, p. 369, no. 35; Mansur, no. 120; Robson, p. 65).

It may be worth noting that in the Gnostic Gospel of Philip it is asserted that soul and spirit "are constituted of water and fire"; see Bentley Layton, *The Gnostic Scriptures*, p. 341, excerpt 58. But this is only a stylistic parallel, since the clearly Gnostic elements in the Muslim gospel are few. There is also some superficial resemblance to Matthew 6:24, and the unattributed saying, which immediately follows this one in Ibn Abi al-Dunya, is in fact a paraphrase of Matthew.

108 A man once accompanied Jesus, saying to him, "I want to be with you and be your companion." They set forth and reached the bank of a river, where they sat down to eat. They had with them three loaves. They ate two loaves, and a third remained. Jesus then rose and went to the river to drink. When he returned, he did not find the third loaf, so he asked the man: "Who took the loaf?" "I do not know," the man replied.

Jesus set forth once more with the man, and he saw a doe with two of her young. Jesus called one of the two, and it came to him. Jesus then slaughtered it, roasted some of it, and ate with his companion. Then he said to the young deer, "Rise, by God's leave." The deer rose and left. Jesus then turned to his companion and said, "I ask you in the name of Him who showed you this miracle, who took the loaf?" "I do not know," the man replied.

The two of them then came to a body of water in a valley. Jesus took the man by the hand and they walked upon the water. When they had crossed over, Jesus said to him, "I ask you in the name of Him who showed you this miracle, who took the loaf?" "I do not know," the man replied.

They then came to a waterless desert and sat down upon the ground. Jesus began to gather some earth and sand, and then said, "Turn to gold, by God's leave," and it did so. Jesus divided the gold into three portions and said, "A third for me, a third for you, and a third for whoever took the loaf." The man said, "It was I who took the loaf." Jesus said, "The gold is all yours."

Jesus then left him. Two men came upon him in the desert with the gold, and wanted to rob and kill him. He said to them, "Let us divide it into three portions among us, and send one of you to town to buy us some food to eat." One of them was sent off, and then said to himself, "Why should I divide the gold with those two? Rather, I shall poison the food and have the gold to myself." He went off and did so.

Meanwhile, the two who stayed behind said to each other, "Why should we give him a third of the gold? Instead, let us kill him when he returns and divide the money between the two of us." When he returned, they killed him, ate the food, and died. The gold remained in the desert with the three men dead beside it. Jesus passed by, found them in that condition, and said to his companions, "This is the world. Beware of it."

Abu Bakr ibn Abi al-Dunya (d. 281/894), *Kitab Dhamm al-Dunya*, in *Mawsuʿat Rasaʾil*, 2:49, excerpt no. 87. Cf. al-Ghazali, *Ihyaʾ*, 3:267 (Asin, pp. 383–384, no. 54; Mansur, no. 136; Robson, pp. 97–99); al-Makki, *Qut*, 1:255 (Asin, pp. 387–388, no. 54 quater; Mansur, no. 26); al-Turtushi, *Siraj*, pp. 79–80; Ibn ʿAsakir, *Sirat*, p. 95, no. 82; al-Abshihi, *al-Mustatraf*, 2:263–264 (Asin, p. 385, no. 54 bis and pp. 386–387, no. 54 ter; slight variation).

A moral fable of perennial interest in many cultures. In the original Arabic, this fable is immediately followed by another, narrated by al-Hasan al-Basri from Muhammad. It is introduced with the words: "You and I and the world are like a group of people lost in a desert and on the point of death." This group then meets a man who guides them to greenery and water. When the man calls on them to move once again to greenery and water unlike what they have had, most disobey him, preferring what they have already enjoyed. The man and his few faithful followers then depart. Those who remain are attacked by enemies and killed or taken captive.

109 Jesus said, "Truly I say to you, just as a sick man looks at food and does not enjoy it because he is in pain, so a lover of this world does not enjoy worship or appreciate its delights because of his love for this world. Truly I say to you, if a beast of burden is left unridden and undisciplined, it grows headstrong and changes its character. So also if the heart is not softened by mention of death and the strain of worship, it grows hard and callous. Truly I say to you, if a water skin is not torn or withered, it may hold honey. So also if the heart is not torn by desires, defiled by avarice, or hardened by luxury, it can be a vessel of wisdom."

Abu Bakr ibn Abi al-Dunya (d. 281/894), *Kitab Dhamm al-Dunya*, in *Mawsuʿat Rasaʾil*, 2:52, excerpt no. 90. Cf. al-Ghazali, *Ihyaʾ*, 3:211 (Asin, p. 377, no. 47; Mansur, no. 129; Robson, pp. 68–69).

In the Islamic literature on prophecy and prophets, Jesus came to be known as the prophet of the heart. This saying is an early example of his teaching on the heart. The wisdom referred to at the end is *hikmah*, a Qurʾanic term denoting the understanding that accompanies faith and makes it possible.

110 Jesus was asked, "Why do you not acquire a house to shelter you?" He replied, "Let us be satisfied with the ruins of those who came before us."

Abu Bakr ibn Abi al-Dunya (d. 281/894), *Kitab Dhamm al-Dunya*, in *Mawsu'at Rasa'il*, 2:68, excerpt no. 129. Cf. al-Ghazali, *Ihya'*, 3:200 (Asin, p. 369, no. 36; Mansur, no. 121; Robson, p. 65).

See Saying 60, above.

111 Jesus said, "The world existed and I was not in it, and it shall exist and I shall not be in it. All I have are my days which I am now living. If I sin in them, I am indeed a sinner."

Abu Bakr ibn Abi al-Dunya (d. 281/894), *Kitab Dhamm al-Dunya*, in *Mawsu'at Rasa'il*, 2:105, excerpt no. 216. Cf. Ibn 'Asakir, *Sirat*, p. 182, no. 213 (variant).

This saying may serve to emphasize the human nature of Jesus by denying his eternity on the one hand and suggesting the possibility of his sinfulness on the other.

112 Jesus said, "It is a mark of the ascetics in this world that they shun the company of any companion who does not desire what they desire."

Abu Bakr ibn Abi al-Dunya (d. 281/894), *Kitab Dhamm al-Dunya*, in *Mawsu'at Rasa'il*, 2:109, excerpt no. 225.

This austere shunning of anyone not desiring what the ascetic desires is more typical of early Muslim ascetics than of the Jesus of the Gospels.

113 Jesus passed by a village and found its people lying dead in its yards and alleys. He turned to his disciples and said, "These men died from divine anger, for otherwise they would have buried one another." "Spirit of God," they said, "would that we could learn what happened to them." Jesus asked God Almighty, and God revealed that he should call upon them when night fell and they would answer him. So when night fell, Jesus walked onto high ground and called out, "O men of the village!" "At your command, Spirit of God," answered one of them. Jesus asked, "What is your state and what is your story?" The man replied, "We went to sleep in good health and woke up to find ourselves in the pit." "How so?" Jesus asked. The man replied, "Because of our love of the world and our subservience to sinners." "How was your love of the world?" Jesus asked. "As the child loves its mother," said the man. "When she approached we were happy, and when she departed we became sad and wept for her." Jesus asked, "Why did your fellow villagers not answer me?" "Because they are fettered with fetters of fire and guarded by harsh and mighty angels," the man replied. "Then how is it that it was you who answered me from among them?" Jesus asked. "Because I was with them but not of them," the man replied. "When the calamity struck them, I too was struck down. I am now suspended on the edge of the precipice of hell, and I do not know whether I shall escape from it or be plunged into it." Then Jesus said to his disciples, "In truth, the eating of barley bread with uncrushed salt, the wearing of haircloth, and going to sleep on dunghills is more than enough if one desires to be safe and secure in this world."

Abu Bakr ibn Abi al-Dunya (d. 281/894), *Kitab Dhamm al-Dunya*, in *Mawsuʿat Rasaʾil*, 2:128–129, excerpt no. 282. Cf. Ibn Babuya, ʿ*Ilal*, 2:151–152; al-Ghazali, *Ihyaʾ*, 3:201 (Asin, pp. 371–372, no. 39; Mansur, no. 123; Robson, pp. 95–96).

A resurrection fable where Jesus interrogates one of the dead. The expression "harsh and mighty angels" is from Qurʾan 66:6. This is also an early description of hell. The fable ends with an admonition we have already encountered; see Sayings 42 and 67, above.

114 Jesus said, "You work for a petty world and you ignore the great afterlife, and upon you all death shall pass."

Abu Bakr ibn Abi al-Dunya (d. 281/894), *Kitab Dhamm al-Dunya*, in *Mawsuʿat Rasaʾil*, 2:129–130, excerpt no. 286.

The image of a "petty" world contrasted with a "great" afterlife occurs also in a saying attributed to an early Muslim ascetic. See the excerpt immediately following this one in Ibn Abi al-Dunya (no. 287).

115 Jesus said, "He who seeks worldly things is like the man who drinks sea water: the more he drinks the more thirsty he becomes, until it kills him."

Abu Bakr ibn Abi al-Dunya (d. 281/894), *Kitab Dhamm al-Dunya*, in *Mawsuʿat Rasaʾil*, 2:146, excerpt no. 342. Cf. Ibn Hamdun, *Al-Tadhkira*, 1:249, no. 638; al-Ghazali, *Ihyaʾ*, 3:212 (Asin, p. 378, no. 48; Mansur, no. 130; Robson, p. 69); Ibn ʿAsakir, *Sirat*, p. 147, no. 150.

The bitter taste of sea water is mentioned twice in the Qurʾan: at 25:53 and 35:12. The saying was also found in Syriac literature; see E. A. Wallis Budge, *The Laughable Stories Collected by Mar Greg-*

ory John Bar-Hebraeus (London: Luzac, 1897), p. 28, no. 110, where it is attributed to an Indian sage.

116 Jesus said, "O Disciples, be ascetics in this world and you will pass through it without anxiety."

Abu Bakr ibn Abi al-Dunya (d. 281/894), *Kitab Dhamm al-Dunya,* in *Mawsu'at Rasa'il,* 2:146, excerpt no. 344.

117 Jesus said, "Woe to you, evil scholars! For the sake of a despicable world and a calamitous desire, you squander the kingdom of paradise and forget the terror of the Day of Judgment."

Abu Bakr ibn Abi al-Dunya (d. 281/894), *Kitab Dhamm al-Dunya,* in *Mawsu'at Rasa'il,* 2:158, excerpt no. 377.

See Sayings 92 and 94, above.

118 It is related that Jesus looked at Satan and said, "Here is the pillar of the world. It is to the world that he went out, and it is the world that he demanded. I do not share anything of it with him, not even a stone to place beneath my head. Nor will I laugh much in it until I have left it."

Abu Bakr ibn Abi al-Dunya (d. 281/894), *Kitab Dhamm al-Dunya,* in *Mawsu'at Rasa'il,* 2:168, excerpt no. 409.

The word *urkun,* translated here as "pillar," is intriguing. The classical dictionaries derive it from the root *rkn* and state that it means a ruler or grandee. But they often equate it with the word *dihqan*, the ancient Persian countryside potentate who continued well into the Islamic period. Hence, doubt remains as to whether it is really of Arabic origin. It is tempting to identify it with the archon or archons of Gnostic gospels, the so-called world rulers of whom the devil was one. The image of the stone beneath the head is repeated in the saying that follows.

119 Satan passed by while Jesus was reclining his head upon a stone. "So, then, Jesus, you have been satisfied with a stone in this world!" Jesus removed the stone from beneath his head, threw it at him, and said, "Take this stone, and the world with it! I have no need of either."

Abu Bakr ibn Abi al-Dunya (d. 281/894), *Kitab Dhamm al-Dunya*, in *Mawsuʿat Rasaʾil*, 2:168, excerpt no. 410. Cf. Miskawayh, *al-Hikma al-Khalida*, 129 (an "idler" instead of Satan); al-Ghazali, *Ihyaʾ*, 4:11 (variant) (Asin, pp. 392–393, no. 63; Mansur, no. 145; Robson, p. 70); Ibn ʿAsakir, *Sirat*, p. 127, no. 112.

In this charming story, Jesus is jeered at by Satan for having finally succumbed to a worldly comfort. For other references to stones, see Sayings 47 and 71, above.

120 Jesus was asked, "Teach us one act through which God may come to love us." He answered, "Hate the world and God will love you."

Abu Bakr ibn Abi al-Dunya (d. 281/894), *Kitab Dhamm al-Dunya*, in *Mawsuʿat Rasaʾil*, 2:170, excerpt no. 415. Cf. al-Ghazali, *Ihyaʾ*, 3:201 (Asin, p. 373, no. 41; Mansur, no. 125; Robson, p. 67).

There are echoes here of John 15:18–19. The commandment to hate the world is also quite common among the sayings of the Egyptian desert fathers; see, e.g., Ward, *The Sayings of the Desert Fathers*, p. 8, no. 33.

121 Jesus said, "O disciples, be satisfied with what is vile in this world while your faith remains whole and sound, just as the people of this world are satisfied with what is vile in religion while their world remains whole and sound."

Abu Bakr ibn Abi al-Dunya (d. 281/894), *Kitab Dhamm al-Dunya*, in *Mawsuʿat Rasaʾil*, 2:179, excerpt no. 449.

A graceful turn of phrase, in the spirit of Adab.

122 Jesus said, "God likes His servant to learn a craft whereby he can become independent of people, and God hates a servant who acquires religious knowledge and then adopts it as a craft."

Abu Bakr ibn Abi al-Dunya (d. 281/894), *Kitab Islah al-Mal*, in *Mawsuʿat Rasaʾil*, 2:95, excerpt no. 316.

For the need to earn a livelihood, see the resurrection story in Saying 247, below. Religious knowledge, in contrast, imposes awesome moral responsibilities, as seen in many sayings above.

123 Among the revelations of God to Jesus is the following: "It is only right and proper for the servants of God to display humility before God when God displays His bounty to them."

Abu Bakr ibn Abi al-Dunya (d. 281/894), *Kitab al-Shukr lillah*, in *Mawsuʿat Rasaʾil*, 3:53–54, excerpt no. 127. Cf. al-Ghazali, *Ihyaʾ*, 3:332 (Asin, p. 391, no. 58; Mansur, no. 140; Robson, p. 78).

The speaker here is the Negus of Ethiopia, who, according to Muslim tradition, granted hospitality to a group of very early Muslims fleeing Meccan persecution. The Muslims found him one day sitting on the ground. In explanation, he told them that he had just received news of a Muslim victory and was duly grateful to God. He then recited to them this saying of Jesus. The Negus is often depicted in Muslim sources as a pious Christian king who nevertheless recognized the truth of Muhammad's mission, thus becoming a type or model of sincerity of faith. That God's favors will be multiplied if man gives thanks for them echoes Qurʾan 14:7.

124 John the son of Zachariah met Jesus the son of Mary, John smiling of face and welcoming while Jesus was frowning and gloomy. Jesus said to John, "You smile as if you feel secure." John said to Jesus, "You frown as if you are in despair." God revealed, "What John does is dearer to Us."

Abu Bakr ibn Abi al-Dunya (d. 281/894), *Kitab al-Ikhwan*, p. 190 (no. 136). Cf. Ibn ʿAbd Rabbihi, *al-ʿIqd*, 6:380 (Asin, p. 544, no. 120; Mansur, no. 21; Robson, p. 108); idem, 6:380–381 (Asin, p. 544, no. 121; Mansur, no. 22; Robson, pp. 108–109); Abu Hayyan, *al-Basaʾir wa al-Dhakhaʾir*, 7:197 (no. 379); idem, *Risala fi al-Sadaqa wa al-Sadiq*, p. 105; Ibn ʿAqil, *Kitab al-Funun*, 2:635–636; Ibn ʿAsakir, *Sirat*, p. 200, no. 246; al-Damiri, *Hayat*, 2:205 (Mansur, no. 233).

This encounter between Jesus and John is perhaps meant as a veiled criticism of excessive asceticism which borders on despair. To a Muslim audience, the saying would be interpreted as a reminder of God's infinite mercy. The words of God at the end imply that in some respects Jesus is less meritorious than John. The story itself recalls the well-known Greek anecdote about the encounter between the philosophers Democritus and Heraclitus; cf. Montaigne, *Essays* (Harmondsworth: Penguin, 1960), p. 132. The same attitudes are reported of two celebrated early Muslim figures, al-Hasan al-Basri and Ibn Sirin (d. 110/728); see Ibn Sa'd, *Tabaqat*, 7:162.

125 They asked Jesus, "Show us an act by which we may enter paradise." Jesus said, "Do not speak at all." They said, "We cannot do this." Jesus replied, "Then speak only good."

Abu Bakr ibn Abi al-Dunya (d. 281/894), *Kitab al-Samt wa Adab al-Lisan*, p. 215 (no. 46). Cf. Miskawayh, *al-Hikma*, p. 123; al-Ghazali, *Ihya'*, 3:107; Ibn 'Asakir, *Sirat*, p. 158, no. 172 (Mansur, no. 110).

The virtue of silence is a common theme in the wisdom literature of the Near East. This saying is taken from a work of Ibn Abi'l Dunya devoted entirely to this subject. Similar sayings are also ascribed to Muhammad; see, e.g., Ibn al-Mubarak, *Kitab al-Zuhd*, p. 125, no. 368.

126 Jesus said, "He who lies much loses his beauty; he who constantly quarrels with men loses his sense of honor; he who worries much grows sick in body; and he whose character is nasty tortures himself."

Abu Bakr ibn Abi al-Dunya (d. 281/894), *Kitab al-Samt wa Adab al-Lisan*, pp. 276–277 (no. 133). Cf. al-Ghazali, *Ihya'*, 3:114; Ibn ʿAsakir, *Sirat*, p. 160, no. 175; Warram, *Majmuʿa*, 2:176 (variant) (Mansur, no. 112).

The sentiment in this saying seems more typical of Adab than of asceticism.

127 Jesus and his disciples passed by a dog's carcass. The disciples said, "How foul is his stench!" Jesus said, "How white are his teeth!" He said this in order to teach them a lesson—namely, to forbid slander.

Abu Bakr ibn Abi al-Dunya (d. 281/894), *Kitab al-Samt wa Adab al-Lisan*, p. 385–386 (no. 297). Cf. al-Ghazali, *Ihya'*, 3:140; Warram, *Majmuʿa*, 1:117; Ibn ʿAsakir, *Sirat*, p. 157, no. 170 (Asin, p. 365, no. 29; Mansur, no. 114; Robson, p. 45).

This and the following saying should perhaps be taken together. They both concern animals distasteful to classical Muslim sensibilities. The pig is of course a totally unclean animal, while contact with a dog necessitates ablution according to most Muslim jurists. Both sayings, therefore, are in some sense offensive to Muslim taste, even if neither saying violates Muslim law in the strict sense. Both sayings, however, carry an editorial explanation of the conduct of Jesus. Does this fact in itself betray the Muslim transmitter's desire to endow Jesus' sayings with credibility by deliberately making them somewhat unpalatable in an Islamic context? In any case, both sayings might well have been uttered by the Jesus of the Gospels. As cited in Warram, above, this saying is supposedly intended as a warning by Jesus to the disciples not to slander even a dead dog.

In his addenda to his collection, Asin, p. 605, quotes from a letter sent to him by the celebrated orientalist Ignaz Goldziher regarding this saying; in the letter, Goldziher informs him that the saying is "undoubtedly" of Buddhist origin. I have not been able to confirm this assertion.

128 A pig passed by Jesus. Jesus said, "Pass in peace." He was asked, "Spirit of God, how can you say this to a pig?" Jesus replied, "I hate to accustom my tongue to evil."

Abu Bakr ibn Abi al-Dunya (d. 281/894), *Kitab al-Samt wa Adab al-Lisan*, p. 392 (no. 308). Cf. al-Ghazali, *Ihya'*, 3:116; Ibn 'Asakir, *Sirat*, p. 157, no. 170 (Asin, p. 365, no. 28; Mansur, no. 113; Robson, p. 45).

See the comments on Saying 127, above.

129 Jesus said to his companions, "What would you do if you passed by a sleeping man whose clothes had been blown away by the wind?" They said, "We would cover him up." Jesus said, "No, you would instead uncover the rest of him." Thus he drew an example of people who hear evil spoken of someone, and add to the evil and mention more.

Abu Bakr ibn Abi al-Dunya (d. 281/894), *Kitab al-Samt wa Adab al-Lisan*, p. 573 (no. 645). Cf. al-Ghazali, *Ihya'*, 2:175; al-Suhrawardi, *'Awarif*, 4:48; Ibn 'Asakir, *Sirat*, p. 154, no. 165 (Asin, p. 358, no. 16; Mansur, no. 101; Robson, p. 44).

For biblical parallels, see the commentaries of Asin. This, too, carries an editorial gloss, designed to make manifest the hidden intention of the challenge posed by Jesus. It shows, once again, the Muslim redactor's desire to unwrap the parable or allegory in the sayings of Jesus. The commandments against backbiting are prominently displayed in the Qur'an and Hadith.

130 Jesus said, "Among the greatest of sins in the sight of God is that a servant of God should say, 'God knows' and God knows it is not so.'"

Abu Bakr ibn Abi al-Dunya (d. 281/894), *Kitab al-Samt wa Adab al-Lisan*, pp. 608–609 (no. 727). Cf. Abu Nuʿaym, *Hilyat*, 6:125 (slight variation) (Mansur, no.78); and al-Ghazali, *Ihya'*, 3:138 (Asin, p. 571, no. 167; Robson, pp. 57–58).

A warning against false witness or false oath.

131 Jesus was asked about sincere counsel. He said, "If two matters arise before you, one of which concerns you and the other of which concerns God, begin with the matter that concerns God."

Al-Hakim al-Tirmidhi (d. 285/898), *al-Salat wa Maqasidiha*, p. 119.

Al-Tirmidhi was a celebrated traditionist whose collection of Hadith was counted among the six canonical collections in Sunni Islam.

Preferring God to self or putting God before self is connected with the sin of pride, a sin prominent in the Gospels as well as the Qur'an. The injunction to "put God first" is common in Sufi writings, and it may be that a Sufi sentiment lurks beneath this saying.

132 It is related that Jesus said, "Scholars are of three kinds: he who knows God and His commandments, he who knows God but not His commandments, and he who knows God's commandments but does not know God."

Al-Hakim al-Tirmidhi (d. 285/898), excerpted in Asin, p. 601 (no. 225), Mansur, no. 239, Robson, p. 61. For a description of the source of this saying, see Asin, p. 534.

Here, too, one might argue that the scholar who knows God's commandments is the lawyer, but he who knows God is the Sufi. Sufism was to make a distinction between intellectual knowledge (*'ilm*) and direct experiential knowledge (*ma'rifa*), and claimed this latter kind as its own special domain.

133 Jesus said, "Multiply what fire cannot consume." "And what is that?" he was asked. "Good works," he replied.

Abu al-'Abbas al-Mubarrad (d. 285/898), *al-Fadil*, p. 35. Cf. al-Ghazali, *Ihya'*, 3:240 (Asin, p. 379, no. 51; Mansur, no. 133; Robson, p. 46).

Al-Mubarrad was a celebrated grammarian and Adab anthologist. The consuming fire is a common biblical and Qur'anic image.

134 It is related that Christ used to say, "If you find yourselves in need of people, eat in moderation and walk to the side."

Abu al-'Abbas al-Mubarrad (d. 285/898), *al-Kamil*, 1:210.

The saying appears to teach humility and good manners. See also Saying 101, above.

135 Jesus was a constant traveler in the land, never abiding in a house or a village. His clothing consisted of a cloak made of coarse hair or camel stub and two hairless shirts (?). In his hand he carried a club. Whenever night fell, his lamp was the moonlight, his shade the blackness of night, his bed the earth, his pillow a stone, his food (?) the plants of the fields. At times, he spent whole days and nights without food. In times of distress he was happy, and in times of ease he was sad.

Abu Rifaʿa al-Fasawi (d. 289/902), *Kitab Badʾ al-Khalq*, p. 333. Cf. Ibn ʿAsakir, *Sirat*, p. 133, no. 120 (variant).

Abu Rifaʿa was an important and early collector of stories of the prophets, which were soon to become a distinct literary and religious genre. On his life and works, see Raif Khuri's introduction to the modern edition of his writings, cited in the Bibliography.

This is an early physical description of Jesus; but see Saying 78, above. In classical Arabic wisdom and prophetic literature, we have numerous descriptions of the physical appearance or daily habits of sages and prophets. The origin of this particular description of Jesus is obscure. On the other hand, it may be that since the physical appearance and daily habits of Muhammad were so well known and so minutely recorded, the Muslim transmitters might have felt inclined to do the same for earlier prophets so that Muhammad's portrait could be seen to be in line with those of his predecessors. In any case, Jesus the wandering ascetic is the dominant image in this description.

There are two places in the text where the reading is uncertain, and indicated here with question marks.

136 Jesus said to his disciples, "You will not gain God's bounty until you wear coarse wool with joy, eat barley with joy, and make the ground your bed with joy."

Abu Rifaʿa al-Fawawi (d. 289/902), *Kitab Badʾ al-Khalq*, p. 337. Cf. Abu Nuʿaym, *Hilyat*, 5:92 (Mansur, no. 71).

The garment of coarse wool *(suf)* was the earliest Sufi badge or uniform, which of course explains the word "Sufi": "wearer of wool." This is a saying which explicitly alerts us to the intrusion of Sufism into the sayings.

137 Jesus was asked, "Who was your tutor?" "No one," he replied. "I saw the ugliness of ignorance and avoided it."

Ibn ʿAbd Rabbihi (d. 328/940), *al-ʿIqd al-Farid*, 2:442 (Mansur, no. 6). Cf. al-Mawardi, *Adab*, 210; and al-Ghazali, *Ihyaʾ*, 3:63 (Asin, p. 361 no. 19; Mansur, no. 104; Robson, p. 44).

Ibn ʿAbd Rabbihi was the author of one of the most celebrated anthologies of classical Arabic Adab. On his life and works, see *EI* 2.

Jesus is presented in this saying as a model Adib, a gentleman scholar, who draws a parallel between ignorance and ugliness—an intellectual or aesthetic analogy, rather than a strictly moral judgment. But the word translated here as "ignorance" *(jahl)* can also mean violence of temper or behavior. Thus, Jesus could also be warning against immoderateness in word or deed. Nevertheless, the shunning of extremism was also quite characteristic of the Adib's way of life.

138 Among the revelations of God to Jesus in the Gospel is the following: "We filled you with yearning but you did not yearn, and we mourned for you but you did not cry. Man of fifty, what have you offered and what have you held back? Man of sixty, your harvest-time approaches! Man of seventy, onward to the reckoning!"

Ibn ʿAbd Rabbihi (d. 328/940), *al-ʿIqd al-Farid*, 3:145 (Asin, p. 543, no. 116; Mansur, no. 14; Robson, p. 52).

Like several other sayings, this one is a composite. The first part echoes Matthew 11:17 and Luke 7:23. The second half appears unconnected with the first, but the Ages of Man motif was a common one in Near Eastern wisdom literature; see, e.g., the Mishnaic tractate *Pirkey Aboth*, in Hertz, *Sayings of the Fathers*, p. 81, no. 24.

139 Jesus said of water, "This is my father," and of bread, "This is my mother." He meant that they nourish the body just as parents do.

Ibn ʿAbd Rabbihi (d. 328/940), *al-ʿIqd al-Farid*, 6:290 (Mansur, no. 20). Cf. Ibn Sida, *al-Mukhassas*, 13:173–174 (Asin, p. 568, 159; Mansur, no. 85; Robson, p. 90).

This appears to be a Muslim recasting of the sacrament of the Eucharist; see Saying 49, above. The "bread of life" and the "bread of heaven" are biblical usages, appearing at their most symbolic in John 6:32–35. Muslim theologians, like Jahiz or the celebrated ʿAbd al-Jabbar (d. 415/1024) often rejected the literal interpretation of the Eucharist and ridiculed the literal transformation of bread and wine into flesh and blood. The saying, with its gloss, appears to give an acceptable Muslim explanation of the event. There is yet another interpretation of the bread brought by Jesus in the Apocryphal Gospel of Philip; see Layton, *The Gnostic Scriptures*, p. 331, excerpt 11.

140 Jesus said, "The evildoer is infectious; the associate of the wicked can kill. Be careful, therefore, with whom you associate."

Muhammad ibn Ya'qub al-Kulayni (d. 329/941), *Al-Usul min al-Kafi,* 2:640.

Al-Kulayni was an important Shi'i Hadith scholar and theologian. On his life and works, see *EI* 2. This saying has an internal rhyme in Arabic which cannot be reproduced in translation and which gives the saying a proverbial character.

141 It is related that Christ said, "He whom God honors from among His worshipers must be honored by all His creation."

Abu Bakr ibn al-Qutiyya (d. 367/977), *Tarikh Iftitah al-Andalus,* p. 60 (Asin, p. 539, no. 107; Mansur, no. 23; Robson, p. 51).

Ibn al-Qutiyya was a historian of the Muslim conquest of Spain, and was most probably of Visigothic Christian origin. This saying appears to echo John 12:26.

142 It is written in the Gospels: "Son of Adam, remember me when you are angry and I will remember you when I am angry. Be content with my support for you, for it is better than your support for yourself."

Abu al-Layth al-Samarqandi (d. 373/983), *Tanbih al-Ghafilin,* p. 73 (Asin, p. 553, no. 133; Mansur, no. 33; Robson, p. 79).

Al-Samarqandi was a distinguished jurist. There does not seem to be any Gospel parallel to this saying. It has the form of a *hadith qudsi,* a divine revelation. There may be echoes here of the exchange between God and Jonah in Jonah 4:1ff. or of the Psalms. That God is the only support of the believer is a very common sentiment in the Qur'an.

143 Jesus said to the Israelites, "Do not reward a wrongdoer with wrongdoing, for this will nullify your virtue in God's sight."

Abu al-Layth al-Samarqandi (d. 373/983), *Tanbih al-Ghafilin*, p. 75 (Asin, p. 553, no. 134; Mansur, no. 34; Robson, p. 55).

This may be an echo of Matthew 5:39.

144 In the time of Jesus, there was a man nicknamed Mal'un (Damned) because of his avarice. One day a man who was going on a military campaign came to him and said, "Mal'un, if you give me some weapons to help me wage war, you will be saved from hell-fire." But Mal'un shunned him and gave him nothing. As the man turned away, Mal'un regretted his decision and called him back to give him his sword. When the man returned home he was met by Jesus, accompanied by a devout man who had worshiped God for seventy years. "Where did you get this sword from?" Jesus asked. The man replied, "Mal'un gave it to me," and Jesus was pleased with his charity. The next time Jesus and the devout man passed by, Mal'un, who was sitting at his doorstep, said to himself, "I will go and look upon Jesus' face and the face of the devout man." When he did so, the devout man said, "I will flee from this Mal'un before he burns me with his fire."

Then God inspired Jesus to say, "Tell this sinful servant of mine, 'I have forgiven you because of your charity with the sword and your love for Jesus, and tell the devout man that you will be his companion in heaven.'" The devout man replied, "As God is my witness! I do not want heaven with him and I do not want a companion like him." God Almighty inspired Jesus to reply, "You are not content with my decree and you have denigrated my servant. Thus, I will see you damned in hell. I have exchanged your places, and have given your station in heaven to my servant and his station in hell to you."

Abu al-Layth al-Samarqandi (d. 373/983), *Tanbih ul-Ghafilin*, p. 114 (Asin, pp. 554–555, no. 137; Mansur, no. 37; Robson, pp. 109–110). Cf. Abu Nu'aym, *Hilyat*, 8:147 (variant); al-Qushayri, *al-Risala*, p. 73 (variant); al-Ghazali, *Ihya'*, 4:150 (variant) (Asin, p. 395, no. 67; Mansur, no. 149; Robson, pp. 99–100); and Ibn Qudama, *Kitab al-Tawwabin*, pp. 80–81.

This is a moral fable in which each character plays a particular moral role. There are Mal'un, the Damned, the man of avarice; the pious warrior; the self-righteous ascetic; and, in the middle, Jesus, who receives God's revelation as to the ultimate fate of the characters. These large moral fables now become more frequent in the corpus of Jesus stories. Their origin remains uncertain. In part, this fable echoes the parable of the Pharisee and the publican in Luke 18:9–14. But the Islamic message is quite clear: first of all, the centrality of *jihad*, or holy war, and, second, the ever-present possibility of repentance or of damnation. Self-righteousness is of course frequently condemned in both the Gospels and the Qur'an. The fable itself may also betray the influence of the preaching style *(wa'z)*, since it appears to be designed as part of a sermon.

145 Jesus passed through a village in which there lived a fuller of clothes. The villagers said to him, "This fuller tears our clothes and keeps them from us. Call on

God not to let him return safely with his bundle." Jesus said, "O God, let him not return with his bundle."

Then the fuller went to full clothes carrying three loaves of bread. He was approached by a holy man who worshiped God in those mountains. The holy man greeted the fuller and said, "Have you any bread to feed me, or even to show me that I might see or smell it, for I have not eaten bread since such-and-such a time!" So he gave him a loaf to eat. The holy man said, "May God forgive your sins and purify your heart." Then the fuller gave him the second loaf and the holy man said, "May God forgive your sins, past and future." Then the fuller gave him the third loaf and the holy man said, "May God build you a mansion in paradise."

The fuller returned that evening safely, and the villagers said, "Jesus, the fuller has returned." So Jesus summoned him and said, "Tell me what you did today." The fuller replied, "I was approached by a holy man who wanders in these mountains. He asked me to feed him so I fed him three loaves, and with each loaf I fed him he prayed for me." Jesus said, "Give me your bundle so that I might examine it." The man gave it to Jesus, who opened it and found a black snake chained in irons. Jesus said, "O black one!" And the snake replied, "At your service, prophet of God!" "Were you not sent to this fuller?" Jesus asked. "Yes," the snake replied, "but a wandering holy man from these mountains came to him and asked him for food. With each loaf he fed him, the holy man prayed for him while an angel standing nearby said, 'Amen!' So God Almighty sent an angel to chain me in irons." Jesus said, "Fuller, go back to work. God has forgiven you through the blessing of your charity."

Abu al-Layth al-Samarqandi (d. 373/983), *Tanbih al-Ghafilin*, p. 116 (Asin, pp. 555–556, no. 138; Mansur, no. 38; Robson, pp. 111–112).

This is another moral fable, similar in spirit and structure to Saying 144. The repentance of a sinner is its major theme. The fullers were the dry cleaners of the ancient world. In premodern Islamic societies they were an unpopular profession, and generally considered deceitful. The wise-serpent motif has a Gospel parallel; see Matthew 10:16.

146 If you want to fast as Jesus did, he would fast all the time and lived on nothing but barley. He always wore [garments of] coarse hair, and wherever he would be at nightfall he would plant his feet and keep praying until he saw the break of dawn. He would never leave a particular place before praying two *rak'as*. If, however, you want to fast as his mother the Virgin did, she used to fast for two days at a time then eat for two days.

Abu al-Layth al-Samarqandi (d. 373/983), *Tanbih al-Ghafilin*, p. 125 (Asin, p. 557, no. 139; Mansur, no. 39; Robson, pp. 74–75).

The fasting habits of various prophets and ascetics were often recorded in ascetic works as examples to ponder or emulate. That Jesus prays in the Muslim manner is, once again, like his pilgrimage and other acts, a confirmation of the fact that he and all earlier prophets were in fact Muslim.

147 It is written in the Gospel: "He who plants evil reaps regret."

Abu al-Layth al-Samarqandi (d. 373/983), *Tanbih al-Ghafilin*, p. 135 (Asin, p. 558, no. 140; Mansur, no. 40; Robson, p. 55).

For biblical but not Gospel parallels, see the comments by Asin.

148 It is written in the Gospels: "Son of Adam, as you have mercy, so shall God have mercy upon you. How do you hope for God's mercy if you do not have mercy upon His servants?"

Abu al-Layth al-Samarqandi (d. 373/983), *Tanbih al-Ghafilin*, p. 139 (Asin, p. 558, no. 141; Mansur, no. 41; Robson, p. 55).

For Gospel parallels, see the comments of Asin.

149 Jesus said, "What avails the blind man if he carries a lamp that only others can see by? And what avails the darkened house if the lamp is placed on its roof? And what avails you who speak words of wisdom but do not act upon them?"

Abu al-Layth al-Samarqandi (d. 373/983), *Tanbih al-Ghafilin*, p. 156 (Asin, p. 562, no. 144; Mansur, no. 45; Robson, p. 56).

Once more, the metaphors of the Gospel are unraveled in the last part of this saying.

150 Jesus was passing by a village where there was a mountain from which came sounds of weeping and wailing. Jesus asked the villagers, "What is this weeping and wailing in this mountain?" The villagers replied, "Ever since we have lived in this village, we have heard the sounds of weeping and wailing coming from this mountain." Jesus said, "O God, let this mountain speak to me." God made the mountain speak and say, "What do you want from me, Jesus?" "Tell me why you weep," asked Jesus. The mountain replied, "I was the mountain from which idols were carved and then worshiped instead of God. I fear that God will cast me into hell-fire, for I have heard God say, 'And fear the flame whose fuel consists of men and stones.'" God inspired Jesus to tell the mountain, "Be at peace, for I have saved you from hell."

Abu al Layth al Samarqandi (d. 373/983), *Tanbih al-Ghafilin*, p. 216 (Asin, p. 564, no. 148; Mansur, no. 49; Robson, pp. 114–5). Cf. al-Turtushi, *Siraj*, p. 466.

A curious story of unknown origin. Jesus interrogates nature and reveals its secrets. It is strange that even mountains feel the need to repent. In Muhammad's biography, certain natural objects like trees and rocks showed signs of life and responded to him. In Qur'an 59:21, it is said that if the Qur'an were made to descend upon a mountain, "you would see it humbled, shattered by the fear of God." In Qur'an 22:18, we are told that the earth, sun, moon, stars, and mountains "bow in prayer" to God. See also 38:18, where mountains are said to "glorify God" *(yusabbihna)*. The phrase uttered by the mountain, "And fear . . . stones," is from Qur'an 2:24, suggesting that judgment will be passed on creation in its entirety, all of which is in some sense animate.

151 Jesus said, "One should not marvel at how they were damned, those who were damned, but rather at how they were saved, those who were saved!"

Abu al-Layth al-Samarqandi (d. 373/983), *Tanbih al-Ghafilin*, p. 220 (Asin, p. 565, no. 150; Mansur, no. 51, Robson, p. 56).

For Gospel echoes, see the comments by Asin. A very similar saying is attributed to al-Hasan al-Basri; see Al-Mubarrad, *al-Kamil*, 1:159.

152 Jesus passed by a town in which a man and his wife were shouting at each other. "What is the matter with you?" Jesus asked. "O prophet of God," the man said, "This is my wife. She is a good enough and virtuous woman, but I want to separate from her." "But tell me, in any case, what is the matter with her," said Jesus. "Her face is worn out, although she is not old," the man replied. Jesus turned to the woman and said, "Woman, do you wish to restore smoothness to your face?" "Yes," she replied. "When you eat," said Jesus, "beware of gluttony, for when food piles up in the stomach and grows excessive, the face loses its smoothness." The woman did so, and her face regained its smoothness.

Ibn Babuya al-Qummi (d. 381/991), *'Ilal al-Shara'i'*, 2:184.

Ibn Babuya was a celebrated Shi'ite jurist and theologian. This and the following two sayings do not resemble anything else in the Muslim gospel. All three depict Jesus as a physician or an experienced farmer offering specific remedies to various diseases. Each remedy is then explained in terms which seem to reflect current medical and other scientific theories of the age of Ibn Babuya. A common Muslim view of that age regarding prophets was that each had been sent to a people particularly adept at a certain skill, and each had then surpassed the skill of his age. Moses, for example, had excelled in magic in an age renowned for its magic, Muhammad in eloquence, and Jesus in healing.

153 Jesus passed by a town whose fruit trees were infested with worms. Its people complained to him of this affliction and he said, "The remedy lies with you, but you do not know it. You are a people who, when planting trees, pour the earth first and then the water. This should not be so. Rather, you ought first to pour water into the root of the trees and then pour the earth so that the worms do not fall into it." They began to do as he had instructed and their affliction ceased.

Ibn Babuya al-Qummi (d. 381/991), *'Ilal al-Shara'i'*, 2:261.

See comments to Saying 152, above.

154 Jesus passed by a town whose people had yellow faces and blue eyes. They cried out to him, complaining about their disease. Jesus said, "The remedy lies with you. When you eat meat, you cook it unwashed. Nothing that is born into this world is ever without pollution." Thereafter they washed their meat, and their diseases disappeared. On another occasion, Jesus passed through a town whose inhabitants suffered from loss of teeth and swollen faces. They complained to him and he said, "You sleep with your mouths shut. The wind in your stomach reaches the mouth but finds no exit, and so turns back to the roots of the teeth, distorting the face. When you sleep, keep your mouths open, and make this a habit." They did so, and their affliction ceased.

Ibn Babuya al-Qummi (d. 381/991), *'Ilal al-Shara'i'*, 2:262.

See comments to Saying 152, above.

155 Jesus said, "The merciful in this world is the one who will be shown mercy in the next world."

Abu al-Hasan al-'Amiri (d. 381/992), *al-Sa'ada wa al-Is'ad*, p. 311.

Al-'Amiri was a philosopher with a particular interest in ethics. On his life and works, see *EI* 2. This saying appears to be a recasting of one of the beatitudes; cf. Matthew 5:7.

156 Jesus would say to the world, "Away from me, you pig!"

Abu Talib al-Makki (d. 386/996), *Qut al-Qulub*, 1:244 (Asin, p. 545, no. 123; Mansur, no. 25; Robson, p. 74). Cf. Ibn Abi al-Dunya, *Kitab Dhamm al-Dunya*, in *Mawsu'at Rasa'il*, 2:147, excerpt no. 347 (the saying is attributed to unnamed early ascetics).

Abu Talib al-Makki was a seminal figure in the development of Sufi doctrine and practice. On his life and works, see *EI* 2. See also Saying 60, above. Abu Talib includes many sayings by Jesus in his major work, *Qut al-Qulub* (The Sustenance of Hearts); these are indicated in the sources cited above. In this saying, we return here to a fiercely ascetic Jesus, one who is more closely akin to the fierce asceticism of Abu Talib himself.

157 Jesus said, "None of you can come to true belief until he no longer cares to be praised for his worship of God Almighty and no longer cares to partake of the goods of this world."

Abu Talib al-Makki (d. 386/996), *Qut al-Qulub,* 1:256. Cf. al-Ghazali, *Ihya',* 4:370 (Asin, p. 419, no. 94; Mansur, no. 176; Robson, p. 49), and al-Ghazali, *Minhaj al-'Abidin,* p. 63.

The total indifference of the true believer to praise and to the things of this world is a sentiment close to the teachings of Abu Talib himself, who is said to have held views bordering on heresy in the closing years of his life.

158 Among God's revelations to Jesus is the following: "Son of Adam, weep all the days of your life the weeping of one who has said farewell to the world and whose desire has been elevated to the world of God. Be content with the bare necessities of this world, and find contentment with what is rough and coarse. In truth I say to you, you are worth no more than your day and hour, and a record is kept of all that you have taken from this world and all that you have spent. Act accordingly, for you will be called to account. If only you knew what I have promised the righteous, you would surrender your spirit."

Abu Talib al-Makki (d. 386/996), *Qut al-Qulub*, 1:256 (Asin, p. 545, no. 124; Mansur, no. 27; Robson, pp. 78–79).

This is a *hadith qudsi*, or divine revelation, enjoining a life of weeping and abnegation bordering on self-destruction. Here, we approach the margins of what would have been acceptable to average Muslim piety of that age.

159 Jesus said, "The lover of God loves hardship." And it is related of him that he once came upon a large group of worshipers who had shriveled up from worshiping, like worn-out water skins. "Who are you?" he asked. "We are worshipers," they answered. "Why do you worship?" he asked. They replied, "God put the fear of hell in us, and we were afraid." So he said, "It is incumbent upon God to save you from what you fear." Then Jesus passed on and came upon others who were even more worshipful. He asked, "Why do you worship?" and they replied, "God gave us a longing for paradise and what He has prepared there for His friends. That is what we hope for." So Jesus said, "It is incumbent upon God to give you what you hope for." Then he passed them by and came upon others who were worshiping and said, "Who are you?" They said, "We are lovers of God. We worship Him not out of fear of hell or longing for paradise, but out of love for Him and to His greater glory." So Jesus said, "You are truly the friends of God, and it is with you that I was commanded to live." And he resided among them.

In another version, it is reported that he said to the first two groups, "It is a created thing that you fear, and a created thing that you love," and to the third group, "You are truly the nearest to God."

Abu Talib al-Makki (d. 386/996), *Qut al-Qulub*, 2:56 (Asin, pp. 411, no. 84 bis; Mansur, no. 30). Cf. al-Ghazali, *Ihya'*, 4:288 (Asin, pp. 410–411, no. 84; Mansur, no. 166; Robson, p. 100), and *Ihya'*, 4:298.

Loving God selflessly, neither out of fear of hell nor out of greed for paradise, was a sentiment ascribed to early Sufis—for example, the famous woman mystic Rabi'a al-'Adawiyya (d. 185/801), who was seen walking the streets of Baghdad with a bucket of water in one hand and a flaming torch in the other. When asked why she did so, she replied, "I want to quench the fires of hell with the water and burn down paradise with the torch, so that people can come to love God selflessly, neither out of fear of the one nor out of greed for the other."

160 Jesus said to his disciples by way of counsel, "If you do what I did and what I told you, you will be with me tomorrow in the Kingdom of Heaven, abiding with my Father and yours, and will see His angels around His throne, extolling His praises and sanctifying Him. There you will partake of every pleasure, without eating or drinking."

Ikhwan al-Safa' (fourth/tenth century), *Rasa'il*, 3:91–92 (Asin, p. 595, no. 214; Mansur, no. 53; Robson, p. 93).

The Ikhwan al-Safa', or Brethren of Purity, were a group of like-minded Neo-Platonist philosophers and scientists of the late fourth/tenth century who produced an encyclopedia of knowledge called *The Epistles,* in which they set forth their views on a diversity of subjects, philosophical, religious, ethical, and scientific. For more information on them, see *EI* 2.

The core of this saying comes from Luke 23:43. The specific denial of any eating or drinking in paradise goes against the commonly accepted Muslim image of paradise, grounded in the Qur'an, where the food and drink of paradise is indeed specified. Such a denial, however, may be a reflection of the views of the Brethren of Purity themselves, who advanced an altogether more allegorical interpretation of the joys of paradise.

161 Jesus once passed by some fullers of clothes on the outskirts of town, and he addressed himself to them saying, "When you have washed, cleaned, and bleached these clothes, would you approve if their owners wore them when their bodies were polluted with blood, urine, excrement, and the stain of dirt?" "No," they replied, "and whoever does so is without shame." "You have done it yourselves," Jesus said. "How so?" they asked. Jesus said, "Because you have cleansed your bodies, bleached your clothes, and worn them, while your souls are polluted with injustice, filled with the garbage of foolishness and blindness, dumbness and ill nature, envy and hatred, slyness and cheating, greed and avarice, infamy and distrust, and the pursuit of ruinous desires. You are miserable in the shame of slavishness, and will have no respite except in death and in the grave."

The fullers answered, "What are we to do? How can we avoid making a living?" Jesus said, "Why not desire the Kingdom of Heaven, where there is neither death nor old age, pain nor illness, hunger nor thirst, fear nor sadness, poverty nor need, weariness nor hardship, grief nor envy among its dwellers, neither hatred nor boasting nor conceit. Rather, they are brothers facing one another on couches, happy and pleased, in ease and plenty, grace and favor, joy and amusement, wandering among the celestial spheres and the wide expanse of the heavens, observing the Kingdom of the Lord of Creation and watching the angels in rows around His throne singing the praises of their Lord in melodies and tunes the like of which have never been heard by man or *jinn*. And you will live eternally with them. You will not age or die, nor will you hunger or thirst, nor will you fall ill, fear, or sorrow."

Ikhwan al-Safa' (fourth/tenth century), *Rasa'il,* 4:95–96 (Asin, p. 547, no. 127; Mansur, no. 54; Robson, pp. 52–54).

On fullers, see Saying 145, above. This is a lengthy homily by Jesus in which some of the views of the Brethren of Purity may be detected. There is, to begin with, the theme of the inward *(batin)* and the outward *(zahir)*, a distinction essential to the symbolic scheme of interpretation devised by the Brethren. There is, second, the long catalogue of filth that the soul harbors, central to the ethics of the Brethren and close to the imagery that they used. Third is the question of slavishness—or, more strictly, slavish imitation of religious authority—which the Brethren attacked as the root of all corruption.

162 Christ used to say to his disciples, "I have come to you from my Father and yours to raise you from the death of ignorance, to cure you from the disease of sin, and to heal you from the sickness of corrupt beliefs, wicked conduct, and evil works, so that your souls will be purified and live through the spirit of wisdom, and you will be raised to the Kingdom of Heaven, to my Father and yours. There you will live the life of the happy ones and will be rid of the prison of this world and the pains of the universe of creation and corruption, which is the abode of villains, the tyranny of devils, and the principality of Satan."

Ikhwan al-Safa' (fourth/tenth century), Rasa'il, 4:172 (Asin, p. 551, no. 129; Mansur, no. 56, Robson, pp. 89–90).

Some of the phrasing here likewise reflects the broader views of the Brethren of Purity—for example, the "death" of ignorance, the "prison" of the world, and the universe of creation and corruption.

163 Jesus came upon his disciples and found them laughing. He said, "He who fears [God] does not laugh." They said, "Spirit of God, we were only jesting." Jesus replied, "A person of sound mind does not jest."

Abu Hayyan al-Tawhidi (d. after 400/1010), al-Basa'ir wa'l Dhakha'ir, 1:21.

Abu Hayyan al-Tawhidi was a scholar with very wide interests in Adab, philosophy, and Sufism. On his life and works, see *EI* 2. In this saying, Jesus is once again seen in a somber mood; see Sayings 124 and 272. A similar story is ascribed to Muhammad; see Ibn al-Mubarak, *Kitab al-Zuhd*, p. 312, no. 892. Al-Hasan al-Basri is also said to have disapproved of laughter; see Ibn Sa'd, *Tabaqat*, 7: 170, 171.

164 Christ said, "O disciples, I have laid the world down flat upon its belly for your sake and made you sit upon its back. Only two groups vie with you for its mastery: kings and devils. As for devils, seek support against them in patience and prayer. As for kings, leave their world to them and they will leave the other world to you."

Abu Hayyan al-Tawhidi (d. after 400/1010), *al-Basaʾir waʾl Dhakhaʾir,* 1:23. Cf. Ibn ʿAsakir, *Sirat,* p. 143, no. 142.

Several elements of this composite saying have been encountered above. The novel part here is the coupling of kings and devils.

165 Jesus said, "Even if God Almighty had not decreed torment for sinning against Him, it would [nonetheless] be fitting that He should not be disobeyed, out of gratitude for His bounty."

Abu Hayyan al-Tawhidi (d. after 400/1010), *al-Basaʾir waʾl Dhakhaʾir,* 2:423. Cf. Ibn Abi al-Dunya, *Kitab al-Shukr,* in *Mawsuʿat Rasaʾil,* 3:78, excerpt no. 204 (attributed to "a wise man"); Al-Abi, *Nathr al-Durr,* 7:28.

An elegant theological formulation, directed perhaps at the believer who is also an intellectual.

166 Jesus said, "A Terror which will overwhelm you at an unpredictable moment: what prevents you from preparing for it before it strikes you suddenly?"

Abu Hayyan al-Tawhidi (d. after 400/1010), *al-Basaʾir waʾl Dhakhaʾir,* 3/1:181.

The Terror alluded to is, of course, the terror of the Day of Judgment.

167 Jesus said, "Be a guest in this world and make the mosque your home."

Abu Hayyan al-Tawhidi (d. after 400/1010), *al-Basa'ir wa'l Dhakha'ir*, 3/2:440.

See Saying 11, above.

168 Jesus said, "Every man slain shall be avenged on the Day of Judgment except the man slain by the world, which shall avenge itself upon him."

Abu Hayyan al-Tawhidi (d. after 400/1010), *al-Basa'ir wa'l Dhakha'ir*, 7:147 (no. 243).

The man "slain" by the world is, of course, he who succumbs to its temptations.

169 Jesus preached to the Israelites. They wept and began to tear their clothes. Jesus said, "What sin have your clothes committed? Turn instead to your hearts and reprove them."

Abu Hayyan al-Tawhidi (d. after 400/1010), *al-Basa'ir wa'l Dhakha'ir*, 7:226 (no. 489).

There is some similarity between this saying and Saying 79, above.

170 Jesus said to his disciples, "The sign that you shall use to recognize each other as my followers is your affection for one another." And Jesus said to his disciple Yashu‘, "As for the Lord, you must love Him with all your heart. Then you must love your neighbor as yourself." Jesus was asked, "Show us, Spirit of God, what difference there is between these two loves, so that we may prepare ourselves for them with clarity of vision." Jesus replied, "You love a friend for your own sake and you love your soul for the sake of your Lord. If you take good care of your friend, you are doing so for your own sake, but if you give your soul away, you do so for the sake of your Lord."

Abu Hayyan al-Tawhidi (d. after 400/1010), *Risala fi al-Sadaqa wa al-Sadiq*, p. 64 (Asin, p. 551, no. 130; Mansur, no. 57; Robson, p. 54).

This saying brings together several Gospel elements, identified by Asin. The last part appears once again to be explicative, drawing out the full meaning of the commandment, as in many such sayings in this volume.

171 Jesus said, "Be modest before God Almighty in your innermost thoughts, as you are in your outward behavior."

Abu Sa‘d al-Kharkushi (d. 406/1015), unpublished manuscript (Asin, p. 569, no. 161; Mansur, no. 59; Robson, p. 91).

The author from whom Asin took this and the following three sayings below was a Sufi preacher, Abu Sa‘d al-Kharkushi, whom Asin mistakenly called Abu Sa‘id. The work remains in manuscript

form, so far as I know. On him and on his other works, see Fuat
Sezgin, *Geschichte der Arabischen Schrifttums* (Leiden: Brill, 1967),
1:670. See also A. J. Arberry, "Khargushi's Manual of Sufism," in
Bulletin of the School of Oriental Studies, 9 (1937–1939), 345–349.
The theme of inward and outward conduct found in this saying
has been encountered in several others above.

172 Jesus said, "The likeness of this world to the
next is like a man who has two wives: if he pleases one,
he arouses the other's resentment."

Abu Saʿd al-Kharkushi (d. 406/1015), unpublished manuscript (Asin, p. 569, no.
162; Mansur, no. 60; Robson, p. 76). Cf. al-Ghazali, *Ihya*ʾ, 3:18. See also Ibn Abi
al-Dunya, *Kitab Dhamm al-Dunya*, in *Mawsuʿat Rasaʾil*, 2:65, excerpt no. 119 (attributed to Wahb ibn Munabbih).

There may be an echo here of Mark 12:18–26. Although the traditional Muslim interpretation of the Qurʾanic passage at 4:3 has
been to permit a man to marry up to four wives, it has often been
pointed out that the term for "co-wife," *durra*, is related to the
root *drr*, meaning "harm."

173 Jesus said, "There are three things which
cause men's feet to slip: a dearth of gratitude for the
gifts of God Almighty, the fear of what is other than
God, and the [false] hope of created beings."

Abu Saʿd al-Kharkushi (d. 406/1015), unpublished manuscript (Asin, p. 569, no.
163; Mansur, no. 61; Robson, p. 57).

The phrase "little thanks do you give" is frequent in the Qurʾan,
to express how seldom man is grateful to the Creator. The fear of
what is other than God is an echo of Qurʾan 39:36.

174 Jesus once passed by a man who was suffering, and he felt pity for him, so he said, "O God, I implore You to relieve him." Then God revealed to him: "How am I to relieve him from what I am relieving him with?"

Abu Saʿd al-Kharkushi (d. 406/1015), unpublished manuscript (Asin, p. 570, no. 164; Mansur, no. 62; Robson, p. 116). Cf. al-Qushayri, *al-Risala*, p. 102 (variant; attributed to "a prophet").

This curious story seems to point to the necessity for patience in suffering as a way of purging the soul.

175 Christ was asked, "Why are the old more attached to the world than the young?" He answered, "Because they have tasted of this world what the young have not."

Al-Raghib al-Isfahani (early fifth / early eleventh century), *Muhadarat al-Udaba'*, 1:525.

Al-Raghib al-Isfahani was the author of a well-known anthology of Adab, carefully organized by topic and much used by literary circles. In the Qur'an, attachment to life is said to be a characteristic of some pagan Arabs who are said to wish to live for a thousand years; see Qur'an 2:96.

176 Christ said, "Flesh eating flesh? How offensive an act!"

Al-Raghib al-Isfahani (early fifth / early eleventh century), *Muhadarat al-Udaba'*, 1:610.

This is an unusual saying, seemingly enjoining abstention from eating meat. There is an echo here perhaps of the Gospel According to Thomas; see Layton, *The Gnostic Scriptures*, p. 395, excerpt no. 87, and p. 399, excerpt no. 112. The saying seems also to have been familiar in Syriac literature; see E. A. Wallis Budge, *The Laughable Stories*, p. 31, no. 131.

177 Jesus said, "O God, who is the most honorable of men?" God replied, "He who when alone knows that I am with him, and so respects my majesty that he would not want me to witness his sins."

Al-Raghib al-Isfahani (early fifth / early eleventh century), *Muhadarat al-Udaba'*, 2:402.

There is a possible parallel here with Matthew 18:20 and John 8:16

178 It is related that Jesus said "God preserve you" to a man who did not deserve to be so addressed. Jesus was asked, "Why do you say this to such as he?" He answered, "A tongue accustomed to good speaks thus to all men."

Abu ʿAli Miskawayh (d. 421/1030), *al-Hikma*, p. 132.

Miskawayh was a celebrated philosopher, historian, and senior state bureaucrat. On his life and works, see *EI* 2 and Tarif Khalidi, *Arabic Historical Thought in the Classical Period* (Cambridge: Cambridge University Press, 1994), pp. 170–176. The work from which these sayings are taken collects wise sayings from various Muslim and non-Muslim sources, its title being an exact translation of *philosophia perennis.* For a similar admonition, see Saying 128, above.

179 Christ said, "Let him who thinks that God is slow with His bounty beware! For God might be angry and open wide to him the bounties of the world."

Abu ʿAli Miskawayh (d. 421/1030), *al-Hikma,* p. 156. Cf. Ibn Maja, *Sunan, Kitab al-Fitan,* 2:1325, no. 3197.

There is a parallel to this saying in the Hadith collection of Ibn Maja, where the Prophet Muhammad says to his followers: "It is not poverty that I fear might befall you; rather, I fear the world's abundance upon you."

180 Jesus said, "Do you desire the world for the sake of virtuous deeds? It is more virtuous for you to forsake the world."

Abu ʿAli Miskawayh (d. 421/1030), *al-Hikma,* p. 192.

181 The disciples said to Jesus: "What do you say about rulers?" He answered: "They have been made into a temptation for you. Let not your love for them lead you into sinning against God, nor your hatred for them lead you out of God's obedience. If you fulfill your obligations towards them, you will escape their evil and your faith will be made whole."

Abu Saʿd al-Abi (d. 421/1030), *Nathr,* 7:33.

Al-Abi was a Shiʿite state secretary and man of letters who served the Buwayhid dynasty (945–1055) of western Iran and Iraq. His important anthology of Adab from which this and the following saying are taken was only recently edited, and its importance in Arabic literature is slowly being recognized.

Injunctions about the proper attitude to rulers are frequent in the Muslim gospel and have been encountered above. Equating rulers with "temptation" suggests that they are a necessary evil, or at least that they should be handled with care. The earlier hostility to them has abated somewhat, and an attitude of resigned acceptance seems to be advocated here.

182 Jesus used to say, "Too much food kills the soul, just as too much water kills a plant."

Abu Saʿd al-Abi (d. 421/1030), *Nathr*, 7:35.

Jesus the physician is to the fore here; see Sayings 152, 153, and 154, above. For some reason that cannot quite be determined, it appears that the Shiʿite tradition contained a sizable number of sayings and stories which depict Jesus as a physician with specific cures for the ills of both man and nature. This saying seems to have been known in Syriac literature; see Budge, *The Laughable Stories*, p. 32, no. 134, where it is attributed to a Hebrew sage.

183 Jesus said to his companions, "Leave yourselves to hunger and thirst, go naked and exhaust yourselves, that your hearts might know God Almighty."

Abu Nuʿaym al-Isbahani (d. 430/1038), *Hilyat al-Awliya'*, 2:370 (Mansur, no. 65). Cf. al-Ghazali, *Ihya'*, 3:79 (Asin, p. 361, no. 21; Mansur, no. 106; Robson, p. 63).

Abu Nuʿaym was the author of one of the earliest and most authoritative biographical dictionaries of the "saints": Sufis and pious men and women of Islamic history. For his life and works, see *EI* 2. The discipline enjoined in this saying is similar to that which is found in many others above. It is also, of course, typical of Sufi discipline.

184 Jesus said, "He who acts without counsel acts in vain."

Abu Nuʿaym al-Isbahani (d. 430/1038), *Hilyat al-Awliya'*, 5:237 (Mansur, no. 72).

This saying appears to belong to the spirit of Adab and, more broadly, to the wisdom literature of the ancient Near East. See, e.g., Proverbs 15:22.

185 Jesus said, "If you are able, be simple-minded before God like doves." It used to be said that there is nothing more simple-minded than a dove; you can take her chicks from under her and kill them, and she will then return to roost in the very same spot.

Abu Nuʿaym al-Isbahani (d. 430/1038), *Hilyat al-Awliya'*, 5:239 (Asin, p. 567, no. 157; Mansur, no. 74; Robson, p. 57). Cf. al-Jahiz, *al-Bayan*, 2:242; idem, *al-Hayawan*, 3:189–190 (partial; not a Jesus saying).

A Gospel core (Matthew 10:16) is glossed with an observation on doves. Jahiz devotes a few pages in his *al-Hayawan* (see citation above) to the simple-mindedness of doves.

186 It is related, and God knows best, that Jesus passed one day through a valley called the Valley of Resurrection and came upon a white skull from which the rest of the bones had decayed. Jesus admired its whiteness. The person had died seventy-two years previously. Jesus said, "O God, I ask You, whom no eye can see, no doubts can confound, and no describer can describe, to allow this skull to tell me to what nation it belonged." God revealed to him, "Jesus, speak to the skull and it shall answer you by my power, for I am powerful over all things." Jesus performed his ablutions, prayed two *rak'a*, approached the skull and said, "In the name of God, Merciful and Compassionate." With eloquent tongue, the skull answered, "Spirit of God, you have called upon the best of names." Jesus said, "I ask you in the name of Almighty God to tell me: Where is your beauty and whiteness, where is your flesh and fat, your bones and your soul?" The skull replied, "Spirit of God, as for beauty and whiteness, the earth has changed them. The flesh and fat have been consumed by the worms. The bones have decayed. As for the soul, it is today in hell-fire, in great torment."

Jesus said, "I ask you in the name of Almighty God: To which nation did you belong?" The skull answered, "I am from a nation upon which descended the anger of God in this worldly abode." Jesus asked, "How did God's anger descend upon you in this worldly abode?" The skull said, "Spirit of God, God sent us a prophet who came with the truth, but we called him a liar. He commanded us to obey God, but we disobeyed him. God then caused rain and lightning to fall upon us for seven years, seven months, and seven days. Then one day angels of torment descended upon us. Each angel carried two whips, a whip of iron and a whip of fire. The angel did not cease to extract my soul from joint to joint and from vein to vein until my soul reached my throat. At that point, the angel of death stretched forth his hand and pulled out my soul."

Jesus said, "I ask you in the name of Almighty God, describe to me the angel of death." The skull answered, "Spirit of God, he has one hand in the West, the other in the East. His head reaches up to the highest heavens, and his legs reach down to the regions of the seventh and lowest earth. The earth itself is between his knees, and all creation is between his eyes." The skull continued, "O Prophet of God, hardly an hour had passed when two pitch-black angels came to me. They spoke like crashing thunder and their eyes flashed like lightning; they were curly haired and furrowed the ground with their fangs. They said to me, 'Who is your God? Who is your prophet? Who is your imam?' Spirit of God, I was terrified and said, 'I have no god, no prophet, no imam except God.' 'You lie,' they said, 'Enemy of God and of yourself.' They struck me a blow with a rod of iron so hard that I felt my bones had broken and my flesh had been torn away. They then cast me in the pit of hell and there tormented me for such time as pleased God. While I was in this state, there came to me the two guardian scribes who inscribe the deeds of all creatures in this world, and they said to me, 'Enemy of God, come with us to the stations of the people of paradise.' So I went with them to the first of the gates of paradise, and found paradise to have eight gates. It is built of bricks, some gold and some silver. Its earth is made of musk. Its grass is saffron. Its pebbles are pearls and rubies. Its rivers are of milk, water, and honey. Its inhabitants are comely maidens, alike in age, chaste, and living in pavilions, servants of the Majestic and Beneficent. Spirit of God, I was delighted. The two scribes then turned to me and said, 'Enemy of God and self, you did not do good in your earthly life to merit all this. But come with us now to the stations of the people of hell.' So I went with them to the first gate of hell, where serpents and scorpions hiss, and asked them, 'For whom is this torment intended?' 'For you,' they replied, 'and for those who consume the wealth of orphans unjustly.' Then I went with them to the second gate, where there were men hanging by their beards, lapping blood and pus off their hands like dogs. I said to them, 'For whom is this torment intended?' 'For you,' they answered, 'and for those who drink wine and eat what is forbidden in this earthly life.' Then I went with them to the third gate and found men with fire entering their mouths and coming out of their rear. 'For whom is this torment?' I asked. 'For you,' they said, 'and for those who libel married women in earthly life.' Then I went with them to the fourth gate and found women hanging by their tongues, with fire coming out of their mouths. 'For whom is this torment?' I asked. 'For you,' they said, 'and for those who fail to perform their prayers in their earthly life.' Then I went with them to the fifth gate, and found women hanging by their hair, with fire over their heads. 'For whom is this torment?' I asked. 'For you,' they replied, 'and for those who adorn themselves for other than their spouses.' I went with them to the sixth gate, and there I found women hanging by their hair and mouths. 'For whom is this torment?' I asked. 'For you,' they replied, 'and for lost sinners in the world.' I went with them to the seventh gate, and found men beneath whom was a well called the Well of Falaq. I was cast into it, Spirit of God. In it I am in greatest torment and have witnessed countless terrors."

Jesus then said to the skull, "O skull, if you so desire, ask anything of me by God's leave." The skull said, "Spirit of God, pray that God would restore me to earthly life." Jesus prayed to God who resurrected the skull and handed it over to Jesus whole and sound, through the power of Almighty God. She then remained twelve years worshiping God with Jesus until certitude—that is to say, death—came upon her. She died a true believer, and God in His mercy placed her among the people of paradise.

Abu Nu'aym al-Isbahani (d. 430/1038), *Hilyat al-Awliya'*, 6:10–12 (Asin, pp. 426–428, no. 102, quinquies; Mansur, no. 263; Robson, pp. 102–107).

This is a long and complex tale. There are two other encounters with skulls; see Sayings 234 and 248, below. For a parallel with other literatures, see the Mishnaic tract *Pirkey Aboth*, in Hertz, *Sayings of the Fathers*, p. 28, no. 7 (R. Hillel and the skull). The initial prayer of Jesus to God is typical of Muslim piety. The number seventy-two is a frequent and symbolic number in Hadith. That Jesus performs the Muslim ablutions and prayers relates, of course, to the fact that he is a Muslim prophet, as does the *basmalah* ("In the name of God, Merciful and Compassionate") which he pronounces. The rain sent upon an ungrateful people echoes Qur'an 7:84 (and several other instances). Falaq is said by some commentators on Qur'an 113:1 to be the name of a prison *(sijn)* or else a pit *(jubb)* of hell. The description of paradise and of hell has several elements in common with visions of the after-life in other religious traditions; see, e.g., Martha Himmelfarb, *Tours of Hell* (Philadelphia: University of Pennsylvania Press, 1983), pp. 82–92, for images of hanging in hell. There are several other elements which appear to echo the accounts of paradise and hell in the Apocryphal *Apocalypse of Peter* and *Apocalypse of Paul;* see M. Rhodes James, *The Apocryphal New Testament*, pp. 505–555.

187 It is written in the Gospels, "The stone in the structure which is there unlawfully is an assurance of its destruction."

Abu Nuʿaym al-Isbahani (d. 430/1038), *Hilyat al-Awliya'*, 6:95 (Mansur, no. 77).

There seems to be an echo here of Matthew 21:42 and Luke 20:17 (cf. Psalms 118:22–23) but while the imagery is similar, the mean-ing is very different. In the Gospels, what is implied is a new cove-nant with a new people of God. In the saying above, the stone in the structure is an ethical metaphor: all human schemes and en-deavors must be founded upon virtue.

188 Jesus said, "Talk much to God, talk little to people." He was asked, "How do we talk much to God?" Jesus answered, "Converse with Him in solitude, pray to Him in solitude."

Abu Nuʿaym al-Isbahani (d. 430/1038), *Hilyat al-Awliya'*, 6:195 ; cf. al-Qushayri, *al-Risala*, p. 69 (attributed to Muʿadh ibn Jabal, a celebrated Companion of Muhammad; variant). (Asin, p. 568, no. 158; Mansur, no. 79; Robson, p. 57).

Asin suggests Matthew 6:5–7 as a parallel. But see also Ecclesiastes 5:1–2. The attribution to Muʿadh ibn Jabal (see reference above) is interesting; one report states, "Jesus was made to ascend to heaven at age thirty-three, and Muʿadh died at age thirty-three" (Ibn Saʿd, *Tabaqat*, 7:389).

189 If you wish, you may repeat what the Possessor of the Word and the Spirit [of God], Jesus the son of Mary, used to say: "Hunger is my seasoning, fear is my garment, wool is my clothing, the light of the dawn is my heat in winter, the moon is my lantern, my legs are my beast of burden, and the produce of the earth is my food and fruit. I retire for the night with nothing to my name and awake in the morning with nothing to my name. And there is no one on earth richer than me."

Abu Nuʿaym al-Isbahani (d. 430/1038), *Hilyat al-Awliya*, 6:314 (Asin, pp. 374–375, no. 44; Mansur, no. 80; Robson, pp. 67–68).

Asin records a similar passage attributed to ʿAli ibn Abi Talib. But there are also some interesting echoes of a letter written by Anacharsis, a Hellenized Scythian who lived circa 600 B.C., who was later regarded as one of the Seven Wise Men and is quoted in Cicero, *On the Good Life* (Harmondsworth: Penguin, 1971), pp. 100–101: "My clothing is a Scythian mantle, my shoes are the hard soles of my feet, my bed is the earth, my food is seasoned only by hunger—and I eat nothing but milk and cheese and meat. Come and visit me and you will find me at peace. You want to give me something. But give it to your fellow-citizens instead, or let the immortal gods have it." The legend of the Seven Wise Men was well known in Arabic Islamic wisdom literature from at least as early as the ninth century.

190 Jesus said, "O Israelites, Moses forbade you to commit adultery, and he did well to forbid it. I forbid you even to contemplate it, for he who contemplates it without acting upon it is like an earthenware house in which a fire is lit: even though it does not burn, it becomes charred from the smoke."

"O Israelites, Moses forbade you to swear by God falsely, and he did well to forbid it. I forbid you to swear by God at all, be it falsely or truly."

Abu Nuʿaym al-Isbahani (d. 430/1038), *Hilyat al-Awliyaʾ*, 8:145–146 (Mansur, no. 82).

The two commandments come from Matthew 5:27–28 and 34–37.

191 Jesus said, "O man of learning, learn of knowledge what you do not know and teach the ignorant what you have learned."

Abu al-Hasan al-Mawardi (d. 450/1058), *Adab al-Dunya wa al-Din*, p. 67.

Al-Mawardi was an important writer on the theory of government and on ethics in Islam. For information on his life and works, see *EI* 2. There are several commandments about knowledge and the importance of imparting it; see, e.g., Sayings 46 and 195.

192 Jesus was asked, "Why are you not married?" He answered, "Only in the abode of eternity is it laudable to multiply."

Abu al-Hasan al-Mawardi (d. 450/1058), *Adab al-Dunya wa al-Din,* pp. 104 and 135.

Jesus has already spoken of marriage above; see Saying 60. The multiplication *(takathur)* of children and of worldly goods is decried in the Qur'an (57:20 and 102:1) as part of the condemnation of boasting and of being too attached to the world.

193 Jesus said, "As you sleep, so shall you die; and as you awake, so shall you be resurrected."

Abu al-Hasan al-Mawardi (d. 450/1058), *Adab al-Dunya wa al-Din,* p. 107.

The figurative use of sleeping and awakening for death and resurrection is common in the Bible; see, e.g., Job 14:11–12 and John 11:11–16.

194 Jesus said, "Beware of glancing at women, and glancing again, for this sows lust in the heart, seduction enough for him who does it."

Abu al-Hasan al-Mawardi (d. 450/1058), *Adab al-Dunya wa al-Din,* p. 294.Cf. Ibn al-Jawzi, *Dhamm al-Hawa,* p. 91.

There is a certain rhyming cadence in the Arabic original, designed no doubt for easy memorization. The core of the saying is clearly Matthew 5:26–28.

195 It is related that Christ was asked, "Until what age is it seemly to acquire knowledge?" He answered, "As long as life itself is seemly."

Ibn ʿAbd al-Barr al-Qurtubi (d. 463/1071), *Jamiʿ Bayan al-ʿIlm*, 1:96.

Ibn ʿAbd al-Barr was an Andalusian traditionist and man of letters. On his life and writings, see *EI* 2. In *Jamiʿ*, he collects a large number of traditions from diverse sources concerning the virtues of knowledge.

196 Jesus said, "O reciters and scholars, how can you go astray after acquiring knowledge, or how can you be blind after acquiring eyesight, and all for the sake of a despicable world and base desires? Woe to you in this world, and woe to this world from you."

Ibn ʿAbd al-Barr al-Qurtubi (d. 463/1071), *Jamiʿ Bayan al-ʿIlm*, 1:190.

The reciters *(qurraʾ)* are of course Qurʾan reciters, a politically prominent group in early Islam. The rebuke addressed to them and to other scholars here is often encountered elsewhere; see Sayings 117, 174, 193, 263.

197 Christ said, "Do not be saddened by what people say about you. If what they say is false, it would be like a good deed that you have not performed. If true, it would be like an evil deed whose punishment has been prematurely exacted."

Ibn ʿAbd al-Barr al-Qurtubi (d. 463/1071), *Bahjat al-Majalis*, 1:405.

This elegant counsel to ignore the opinions of mankind may be a distant echo of Matthew 5:11–12.

198 Jesus was passing by a cemetery. He called one of the dead and God resurrected him. Jesus asked him, "Who are you?" "I was once a porter," the man replied, "I was carrying some firewood for a man and broke off a twig to clean my teeth. Since I died I have been asked about this twig."

Abu al-Qasim al-Qushayri (d. 465/1073), *Al-Risala al-Qushayriyya fi ʿIlm al-Tasawwuf*, p. 65 (Asin, p. 565, no. 151; Mansur, no. 88; Robson, p. 115). Cf. Asin, p. 566, no. 152; Robson, pp. 115–116 (fuller version).

Al-Qushayri was a celebrated Sufi author who was also a learned lawyer and accomplished man of letters. The work from which this story is taken is a guide to Sufi terminology, the major Sufi figures, and Sufi lore and conduct. On his life and works, see *EI* 2.

That a divine record is kept of even the most trivial of sins is consonant with Qurʾan 99:7–8, "Whoever does an atom's weight of good shall see it, and whoever does an atom's weight of evil shall see it."

199 Jesus said, "How many trees there are but not all bear fruit! How many fruits there are but not all are good to eat! How many sciences there are but not all are useful!"

Abu Hamid al-Ghazali (d. 505/1111), *Ihya' 'Ulum al-Din*, 1:38 (Asin, p. 349, no. 2; Mansur, no. 90; Robson, p. 42).

Al-Ghazali was a towering figure of classical Islam. His objective was nothing less than the complete redefinition of the diverse sciences of Islamic civilization, with the aim of endowing them all with the spirituality of Sufism. His immense knowledge of law, theology, philosophy, and Hadith and his own fascinating record of his intellectual and spiritual journey make him one of the most attractive intellects of world culture. The work from which most of the following sayings and stories are taken, *Ihya' 'Ulum al-Din* (The Revival of the Sciences of Religion), is an encyclopedic treatment of the various aspects of Muslim devotion, and quickly came to occupy a very prominent place in the Islamic canon of religious literature. Ghazali had a particular and pronounced interest in Jesus, whom he designated "Prophet of the Heart," enshrining him as one of the central figures of Sufi spirituality. On Ghazali's life and works, see *EI* 2.

The core of this saying comes from Matthew 7:16–20. The appended criticism of useless sciences occurs in the context of an attack by Ghazali on lawyers preoccupied with useless minutiae of the law. This is a theme found quite often in other sayings and stories below. Ghazali believed that many scholars of law were a hindrance to the development of a truly spiritual life.

200 Jesus said, "To dispense wisdom to other than those worthy of it is to do it an injustice, and to bar it from those worthy of it is to do them an injustice. Be like the gentle physician who applies medication to the place of illness." In another version, he said, "He who dispenses wisdom to other than those worthy of it is ignorant, and he who bars it from those worthy of it has done an injustice. Wisdom has its due, and it has people who are worthy of it, so give every man his due."

Abu Hamid al-Ghazali (d. 505/1111), *Ihya³ ʿUlum al-Din*, 1:43 (Asin, p. 349, no. 3; Mansur, no. 91; Robson, p. 42). Cf. al-Jahiz, *al-Bayan*, 2:35; Ikhwan al-Safa³, *Rasaʾil*, 4:215 (partial); al-Mawardi, *Adab*, p. 127; Ibn ʿAbd al-Barr, *Jamiʿ*, 1:109 (partial); Ibn ʿAsakir, *Sirat*, p. 187, no. 225 (variant).

An echo of Matthew 7:6. Like many other Islamic thinkers of his age, Ghazali held that individuals differed greatly in their intellectual abilities and natural dispositions. Accordingly, not all sciences should be made accessible to all people; to each his level of knowledge of the sciences that stands to benefit him most. Otherwise, there would be a distinct danger of misunderstanding and even of heresy. Sciences such as mathematics were seductive, in Ghazali's opinion, for anyone who demanded the same mathematical standards of accuracy from other sciences (e.g., theology) ran the risk of falling into unbelief. In sum, Ghazali was an intellectual elitist.

201 Jesus said, "The scholars of evil are like a rock which has fallen into the mouth of a river: it neither drinks the water nor allows the water to pass to the crops. The scholars of evil are also like the channels of a sewer: their exterior is white plaster and their interior is foul; or like tombs which are grand on the outside and full of dead bones inside."

Abu Hamid al-Ghazali (d. 505/1111), *Ihya³ ʿUlum al-Din*, 1:66. Cf. Warram, *Majmuʿa*, 1:84 (Asin, p. 351, no. 5; Mansur, no. 93; Robson, p. 43).

The context is still the attack on narrow-minded scholars. Asin suggests some Gospel parallels. For another parallel, see J. Sadan, "Some Literary Problems concerning Judaism and Jewry in Medieval Arabic Sources," in M. Sharon, ed., *Studies in Honour of Professor David Ayalon* (Leiden: Brill, 1986), pp. 353–398, at 389–390, no. S6. In this article, Sadan summarizes an Islamic version of the supposedly genuine Torah revealed to Moses, and discusses this text at pp. 370ff.

202 Jesus said, "How can someone be considered a man of learning if he deliberately travels down the road of this world while his destination is the afterlife? And how can someone be considered a man of learning if he desires speech in order to relay it to others rather than to act upon it?"

Abu Hamid al-Ghazali (d. 505/1111), *Ihya' 'Ulum al-Din*, 1:67 (Asin, p. 352, no. 6; Mansur, no. 94; Robson, p. 63).

Compare with Saying 191, above.

203 Jesus said, "One who acquires knowledge but does not act in accordance with it is like a woman who commits adultery in secret and becomes pregnant, and her shame is known to all. So, also, he who does not act in accordance with his knowledge shall be shamed by God before all men on the Day of Judgment."

Abu Hamid al-Ghazali (d. 505/1111), *Ihya' 'Ulum al-Din*, 1:69 (Asin, p. 353, no. 8; Mansur, no. 95; Robson, p. 43).

See Saying 43, above.

204 It is told that Jesus went out one day to pray for rain. When those around him became restless, Jesus said, "Whoever among you who has committed a sin must return." So they all went back, except for one man who stayed behind with him in the desert. Jesus said to him, "Have you not committed any sins?" "As God is my witness," he answered, "none that I know of. Except that one day, while I was praying, a woman passed near me and I looked at her with this eye. As she passed by, I put my finger into my eye and plucked it out, and flung it at the woman." Then Jesus said to him, "Pray to God, so that I may call 'Amen' to your prayer." The man prayed to God, the sky became covered with clouds, and it poured. And so they were quenched.

Abu Hamid al-Ghazali (d. 505/1111), *Ihya' 'Ulum al-Din*, 1:316 (Asin, p. 354, no. 10; Mansur, no. 97; Robson, p. 95). Cf. Asin, p. 587, no. 201; Robson, pp. 121–122 (fuller version); and Ibn al-Jawzi, *Dhamm al-Hawa*, p. 131 (slightly variant).

There is a special Muslim prayer for rain *(Salat al-Istisqa')*. The image of the offending eye being plucked out comes from Matthew 18:9.

205 While seeking Jesus, Mary passed by some weavers and asked the way. When they pointed her to the wrong road, she said, "O God! Strip their gain of blessing, let them die poor, and demean them in the eyes of people." And her prayer was answered.

Abu Hamid al-Ghazali (d. 505/1111), *Ihya' 'Ulum al-Din*, 2:85 (Asin, p. 357, no. 13; Mansur, no. 99).

Some classical Muslim writers, such as Jahiz, considered certain professions and crafts (e.g., weaving) to be ignoble; see Jahiz, *Rasaʾil*, 1:51–52, and compare Saying 145, above, for fullers. Such stories helped, of course, to "explain" the low standing of these professions. This story was also known in Syriac literature; see Budge, *The Laughable Stories*, p. 123, no. 475.

206 It is related that Satan once appeared before Jesus and said to him, "Say: 'There is no god but God.'" Jesus replied, "Righteous words which I will not repeat after you." This is because Satan's deceptions can lurk even beneath good.

Abu Hamid al-Ghazali (d. 505/1111), *Ihyaʾ ʿUlum al-Din*, 3:29 (Asin, p. 359, no. 17; Mansur, no. 102; Robson, p. 81).

The temptation of Jesus in the wilderness in Matthew 4:1–11 may be the inspiration for this episode. Note that Satan wants Jesus to repeat the *Muslim* confession of faith. The last sentence is a gloss, probably by Ghazali himself.

207 When Jesus was born, the devils came to Satan and said, "The idols today have all bowed their heads." Satan said, "Something has happened in your world." Satan then flew all over the world but found nothing. At last he found the infant Jesus, surrounded by the angels. He returned to the devils and said, "A prophet was born yesterday. No female ever conceived or gave birth without my being present, except this one. Therefore, despair of idol worship after this night.

Henceforth, seduce men by exploiting their hastiness and superficiality."

Abu Hamid al-Ghazali (d. 505/1111), *Ihya' 'Ulum al-Din*, 3:32 (Asin, pp. 359–360, no. 18; Mansur, no. 103, Robson, pp. 81–82). Cf. Ibn 'Asakir, *Sirat*, p. 37, no. 18.

There are several apocryphal texts which speak of idols falling shortly after the birth of Jesus; see James, *The Apocryphal New Testament*, pp. 75, 80, 83. Haste and superficiality are often condemned in the Qur'an.

208 Jesus said, "Blessed is he who abandons a present desire for the sake of an absent, invisible promise."

Abu Hamid al-Ghazali (d. 505/1111), *Ihya' 'Ulum al-Din*, 3:64; Ibn 'Asakir, *Sirat*, p. 150, no. 157 (Asin, p. 361, no. 20; Mansur, no. 105; Robson, p. 63).

The form of this saying bears a strong resemblance to the apocryphal letter of Christ to Abgarus (Al-Abjar). See James, *The Apocryphal New Testament*, p. 477.

209 It is told that Jesus spent sixty days in intimate conversation with his Lord without eating. Then the thought of bread occurred to him and his intimacy was interrupted. At once a loaf of bread appeared in his hands, so he sat down and wept for the loss of intimacy. At that moment, an old man cast his shadow upon him and Jesus said to him, "God bless you, friend of God. Pray to God for me, for I was in a trance and the thought of bread occurred to me, and so my trance was interrupted." The old man prayed, "O God! If you know that the thought of bread has occurred to me since I have known You, do not forgive me. On the contrary, if anything was brought before me, I would eat it without any thought of it."

Abu Hamid al-Ghazali (d. 505/1111), *Ihya' 'Ulum al-Din*, 3:81 (Asin, p. 362, no. 22; Mansur, no. 107; Robson, pp. 63–64).

A curious exchange, bearing some relation to the fasting and meditation of the Sufis but also to early Christian ascetic practice. Here, too, Jesus is seen as manifesting a human weakness when compared to the total godly communion of the "old man," who may perhaps be a model Sufi master.

210 Jesus said, "Piety is nine-tenths silence, and one-tenth fleeing from people."

Abu Hamid al-Ghazali (d. 505/1111), *Ihya' 'Ulum al-Din*, 3:107 (Asin, p. 364, no. 26; Mansur, no. 111; Robson, p. 64).

A similar commandment was revealed to an Egyptian desert father; see Ward, *The Sayings of the Desert Fathers*, p. 9, no. 2.

211 It is written in the Gospels, "He who prays for those who treat him badly defeats Satan."

Abu Hamid al-Ghazali (d. 505/1111), *Ihya' 'Ulum al-Din*, 3:180 (Asin, p. 367, no. 33; Mansur, no. 118; Robson, p. 46).

To a Gospel core (Luke 6:28) is added the defeat of Satan.

212 Jesus said, "Woe to the man of this world! How he dies when he leaves it and all that is in it behind him! How the world deceives him, yet he still trusts it! How it lets him down, yet he still has faith in it! Woe to the deceived! How the world showed them what they hate! How those things they loved have forsaken them! How they have encountered what they have been threatened with! Woe to him who makes the world his concern, and sin his pursuit! How soon his sin will be revealed!"

Abu Hamid al-Ghazali (d. 505/1111), *Ihya' 'Ulum al-Din*, 3:200 (Asin, p. 371, no. 38; Mansur, no. 122, Robson, pp. 66–67). Cf. al-Zabidi, *Ithaf*, 8:87.

Imprecations against the world are very common in Muslim ascetic writings; see especially Ibn Abi'l Dunya's *Kitab Dhamm al-Dunya*, in *Mawsu'at Rasa'il*, which contains an unusually large number of sayings attributed to Jesus.

213 It is reported that Jesus said, "O scholars of evil! You fast and pray and give alms but do not do what you order others to do, and you preach what you do not practice. Wretched indeed is your judgment! You repent in word and false hope, but you act according to your whims. What does it avail you if you keep your skins clean while your hearts are sullied? In truth I say to you, do not be like the sieve through which the tasty flour falls while the residue is left behind, for so are you when you pass judgment with your mouths but malice is left behind in your hearts. Slaves of the world, how can a man attain the other world when his lust for this world is unceasing, his desire for it unsatisfied? In truth I say to you, your hearts weep because of your deeds. You have placed the world under your tongues and the deed under your feet. In truth I say to you, you have corrupted your afterlife, since the good of this world is dearer to you than the good of the next. Who among men is more lost than you are—if only you knew!

Woe to you! How long will you continue to describe the road for travelers by night and take up your stations among men who are bewildered, as though you were calling upon the people of this world to leave the world to you? Go slow! Go slow! Woe to you—what does it avail the dark house if the lantern is placed on the roof while the inside is dark and desolate? Likewise will it be no avail to you if the light of wisdom is in your mouths while inside you all is desolate and void. Slaves of the world—but not indeed like pious slaves nor like honorable freemen! The world is about to pull you out by the roots, throw you down upon your faces, and grind your noses into the dust. It will then seize you by your forelocks because of your sins and propel you from behind until it delivers you naked and alone to the King and Judge, who shall acquaint you with your sins and then punish you for your evil deeds."

Abu Hamid al-Ghazali (d. 505/1111), *Ihya' 'Ulum al-Din*, 3:258–259 (Asin, pp. 380–381, no. 53; Mansur, no. 135; Robson, pp. 82–83). Cf. Ibn 'Asakir, *Sirat*, p. 191, no. 233.

This imprecation against evil scholars has appeared earlier; see Sayings 93, 94, 117, 196, and 201. In several places it is reminiscent of Jesus' indictment of the scribes and Pharisees in Matthew

23:13–36. Seizing by the forelock is a Qur'anic image; see Qur'an 96:15.

214 Christ said, "Seeds grow in a plain but not among rocks. So, also, wisdom flourishes in the heart of a humble man but not in the heart of the proud. Do you not see how the man who flaunts his head to the ceiling will dash it, while he who lowers his head shelters and protects it?"

Abu Hamid al-Ghazali (d. 505/1111), *Ihya' 'Ulum al-Din,* 3:336 (Asin, p. 391, no. 59; Mansur, no. 141; Robson, p. 47).

Asin suggests the parable of the sower (Matthew 13:4–9) as a possible origin for part of this saying. The conjunction of wisdom and humility is common in religious literatures of the Near East; see, e.g., Proverbs 11:2.

215 Jesus said, "Fine clothes, proud hearts."

Abu Hamid al-Ghazali (d. 505/1111), *Ihya' 'Ulum al-Din,* 3:345–346 (Asin, p. 391, no. 60; Mansur, no. 142; Robson, p. 70).

Asin suggests Luke 7:25 as a possible parallel. To this, one might add Luke 20:45–47, as perhaps a closer parallel.

216 Jesus said, "Why do you come to me dressed like monks, though your hearts are the hearts of wolves and predators? Wear the clothes of kings but mortify your hearts with the fear of God."

Abu Hamid al-Ghazali (d. 505/1111), *Ihya' 'Ulum al-Din*, 3:346 (Asin, p. 391, no. 61; Mansur, no. 143; Robson, pp. 83–84). Cf. al-Raghib al-Isfahani, *Muhadarat*, 2:402.

The "false prophets" who come disguised as sheep in Matthew 7:15 are transformed here into monks. The Qur'an mentions monks *(ruhban)* in four places, but expresses a certain admiration for them in only one place, the passage at 5:82, where it praises their humility.

217 Christ said, "You shall not attain what you desire except by suffering what you do not desire."

Abu Hamid al-Ghazali (d. 505/1111), *Ihya' 'Ulum al-Din*, 4:61; cf. Jahiz, *Bayan*, 3:164 (attributed to al-Hasan al-Basri); Ibn Hamdun, *Al-Tadhkira*, 1:201, no. 475 (Asin, p. 394, no. 64; Mansur, no. 146; Robson, p. 47).

See Ward, *The Sayings of the Desert Fathers*, p. 70, no. 7.

218 It is related that Jesus said, "You disciples are afraid of sin. We prophets are afraid of unbelief."

Abu Hamid al-Ghazali (d. 505/1111), *Ihya' 'Ulum al-Din*, 4:169 (Asin, p. 397, no. 68; Mansur, no. 150; Robson, p. 48).

A curious saying, perhaps to be understood as referring to Sufi disciples in contrast to Sufi masters. This interpretation is supported by a saying cited immediately before this one and ascribed to the Sufi master Sahl al-Tustari (d. 283/896): "The *murid* [Sufi disciple] fears the affliction of sins; the *'arif* [Sufi master] fears the affliction of unbelief." The general context of this saying is a discussion by Ghazali of how one's fear of God increases as one's knowledge of God increases.

219 It is related that on one of his journeys Jesus passed by a man asleep, wrapped in his cloak. Jesus woke him up and said, "Sleeper, get up and mention God Almighty." "What do you want from me?" said the sleeper, "I have abandoned this world to its people." Jesus said, "Sleep on, my beloved."

Abu Hamid al-Ghazali (d. 505/1111), *Ihya' 'Ulum al-Din*, 4:190 (Asin, p. 401, no. 71; Mansur, no. 153; Robson, p. 70).

Although there seems to be no Gospel parallel to this exchange, it appears to belong in spirit to the stories one encounters in early ascetic Christian and Muslim literature. Waking up in order to pray was considered an especially meritorious deed in Jewish and Muslim practice; see, e.g., Proverbs 6:9–11, and Hertz, *Sayings of the Fathers*, p. 45, excerpt no. 14. The Muslim call to dawn prayer includes the phrase, "Prayer is more virtuous than sleep." The image of the man wrapped up in his cloak recalls the figure described in Qur'an 73 and 74. This was an image found particularly meaningful by the Sufis, who saw the cloak-swathed man as a model of the meditative solitary.

220 Christ said, "The world is a bridge. Cross this bridge, but do not build upon it." He was once asked, "Prophet of God, would that you ordered us to build a house where we can worship God." He said, "Go and build a house on water." They asked him, "How can anything sound be built on water?" He answered, "How can there be sound worship if it is joined with love of the world?"

Abu Hamid al-Ghazali (d. 505/1111), *Ihya' 'Ulum al-Din*, 4:218 (Asin, p. 404, no. 75; Mansur, no. 156; Robson, p. 71). Cf. al-Makki, *Qut*, 1:256.

A composite saying, elements of which are found elsewhere in this volume. See Sayings 41, 60, 99, 110, and 302.

221 As Jesus sat in the shade of a wall belonging to a man, the man came and made him leave the spot. Jesus said, "It was not you who made me leave, but rather He who did not want me to enjoy the shade."

Abu Hamid al-Ghazali (d. 505/1111), *Ihya' 'Ulum al-Din*, 4:224 (Asin, p. 407, no. 79; Mansur, no. 160; Robson, p. 71–72). Cf. Ibn 'Asakir, *Sirat*, p. 132, no. 118.

Asin sees here an echo of Matthew 8:20. It is clearly an exchange which emphasizes the total renunciation of the world we saw above in, for example, the story of the stone pillow in Sayings 118 and 119.

222 Jesus owned nothing but a comb and a cup. He once saw a man combing his beard with his fingers, so Jesus threw away the comb. He saw another drinking from a river with his hands cupped, so Jesus threw away the cup.

Abu Hamid al-Ghazali (d. 505/1111), *Ihya' 'Ulum al-Din*, 4:231–232 (Asin, p. 408, no. 81; Mansur, no. 162; Robson, p. 72).

Physical descriptions of Jesus and his mode of life have been encountered above; see Sayings 77 and 78.

223 Jesus said, "He is not wise who does not rejoice when calamities and diseases befall his body and riches, for then he can look forward to doing penance for his sins."

Abu Hamid al-Ghazali (d. 505/1111), *Ihya' 'Ulum al-Din*, 4:281 (Asin, p. 410, no. 83; Mansur, no. 165; Robson, p. 48).

Cf. Ibn Abi al-Dunya, *Kitab al-Shukr*, in *Mawsu'at Rasa'il*, 3:36, excerpt no. 80, a saying attributed to Sufyan al-Thawri (d. 161/778), a celebrated traditionist and ascetic: "He is no scholar who does not count calamity a divine favor nor prosperity a calamity."

224 Among the sayings of Jesus is the following: "If you see a youth enamored with the pursuit of God, [know that] this makes him oblivious to everything else."

Abu Hamid al-Ghazali (d. 505/1111), *Ihya' 'Ulum al-Din*, 4:302 (Asin, p. 413, no. 85; Mansur, no. 167; Robson, p. 48).

See Saying 238, below. For other stories of youths devoting themselves to God, see Ward, *The Sayings of the Desert Fathers*, pp. 145–146 and passim.

225 It is related that Jesus passed by a man who was blind, leprous, crippled, paralyzed on both sides of his body, and mutilated with lesions from leprosy. The man was saying, "Praise be to God, who healed me from what He has inflicted upon so many of His creatures." Jesus asked him, "You there—what kind of affliction can I see that has not been visited upon you?" The man replied, "Spirit of God, I am better than him in whose heart God has not planted the share of His knowledge that He has planted in mine." "You have spoken truly," said Jesus, "Give me your hand." The man stretched forth his hand—and behold, his face and form were transformed into the fairest and most comely, for God had cured him of his affliction. Thereafter, he accompanied Jesus and worshiped with him.

Abu Hamid al-Ghazali (d. 505/1111), *Ihya᾽ ʿUlum al-Din*, 4:339 (Asin, p. 415, no. 88; Mansur, no. 170; Robson, p. 101).

The cure of the leper in Matthew 8:1–3 is transformed here into an exchange where the leper most probably uses the term "knowledge" *(maʿrifa)* to designate that higher or immediate and experiential knowledge of God which the Sufis claimed as their prerogative.

226 Jesus asked the Israelites, "Where does seed grow?" "In the soil," they answered. Jesus said, "Truly I say to you, wisdom grows only in a soil-like heart."

Abu Hamid al-Ghazali (d. 505/1111), *Ihya᾽ ʿUlum al-Din*, 4:347 (Asin, p. 416, no. 89; Mansur, no. 171; Robson, p. 49).

See Saying 214, above.

227 God revealed to Jesus, "If I look into the secret thought of a servant and find in it no love of this world or the next, I fill it with love of me and take charge of guarding it."

Abu Hamid al-Ghazali (d. 505/1111), *Ihya' 'Ulum al-Din,* 4:349. Cf. al-Qushayri, *al-Risala,* p. 173 (slightly variant) (Asin, p. 417, no. 90; Mansur, no. 172; Robson, p. 78).

The "secret thought" of a servant of God and the heart filled with God's love suggest Sufi images.

228 Jesus was asked to name the best of all works. He said, "Contentment with God Almighty and love of Him."

Abu Hamid al-Ghazali (d. 505/1111), *Ihya' 'Ulum al-Din,* 4:349 (Asin, p. 417, no. 91; Mansur, no. 173; Robson, p. 49).

Contentment with God *(al-Rida 'an Allah)* is the subject of one of the Epistles of Ibn Abi al-Dunya. There are several parallels to this saying attributed to early and pious Muslims; see, e.g., *Kitab al-Rida 'an Allah,* in *Mawsu'at Rasa'il,* 3:22, excerpt no. 6; 3:25, excerpt no. 9; and 3:42, excerpt no. 31.

229 Jesus said, "Blessed is the eye that sleeps with no intention of sinning and awakens to other than sinning."

Abu Hamid al-Ghazali (d. 505/1111), *Ihya' 'Ulum al-Din,* 4:353 (Asin, p. 417, no. 92; Mansur, no. 174; Robson, p. 49).

The image of the offending eye comes from Matthew 6:22–23 and 18:9. The reference to the blessed eye comes from Luke 10:23.

230 The disciples asked Jesus, "Spirit of God, is there anyone on earth now who is like you?" Jesus answered, "Yes, he whose speech is a mention [of God], whose silence is contemplation [of God], and whose every glance derives a lesson—such a man is like me."

Abu Hamid al-Ghazali (d. 505/1111), *Ihya' 'Ulum al-Din*, 4:411 (Asin, p. 420, no. 97; Mansur, no. 179; Robson, pp. 49–50).

See Sayings 10 and 13, above.

231 It is said that once when Jesus was sitting, an old man was working with a shovel scooping up the earth. Jesus said, "O God, remove hope from him." The old man put aside his shovel and lay down, remaining thus for an hour. Then Jesus said, "O God, restore hope to him." The man got up and began to work. Jesus asked him about this, and the man said, "While I was working, my spirit said to me, 'How long must you work—you, an old man?' I threw the shovel away and lay down. Then my spirit said to me, 'It's God's truth: you must earn a living as long as you live.' So I went back to my shovel."

Abu Hamid al-Ghazali (d. 505/1111), *Ihya' 'Ulum al-Din*, 4:438 (Asin, p. 421, no. 99; Mansur, no. 181; Robson, pp. 101–102). Cf. Ibn 'Asakir, *Sirat*, p. 202, no. 248.

For the importance of earning a living, see Saying 247, below. There is an echo here of the ethics practiced by the Egyptian desert fathers; see Ward, *The Sayings of the Desert Fathers*, p. 70, no. 5.

232 Jesus said, "Have no care for tomorrow's gain. If tomorrow is one of your appointed times, your gain will come with your appointed time. If it is not, have no care for the appointed times of others."

Abu Hamid al-Ghazali (d. 505/1111), *Ihya' 'Ulum al-Din*, 4:442 (Asin, p. 422, no. 100; Mansur, no. 182; Robson, p. 50).

See Sayings 44 and 73, above.

233 Jesus said to his disciples, "Pray God that He may make this agony—meaning death—easy for me, for I have come to fear death so much that my fear of death has made me acquainted with death."

Abu Hamid al-Ghazali (d. 505/1111), *Ihya' 'Ulum al-Din*, 4:446 (Asin, p. 423, no. 101; Mansur, no. 183; Robson, p. 84).

The core of this saying comes probably from the agony in the Garden of Gethsemane in Matthew 26:39 and Luke 22:44. The saying, like many others, underlines the human frailty of Jesus.

234 It is related that Jesus passed by a skull, which he kicked with his foot and addressed with the words, "Speak, by God's leave!" The skull answered, "Spirit of God, I am the king of such-and-such time. As I was sit-

ting on my throne, with the crown on my head and surrounded by my soldiers and courtiers, the angel of death
appeared before me. All of my limbs fell away from me
one by one, and then my spirit came out to him. Would
that all those crowds had been replaced with solitude!
Would that all that joy had been replaced with gloom!"

Abu Hamid al-Ghazali (d. 505/1111), *Ihya' 'Ulum al-Din*, 4:448 (Asin, p. 423, no.
102; Mansur, no. 184; Robson, p. 102). Cf. Asin, p. 423, no. 102 bis; p. 424, no. 102
ter; pp. 424–425, no. 102 quater (variant).

For encounters with skulls, see Sayings 186 and 248. For parallels
with other traditions, see the commentary on Saying 186, and also
Ward, *The Sayings of the Desert Fathers*, p. 136, no. 38.

235 Jesus said, "How many there are of sound
body, beautiful face, and eloquent tongue who end up
screaming in the tiers of hell!"

Abu Hamid al-Ghazali (d. 505/1111), *Ihya' 'Ulum al-Din*, 4:518 (Asin, p. 431, no.
103; Mansur, no. 185; Robson, p. 73).

There is a rhyming cadence to the Arabic which is meant to convey a proverb-like tone.

236 Jesus said to John the son of Zachariah, "If a
man makes mention of you and speaks the truth, give
thanks to God. If he is lying, multiply your thanks, for
God will increase the register of your good deeds without exertion from you."

Abu Hamid al-Ghazali (d. 505/1111), *al-Tibr al-Masbuk*, p. 21 (Mansur, no. 186). The attribution of this work to Ghazali is in doubt.

Suffering the calumnies of mankind is, of course, at one with the ethics of suffering insults, as in Sayings 80, 100, and 197.

237 Jesus said, "Between the moment a man is carried out for his funeral and the moment he is placed on the edge of his grave, God Almighty, in His glory over him, asks him forty questions. In the first, God says, 'My servant, you have cleansed the image of my creatures for years, but have not cleansed my own for even one hour.' Every day that Almighty God examines your heart, He says, 'What are you doing for what is other-than-me, while you yourself are enveloped in my bounty? Are you deaf? Can you not hear?'"

Abu Hamid al-Ghazali (d. 505/1111), *Ayyuha al Walad*, p. 108 (Asin, p. 570, no. 165; Mansur, no. 188; Robson, p. 91).

According to the usual Muslim account of the interrogation of the soul after death, the questioning is carried out by two angels that God has assigned to the task, rather than by God himself.

238 Jesus passed by a young man who was watering a garden. The young man said to Jesus, "Ask your God to grant me an atom's weight of love for Him." Jesus said, "You cannot bear an atom's weight." The young man said, "Then half an atom's weight." Jesus prayed, "O God, grant him half an atom's weight of love for You." Jesus then passed on. A long time later

Jesus was passing through the place where the young man used to be and, asking about him, was told, "He has gone mad and left for the mountains."

Jesus prayed to God to reveal his place, and saw him up in the mountains. He found him standing on a rock, staring up at the sky. Jesus greeted him, but the young man did not return his greeting, and so he said, "I am Jesus." God then revealed to Jesus, "How can he whose heart has half an atom's weight of love for me hear the words of human beings? By my glory and might, even if you were to saw him through, he would not be aware of it."

Abu Hamid al-Ghazali (d. 505/1111), *Mukashafat al-Qulub*, p. 25 (Asin, p. 572, no. 170; Mansur, no. 191; Robson, pp. 116–117). Cf. Asin, pp. 581–582, no. 189; Robson, pp. 120–121 (partial and variant).

Such feats of asceticism were much admired and held up as moral examples by the early Christian hermits, as well as by the early Muslim Sufis.

239 It is reported that John and Jesus were walking in the marketplace. A woman bumped into them, and John said, "As God is my witness, I did not feel it." Jesus said, "God be praised! Your body is with me, but where is your heart?" John answered, "Cousin, if my heart were to feel secure about anything other than God for the twinkling of an eye, I would think I had not known God."

Abu Hamid al-Ghazali (d. 505/1111), *Mukashafat al-Qulub*, p. 30 (Asin, p. 573, no. 171; Mansur, no. 192; Robson, p. 117).

A story which in spirit echoes Saying 238 in its advocacy of total preoccupation with God. It emulates the spiritual exercises of certain Sufi masters who at this time "adopted" both Jesus and John as heroes of the spirit and prophets of the heart—as Sufis before Sufism, so to speak.

240 It is related that Jesus went out one day and met Satan, who was carrying honey in one hand and ashes in the other. Jesus said, "Enemy of God, what are you doing with this honey and these ashes?" Satan replied, "The honey I put on the lips of backbiters so that they achieve their aim. The ashes I put on the faces of orphans so that mankind comes to dislike them."

Abu Hamid al-Ghazali (d. 505/1111), *Mukashafat al-Qulub*, p. 53 (Asin, p. 573, no. 172; Mansur, no. 193, Robson, p. 91).

See Saying 285 for a similar Satan story. Backbiting and gossip are frequently condemned in the Qur'an, which assigns a special punishment for those who spread slander about married women. The Qur'an also often laments the orphan's lot, and in many places enjoins kindness and generosity toward them. For similar encounters between Satan and the desert fathers, see Ward, *The Sayings of the Desert Fathers*, p. 126, no. 3, and pp. 129–130, no. 11.

241 Jesus said, "Earthly life consists of three days: a yesterday over which you have no control, a tomorrow which you do not know whether you will attain, and a today which you should put to good use."

Abu Hamid al-Ghazali (d. 505/1111), *Minhaj al-ʿAbidin*, p. 29 (Asin, p. 574, no. 173; Mansur, no. 195; Robson, p. 58).

See Sayings 44, 73, and 232.

242
Jesus said, "By recollecting the immortality of immortals, the hearts of the fearful are calmed."

Abu Hamid al-Ghazali (d. 505/1111), *Minhaj al-ʿAbidin*, p. 61 (Asin, p. 575, no. 175; Mansur, no. 197; Robson, p. 58).

The rhyming prose of this saying has the same proverbial ring to it as that of Saying 235, above.

243
Jesus said to his disciples, "Many a lamp has been extinguished by the wind, and many a devout man has been destroyed by vanity."

Abu Hamid al-Ghazali (d. 505/1111), *Minhaj al-ʿAbidin*, p. 65 (Asin, p. 575, no. 176; Mansur, no. 198; Robson, p. 58).

See Saying 68, above.

244
It is reported that Jesus passed by a man sleeping on the ground, a brick under his head, his face and beard in the dust, his body wrapped in a cloak. Jesus said, "O God, this servant of yours is lost in this world." God then revealed to him, "Jesus, do you not know that

if I turn my whole face upon one of my servants, I avert
the entire world from him?"

Abu Hamid al-Ghazali (d. 505/1111), excerpted in Asin, p. 571 no. 168; Mansur,
no. 199; Robson, p. 76. I was unable to trace the Arabic original of this saying.

See Saying 237, above.

245 Jesus said, "I have two loves—whoever loves
them loves me, and whoever hates them hates me: poverty and pious exertion."

Abu Hamid al-Ghazali (d. 505/1111), excerpted in Asin, p. 572, no. 169; Mansur,
no. 200; Robson, p. 76. I was unable to trace the Arabic original of this saying.

The term translated here as "pious exertion" *(jihad)* has the more
general and common meaning of "holy war." It was probably the
Sufis who popularized the use of this term to denote the struggle
of the soul against evil desires.

246 One day Jesus went out with his disciples. At
noon they passed by a field of wheat ready for harvest.
"Prophet of God," they said, "we are hungry." God inspired him to allow them to eat, so they dispersed among
the wheat, rubbing it and eating. While they were eating, the owner came up and cried, "This is my field and
my land, inherited from my father and grandfather. By
whose permission do you eat it?" Jesus prayed God to
resurrect all who had ever owned that field, from the
days of Adam until that very hour. And so at each blade
of wheat a multitude of men and women appeared, each

of them crying, "This is my field and my land, inherited from my father and grandfather!" The man fled in fear. He had heard about Jesus but had not met him. When he recognized Jesus, he said, "I apologize, O Prophet of God. I did not recognize you. My land and wealth are at your disposal." Jesus wept and said, "Woe unto you! All these people inherited this land and cultivated it and then departed. You too, following them, shall depart, without land or wealth."

Ibn Abi Randaqa al-Turtushi (d. 520/1126), *Siraj al-Muluk*, pp. 73–74 (Asin, p. 576, no. 178; Mansur, no. 201; Robson, pp. 117–118). Cf. al-Zubayr ibn Bakkar, *Jamharat*, 1:294 (much shorter variant; not ascribed to Jesus); al-Abshihi, *al-Mustatraf*, 2:262–263.

Al-Turtushi was the author of a celebrated work of political theory of the Adabi type, a type which some modern writers call the "mirrors of princes" genre. In this work, Turtushi, an Andalusian, reflects upon history and derives from it rules for statecraft.

The story appears to have had its Islamic origin in the biographical compendium of the ninth-century genealogist al-Zubayr ibn Bakkar (d. 256/870), where, in truncated form, it is reported as a story involving "some Israelites." It may ultimately go back to a curious saying by Jesus in the Gospel of Thomas; see the Gospel of Thomas, in Layton, *The Gnostic Scriptures*, p. 384, excerpt no. 21. It does, of course, bear a superficial resemblance to the story in Matthew 12:1–8, in which the disciples are allowed by Jesus to pick corn on the Sabbath; but the moral of our story is quite different and has to do with the transience of life and property.

247 Two women came to Jesus and said, "Spirit of God, ask God to resurrect our father, for he died while we were away." Jesus asked, "Do you know his grave?" They said, "Yes." So he went with them, and the women came to a grave and said, "This is it." Jesus prayed and the dead man was resurrected, but it turned out not to be their father. So Jesus prayed and the man was returned to the dead. The two women then showed Jesus another grave. Jesus prayed and the man was resurrected and turned out to be their father. The two women approached, greeted him and then said to Jesus, "Prophet of God and teacher of virtue, pray God to leave him with us." Jesus replied, "How can I pray for him, seeing that he no longer has any means of subsistence?" So he returned him to the dead and went away.

Ibn Abi Randaqa al-Turtushi (d. 520/1126), *Siraj al-Muluk*, p. 76 (Asin, p. 577, no. 179; Mansur, no. 202; Robson, pp. 118–119).

See the commentary on Saying 231, above.

248 While on his travels, Jesus passed by a rotting skull. He commanded it to speak. The skull said, "Spirit of God, my name is Balwan ibn Hafs, king of Yemen. I lived a thousand years, begat a thousand sons, deflowered a thousand virgins, routed a thousand armies, killed a thousand tyrants, and conquered a thousand cities. Let him who hears my tale not be tempted by the world, for it was like nothing so much as the dream of a sleeper." Jesus wept.

Ibn Abi Randaqa al-Turtushi (d. 520/1126), *Siraj al-Muluk*, p. 82. (Asin, p. 423, no. 102 bis). Cf. *Siraj*, pp. 83–84; and al-Abshihi, *al-Mustatraf*, 2:264.

See Saying 186, above. Jesus is found weeping or crying in a number of sayings and stories; see Sayings 6, 38, and 246. Sorrow was a mark of the true Sufi. The weeping of Jesus emphasizes, once again, his human frailty. Legends of Yemeni kings were an important part of Arabic popular folklore.

249 Jesus said, "God addressed the world in the following words: 'Serve him who serves me, enslave him who serves you. O world, pass quickly before my saints and do not trick them so that they are seduced by you.'"

Ibn Abi Randaqa al-Turtushi (d. 520/1126), *Siraj al-Muluk,* p. 91 (Asin, p. 578, no. 180; Mansur, no. 205; Robson, p. 58). Cf. al-Mawardi, *Adab,* p. 102; and al-Abshihi, *Mustatraf,* 2:265.

The "saints" *(awliya')* is the favored term employed by the Sufis to denote themselves.

250 It is related that Jesus arrived at a town. Its fortifications had fallen into ruin, its streams had run dry, and its trees had withered. Jesus called out, "O ruin, where is your people?" No one answered. He called out again, "O ruin, where is your people?" A voice then called out to Jesus, "They have perished, and the earth now holds them. Their works have become necklaces around their necks until the Day of Judgment. O Jesus son of Mary, exert yourself."

Ibn Abi Randaqa al-Turtushi (d. 520/1126), *Siraj al-Muluk,* p. 93 (Asin, p. 578, no. 181; Mansur, no. 207; Robson, p. 119).

See Saying 14, above. The image of chains hung around the necks of the unbelievers comes from Qur'an 34:33. See also Qur'an 13:5, 36:8, and 40:71.

251 Jesus said, "A ruler should not be vicious, since it is to him that mankind looks for self-restraint; nor should he be tyrannical, since it is from him that mankind demands justice."

Ibn Abi Randaqa al-Turtushi (d. 520/1126), *Siraj al-Muluk*, p. 182.

A saying which belongs more to the literature of the "mirror of princes" than to the range of sentiments expressed by Jesus in this volume. "Self-restraint" *(hilm)* was a quality much admired in pre-Islamic as well as Islamic rulers and elites.

252 One of the disciples of Christ died and the others mourned him greatly. They conveyed their distress to Christ, who stood by his grave and prayed. God resurrected him, and his feet were in sandals of fire. Christ asked him about this, and he said, "I swear to God that I have never sinned, but I once passed by a man who was unjustly treated and did not go to his aid; and so I was made to wear these sandals."

Ibn Abi Randaqa al-Turtushi (d. 520/1126), *Siraj al-Muluk*, p. 447 (Asin, p. 579, no. 183; Mansur, no. 209; Robson, p. 120).

The Qur'an repeatedly enjoins the duty of going to the aid of those unjustly treated: see, e.g., Qur'an 2:270, 3:192, 8:72, 42:8.

253 Christ said, "What is forbearance if one is impatient with ignorance? What is strength if one cannot restrain anger? What is worship if one is immodest before God Almighty? When fools come to worship, they come at an inopportune time and sit above their station. When a crisis occurs, wise counsel departs."

Ibn Abi Randaqa al-Turtushi (d. 520/1126), *Siraj al-Muluk*, p. 577 (Asin, p. 579; no. 185; Mansur, no. 210; Robson, p. 59). Cf. *Siraj* , p. 260.

The term translated as "ignorance" *(jahl)* can also mean "violence." The last phrase is in rhymed prose and sounds like a proverb. Sitting above one's station recalls Matthew 23:6. The whole saying appears to be a composite and to belong to the spirit of Adab.

254 Jesus looked down upon the Ghuta of Damascus from a high place and said, "O Ghuta, even if the wealthy man is unable to reap a fortune from you, the poor man will not fail to get his fill of bread from you."

Abu al-Qasim ibn ʿAsakir (d. 571/1175), *Tarikh Madinat Dimashq*, 2/1:117. Cf. Zamakhshari, *Rabiʿ al-Abrar*, 1:259.

Ibn ʿAsakir, like many other Muslim city historians, was eager to establish associations between his native city and prophets or other spiritual figures of early days in order to underline the sanctity of the city's territory to friend and foe alike. The Ghuta is a rich agricultural area to the west of Damascus.

255 Jesus said, "Accept the truth from those who speak falsehood, but do not accept falsehood from those who speak the truth. Be discriminating in your speech so as not to admit into it anything which may be counterfeit."

Abu al-Qasim ibn ʿAsakir (d. 571/1175), *Sirat al-Sayyid al-Masih*, p. 161, no. 176.

An elegant saying which emphasizes the acceptance of truth irrespective of its source. The counterfeiting image was common among Hadith scholars, who are sometimes enjoined to be as discriminating in judging the veracity of traditions as an expert money-changer in judging true coin. See, further, Tarif Khalidi, *Arabic Historical Thought in the Classical Period* (Cambridge: Cambridge University Press, 1994), p. 22 and note 11.

256 Jesus used to say, "He who prays and fasts but does not abandon sin is inscribed in the Kingdom of God as a liar."

Abu al-Qasim ibn ʿAsakir (d. 571/1175), *Sirat al-Sayyid al-Masih*, p. 172, no. 196.

The hypocrisy condemned in this saying is couched in Gospel-like terms.

257 Jesus said, "No man can ever know what faith truly means unless he comes to dislike being praised for his obedience to God."

Abu al-Qasim ibn ʿAsakir (d. 571/1175), *Sirat al-Sayyid al-Masih*, p. 175, no. 200.

Shunning the praises of mankind appears as a mark of the true believer. Cf. John 12:43; Romans 2:29.

258 Jesus said, "Let him who works good expect a good reward, and let him who works evil not be surprised when punished. He who seizes power unjustly— God will justly make him inherit humiliation; and he who unjustly seizes wealth—God will justly make him inherit poverty."

Abu al-Qasim ibn ʿAsakir (d. 571/1175), *Sirat al-Sayyid al-Masih*, p. 176, no. 203.

A well-crafted saying, with its various parts neatly balanced to facilitate memorization.

259 A man asked Jesus, "Who among men is the most virtuous?" Jesus picked up two handfuls of dust and said, "Which of these two is more virtuous? Men are born from dust, and the most honorable are the most God-fearing."

Abu al-Qasim ibn ʿAsakir (d. 571/1175), *Sirat al-Sayyid al-Masih*, p. 176, no. 204. Cf. al-Abshihi, *al-Mustatraf*, 2:12. (Asin, p. 586, no. 200; Mansur, no. 240; Robson, p. 60).

For Biblical parallels to this saying, see the comments by Asin.

260 Jesus used to say, "No good can come from any knowledge that does not cross the valley [of life] with you or make you improve the assembly of men."

Abu al-Qasim ibn ʿAsakir (d. 571/1175), *Sirat al-Sayyid al-Masih*, p. 187, no. 224.

The context in which this saying is found suggests that the saying, which has an internal rhyme, encourages memory at the expense of book learning.

261 God revealed to Jesus, "When idlers laugh, paint your eyes with the antimony of sadness."

Abu al-Qasim ibn ʿAsakir (d. 571/1175), *Sirat al-Sayyid al-Masih*, p. 82, no. 73.

Antimony *(kuhl)* is more often used for festive rather than sad occasions. Jesus is being enjoined here to display sorrow in the presence of idle merriment.

262 Mary said, "In the days I was pregnant with Jesus, whenever there was someone in my house speaking with me, I would hear Jesus praising God inside me. Whenever I was alone and there was no one with me, I would converse with him and he with me, while he was still in my womb."

Abu al-Qasim ibn ʿAsakir (d. 571/1175), *Sirat al-Sayyid al-Masih*, p. 30, no. 6.

This unusual story about the infant Jesus may be related to the Qur'anic narrative of Jesus' speaking in his cradle.

263 It is reported that Jesus said, "O God, how can I thank You when my thanks are a blessing bestowed

by You for which I must render thanks?" God answered, "If you know this, then you have thanked me."

Abu al-Hajjaj al-Balawi (d. 604/1207), *Kitab Alif Baʾ*, 1:370–371 (Asin, p. 580, no. 186; Mansur, no. 213; Robson, p. 92). Cf. Ibn Abiʾl Dunya, *Kitab al-Shukr*, in *Mawsuʿat Rasaʾil*, 3:11–12, nos. 5 and 6 (slightly variant; attributed to David and Moses).

Al-Balawi was an Andalusian man of letters. His literary anthology was addressed to his son and arranged alphabetically (hence its title: *A, B*) to serve as an educational primer.

This saying resembles a theological conundrum having to do with the problem of free will and predestination. If God is the benevolent author of all human acts, what merit does thanksgiving have? Nevertheless, a pious acceptance of this "mystery" by the true believer is rewarded by God.

264 With Mary in the sanctuary was a cousin of hers called Yusuf who served her and conversed with her from behind a screen. He was the first to learn of her pregnancy and was concerned and saddened by it, fearing too that he might be thought sinful and of ill repute. So he said to her, "Mary, can there be a plant without seed?" "Yes," she replied. "How so?" he asked. "God," she said, "created the first seed without a plant. But then you might say, 'If He had not sought the aid of the seed, the matter would have been too difficult for Him.'" "God forbid!" said Yusuf. Then he said to her, "Can a tree grow without water or rain?" Mary answered, "Do you not know that seeds, plants, water, rain, and trees have a sole creator?" Then again he asked her, "Can there be children or pregnancy without a male?" "Yes," she answered. "How so?" he asked. "Do you not know," she said, "that God created Adam and his wife Eve without pregnancy, without a male and without a mother?" "Yes," he answered, and added, "Tell me, then, what happened to you." Mary said, "God has brought me glad tidings of a word from Him, whose name is the Messiah Jesus son of Mary."

Abu al-Hajjaj al-Balawi (d. 604/1207), *Kitab Alif Ba'*, 1:406 (Asin, p. 580, no. 187; Mansur, no. 214).

This exchange between Joseph and Mary also appears to have theological implications, and echoes some of the arguments used by Muslim theologians to defend the Virgin Birth. Qur'an 3:59 specifically compares the creation of Jesus with that of Adam: both were formed of "earth" and then the divine "Be!" gave them life.

In some Coptic apocryphal writings, particularly a tract called *The Death of Joseph*, there is an exchange between Joseph and Jesus where Joseph confesses to his perplexity regarding the Virgin Birth: "I did not know, my lord, neither do I understand, the mystery of thy strange birth, neither did I ever hear that a woman was pregnant without a man, or that a virgin bare, sealed in her virginity." See Forbes Robinson, *Coptic Apocryphal Gospels*, in J. Armitage Robinson, ed., *Texts and Studies: Contributions to Biblical and Patristic Literature*, vol. 4, no. 2 (Cambridge: Cambridge University Press, 1896), pp. 137 and 154.

265 Jesus said, "Bear with patience one word from the impudent and you shall gain tenfold."

Abu al-Hajjaj al-Balawi (d. 604/1207), *Kitab Alif Ba*', 1:464 (Asin, p. 581, no. 188; Mansur, no. 215; Robson, p. 59).

See Sayings 80 and 100, above.

266 Jesus said, "O Israelites, do not eat to excess, for he who eats to excess sleeps to excess, and he who sleeps to excess prays little, and he who prays little is inscribed among the negligent."

Abu al-Husayn Warram ibn Abi Firas (d. 605/1208), *Majmu'a*, 1:47.

Warram was a Shi'i traditionist, a descendant of one of 'Ali's closest companions, Malik al-Ashtar, and described in the sources as an ascetic. His anthology of ethical and ascetic sayings was widely known. In company with many Shi'i authors, Warram includes several sayings that bear on matters of diet and health, reflecting an image of Jesus as a healer; see Saying 152, above.

267 God revealed to Jesus, "Be in gentleness toward people like the earth beneath their feet, in generosity like flowing water, and in mercy like the sun and the moon, for they rise upon both the good and the evil."

Abu al-Husayn Warram ibn Abi Firas (d. 605/1208), *Majmu'a*, 1:80.

An echo of Matthew 5:45.

268 Jesus said, "How can someone be a scholar if the afterlife is indicated to him while he remains preoccupied with this life, and if what harms him is more desirable to him than what benefits him?"

Abu al-Husayn Warram ibn Abi Firas (d. 605/1208), *Majmuʿa*, 1:83.

A rebuke directed against worldly scholars.

269 Jesus prepared food for his disciples. When they had eaten, he himself washed their hands and feet. They said to him, "Spirit of God, it is we, rather, that should do this." He replied, "I have done this so that you would do it to those whom you teach."

Abu al-Husayn Warram ibn Abi Firas (d. 605/1208), *Majmuʿa*, 1:83.

See John 13:1–16.

270 Jesus said, "The burdens of this life and of the afterlife have become severe. As for the burdens of this life, you will not stretch forth your hand toward anything in it without finding that a dissolute person has preceded you to it. As for the burdens of the afterlife, you will not find anyone to help you with them."

Abu al-Husayn Warram ibn Abi Firas (d. 605/1208), *Majmuʿa*, 2:146.

The immediate context of this saying is a description of the terrors and travails of the Day of Judgment, which are said to have fifty "stations" *(mawaqif)*, each lasting one thousand years. It is also preceded by several pages of advice and admonishments from God to Jesus.

271 Jesus said, "O Lord, tell me about this nation that will obtain Your mercy." God said, "It is the nation of Muhammad, a nation of scholars, god-fearing, pious, self-restrained, pure of heart, and wise, as though they were prophets. They are satisfied with a little bounty from me and I am satisfied with a little of good works from them. I lead them into paradise because they say, 'There is no god but God.' O Jesus, they are the majority of the inhabitants of paradise, for no people's tongues have ever been more humbled by uttering 'There is no god but God' than theirs, and no people's necks have ever been more humbled by prostration than theirs."

Shihab al-Din ʿUmar al-Suhrawardi (d. 632/1234), *ʿAwarif al-Maʿarif*, 2:159.

Al-Suhrawardi was a celebrated Sufi theorist, whose principal work bears a resemblance to Ghazali's. This saying is, in form, a *hadith qudsi* (a divine revelation to Jesus) which is meant, as is clear, to extol the praises of the "nation" of Muhammad. It has been a common Muslim view that a person is potentially saved from hell by making the confession of faith "There is no god but God."

272 It is related that Jesus said, "God Almighty hates the man who laughs much without cause and walks much without aim, and hates the mention of a holy book in between pleasantries and joking."

Shihab al-Din ʿUmar al-Suhrawardi (d. 632/1234), *ʿAwarif al-Maʿarif*, 2:243 (Asin, p. 583, no. 191; Mansur, no. 217; Robson, pp. 59–60).

See Saying 163, above. The dislike of laughter and jesting is common among the pious and ascetic figures of Near Eastern religions; see, e.g., Hertz, *Sayings of the Fathers*, p. 47, no. 17; and Ward, *The Sayings of the Desert Fathers*, p. 87, no. 9.

273 It is related that Jesus said, "He who has not been born twice shall not enter the Kingdom of Heaven."

Shihab al-Din ʿUmar al-Suhrawardi (d. 632/1234), *ʿAwarif al-Maʿarif*, 1:174 (Asin, p. 583, no. 190; Mansur, no. 216; Robson, p. 59. Cf. Asin, p. 592, no. 207; Robson, p. 61 [fuller version]).

Asin suggests John 3:3–8 by way of a parallel. Spiritual rebirth is of course a central concept of Gnostic Christianity, and a Gnostic inspiration cannot be excluded.

274 A group of people came to stay with Jesus as guests. He offered them bread and vinegar and said, "Had I been in the habit of affecting hospitality for anyone, I would have affected hospitality for you."

Abu al-Faraj ibn al-Hanbali (d. 634/1236), *al-Istisʿad bi-man Laqaytuhu mina al-ʿIbad*, p. 180.

Ibn al-Hanbali was a Damascene legal scholar, Hadith expert, preacher, and member of a distinguished family of scholars. This saying appears to underline the ascetic simplicity of Jesus' mode of life.

275 Jesus said, "Conduct yourselves with people in such a manner that while you live they long for you and after you die they weep for you."

Muhyi al-Din ibn ʿArabi (d. 638/1240), *Muhadarat al-Abrar*, 2:2 (Asin, p. 585, no. 196; Mansur, no. 219; Robson, p. 60).

Ibn ʿArabi was one of the most celebrated Sufi theorists of all time. Prolific author and controversial public figure, he developed Sufi doctrine in new directions and created a highly complex mystical-philosophical system. In Ibn ʿArabi's ethical system, the concept of longing *(shawq)* plays a central role in a human being's relationship to God as well as to other human beings.

276 Jesus said to the religious lawyers, "You sit on the road to the afterlife—but you have neither walked this road to its end, nor allowed anyone else to pass by. Woe to him who is beguiled by you!"

Muhyi al-Din ibn ʾArabi (d. 638/1240), *Muhadarat al-Abrar*, 2:30 (Asin, p. 585, no. 197; Mansur, no. 220; Robson, p. 92).

The age of Ibn ʿArabi saw increasing tension between Sufis and legal scholars. For further details, see Tarif Khalidi, *Arabic Historical Thought*, pp. 210–215. Jesus was conveniently inducted into this struggle on the side of the Sufis because of his perceived disapproval of narrow-minded legalism.

277 It is reported that Jesus passed by 400,000 women whose color had changed and who were wearing tunics of haircloth and wool. Jesus asked, "What is it that has changed your color, you crowds of women?"

They replied, "It is the remembrance of hell-fire which has changed our color, son of Mary. He who enters hell-fire tastes neither cold nor drink."

Muhyi al-Din ibn ʿArabi (d. 638/1240), *Muhadarat al-Abrar*, 2:253 (Asin, p. 412, no. 84 ter; Mansur, no. 221; Robson, pp. 100–1).

The encounter between Jesus and the women in penitential garb suggests that women, commonly viewed as temptresses, can indeed, and in their great majority (400,000 suggests their "astronomical" numbers), be induced to turn away from sin.

278 Satan appeared to Jesus in the visible form of an old man. "Spirit of God, say: 'There is no god but God,'" he bade him, hoping that he [would repeat this after him and thus] would have obeyed him to that extent. Jesus answered, "I say it—but not because you said it: there is no god but God." Satan departed in disgrace.

Muhyi al-Din ibn ʿArabi (d. 638/1240), *al-Futuhat al-Makkiyya*, 1:368–369 (Mansur, no. 222).

See Saying 206, above. Jesus outsmarts Satan in a theological exchange which illustrates a commonly cited maxim: "Man is judged by the truth and not the truth by man"—a maxim often resorted to by, for instance, al-Ghazali, who uses it in his polemics against the blind imitation of authority among various sectarian groups.

279 Jesus said to the Israelites, "Know that your present life is to your afterlife as your sunrise is to your sunset. The closer you approach to the east, the farther you are from the west, and the closer you approach to the west, the farther you are from the east." He exhorted them in this example to draw closer to the afterlife through good deeds.

Muhyi al-Din ibn ʿArabi (d. 638/1240), *al-Futuhat al-Makkiyya*, 4:662 (Asin, p. 583, no. 193; Mansur, no. 224; Robson, p. 77). Cf. Ibn Hamdun, *al-Tadhkira al-Hamduniyya*, pp. 58–59; Al-Zamakhshari, *Rabiʿ al-Abrar*, 1:45 (attributed to ʿAli); Warram, *Majmuʿa*, 2:24.

The phrase "as far as the east is from the west" is at least as old as Psalms 103:12.

280 Jesus exhorted some of his companions as follows: "Fast from the world and break your fast with death. Be like him who treats his wound with medicine lest it oppress him. Remember death often—for death comes to the man of faith bringing good with no evil to follow; but to the evil man, it brings evil with no good to follow."

Muhyi al-Din ibn ʿArabi (d. 638/1240), *al-Futuhat al-Makkiyya*, 4:663 (Asin, p. 584, no. 194; Mansur, no. 225; Robson, p. 60).

The graceful phrasing of this saying, the exhortation to a totally ascetic life, and the admonition to remember death constantly are all typical of the Sufi spirit.

281 Jesus met Satan and said to him, "I ask you, in the name of God the Living and Everlasting, what is it that truly breaks your back?" He said, "The neighing of horses in the cause of God."

Sibt ibn al-Jawzi (d. 654/1256), *Mir'at al-Zaman*, 8:494.

Sibt ibn al-Jawzi was a historian and member of a distinguished scholarly family. This saying reflects an age of war when both Crusaders and Mongols threatened the central Islamic world. Jesus is brought in to urge the faithful to fight in the cause of God.

282 Al-ʿUris saw in his sleep Christ Jesus Son of Mary, who seemed to turn his face toward him from heaven. Al-ʿUris asked him, "Did the crucifixion really happen?" Jesus said, "Yes, the crucifixion really happened." Al-ʿUris then related his dream to an interpreter, who said, "The man who saw this dream shall be crucified. For Jesus is infallible and can speak only the truth, yet the crucifixion he spoke of cannot refer to his own, because the Glorious Qur'an specifically states that Jesus was not crucified or killed. Accordingly, this must refer to the dreamer, and it is he who shall be crucified." The matter turned out as the interpreter said.

Jamal al-Din ibn Wasil (d. 697/1298), *Mufarrij al-Kurub*, 1:248. Cf. al-Abshihi, *al-Mustatraf*, 2:83 (variant).

This is a curious story, included here as an instance where the Islamic Jesus appears, at least in a dream, to assert the truth of his crucifixion. Al-ʿUris was a historical person, and the source in which this story is found is an important chronicle of the Ayyubids (the family of Saladin) and of their wars against the Crusaders.

283 Jesus said, "O disciples, gold is a cause of joy in this world and a cause of harm in the afterlife. Truly I say to you, the rich shall not enter the Kingdom of Heaven."

Taj al-Din al-Subki (d. 771/1370), *Tabaqat al-Shafiʿiyya*, 4:134.

Al-Subki was an important biographer of prominent people who belonged to the Shafiʿi school of law. This saying is a composite of Gospel and non-Gospel elements.

284 Historians and biographers relate that in the time of Jesus there lived a man of the Israelites called Ishaq, whose wife—his cousin—was among the prettiest women of her age. He was in love with her, but she died; so he was constantly at her graveside, tirelessly visiting it for long periods.

One day Jesus passed by and found him weeping by her grave. "Why are you weeping, Ishaq?" Jesus asked. He answered, "Spirit of God, I had a cousin who was my wife and whom I loved very much. She died—this is her grave—and I cannot bear to be separated from her. Her departure has been the death of me." Jesus asked him, "Would you like me to resurrect her for you, by God's leave?" "Yes, Spirit of God," the man replied.

So Jesus stood by the grave and said, "Rise, by God's leave, you who are in this grave!" The grave was split open and a black slave emerged, fire blazing from his nostrils, eyes, and other orifices in his face, and said, "There is no god but God, and Jesus is God's Spirit,

Word, Servant, and Prophet." Ishaq said, "Spirit and Word of God, this is not the grave of my wife, but rather this one," and pointed to another grave.

Jesus said to the black man, "Go back to where you were." The man fell dead and Jesus buried him in his grave. Jesus then stood at the other grave and said, "Rise, by God's leave, you who are in this grave!" The woman rose, shaking the dust from her face. "Is this your wife?" Jesus asked. "Yes, Spirit of God," he answered. "Take her hand and go," Jesus said. So he took her and departed. Then sleep came upon him and he said to her, "The vigil at your graveside has exhausted me and I would like to rest a while." "Do so," she replied. So, resting his head upon her thigh, he fell asleep.

As he slept, the son of the king passed by. He was beautiful and very imposing and rode a fine horse. When she saw him, she was infatuated and rose and went quickly to him. He too, when he saw her, fell in love with her. Approaching him, she said, "Take me!" He drew her up to sit behind him on his horse, and rode away.

When her husband woke up, he looked around but did not see her, so he went looking for her, and, tracking the horse, he caught up with them. Addressing the king's son, he said, "Give me back my wife and cousin." She in turn denied knowing him and said, "I am the slave girl of the king's son." "No," he said, "You are my wife and my cousin." "I do not know you," she said. "I am but the slave girl of the king's son." The king's son said to him, "Do you intend to corrupt my slave girl?"

The man said, "I swear by God that she is my wife and that Jesus the son of Mary resurrected her for me by God's leave after her death."

While they were arguing Jesus passed by, so Ishaq said to him, "Spirit of God, is this not my wife whom you resurrected for me by God's leave?" "Yes," Jesus replied. The woman said, "Spirit of God, he is lying—I am the slave girl of the king's son." The king's son added, "This is my slave girl." Jesus asked the woman, "Are you not the woman I resurrected by God's leave?" "No, Spirit of God—as God is my witness," she replied. Jesus said, "Then give us back what we gave you," and the woman fell down dead.

Jesus said, "Whoever wishes to see a man whom God caused to die an unbeliever, then resurrected and caused to die again as a Muslim, let him look at the black man; and whoever wishes to see a woman whom God caused to die a believer, then resurrected and caused to die again as an unbeliever, let him look at this woman." As for Ishaq the Israelite, he vowed before God that he would never marry again, and wandered aimlessly in the wilderness, weeping.

Kamal al-Din al-Damiri (d. 808/1405), *Hayat al-Hayawan al-Kubra*, 1:202–203 (Asin, pp. 588–589, no. 203; Mansur, no. 231; Robson, pp. 122–125).

Al-Damiri was the author of a celebrated work on animals. His spirit and message, however, were predominantly literary and ethical rather than zoological. The lengthy story of Jesus and Ishaq the Israelite has several elements which seem to be similar in spirit to the stories encountered in the apocryphal acts of the apostles. For the black man see, for example, the Acts of Philip, in James,

The Apocryphal New Testament, p. 451. The story of Ishaq's wife bears some resemblance to the story of the Gardener's Daughter (ibid., p. 303). Once again, the story is given an explicit moral at the end by Jesus, rather than being left to stand by itself as a parable of salvation and damnation.

285 Jesus met Satan leading five asses bearing loads. Jesus asked him what these loads were, and Satan replied, "Merchandise for which I am seeking buyers." "What is this merchandise?" Jesus asked. "One is oppression," Satan replied. "Who buys it?" Jesus asked. "Rulers," he answered. "And the second is pride." "Who buys it?" Jesus asked. "Provincial notables," he answered. "And the third is envy." "Who buys it?" Jesus asked. "Religious scholars," he answered. "And the fourth is dishonesty." "Who buys it?" Jesus asked. "Merchants' agents," he answered. "And the fifth is guile." "Who buys it?" Jesus asked. "Women," he answered.

Kamal al-Din al-Damiri (d. 808/1405), *Hayat al-Hayawan al-Kubra*, 1:225 (Mansur, no. 229). Cf. al-Abshihi, *al-Mustatraf*, 2:215.

This question-and-answer exchange between Jesus and Satan is typical of the Adab style. Many anthologies of Adab preserve similar exchanges between celebrated individuals, most often between rulers and scholars.

286 Jesus was once passing by a snake charmer chasing a snake. The snake said, "Spirit of God, tell this man that if he does not leave me alone, I will cut him to pieces." Passing by again, Jesus saw the snake in the charmer's basket. "Did you not tell me you would cut this man to pieces? How did you end up where you are?" "Spirit of God," the snake replied, "He swore an oath to me and then betrayed his oath. The venom of his treachery is worse for him than my poison."

Kamal al-Din al-Damiri (d. 808/1405), *Hayat al-Hayawan al-Kubra*, 1:252 (Mansur, no. 230).

Jesus has already appeared in several stories as an interrogator of natural objects and animals. The snake as a wise creature appears in the Gospels; see Matthew 10:16. See also Jesus and the snake in Saying 123, above.

287 As Jesus the son of Mary and John the son of Zachariah were walking, they saw a wild goat calving. Jesus said to John, "Say these words: 'Hannah begat John and Mary begat Jesus. The earth calls you, child. Come out, child.'"

Any woman in labor to whom these words are spoken will straightway deliver, by God's leave.

John was the first to believe in Jesus and trust him. They were cousins, sons of maternal aunts, John being six months older than Jesus. Then John was killed before Jesus was raised to heaven.

Kamal al-Din al-Damiri (d. 808/1405), *Hayat al-Hayawan al-Kubra*, 2:40 (Mansur, no. 232).

The first half of this story bears some resemblance to the tale of the cow calving in Saying 103, above. The second half is a commentary by the Muslim transmitter of the story.

288 Jesus said, "When someone turns a beggar away empty-handed, the angels will not visit his house for seven days."

Baha' al-Din al-Abshihi (d. 892/1487), *al-Mustatraf,* 1:9.

Al-Abshihi was one of the last in a long line of Arabic literary anthologists. His anthology of Adab was widely popular in the later medieval period. In form and spirit, this saying resembles a Muhammadan Hadith.

289 Jesus said, "I treated the leper and the blind man and cured them both. I treated the fool and he made me despair. Silence is the [best] reply to the fool."

Baha' al-Din al-Abshihi (d. 892/1487), *al-Mustatraf,* 1:16. Cf. al-Ghazali, *Ayyuha al-Walad,* p. 138 (shorter version) (Mansur, no. 189).

In this saying, Jesus is made to echo a piece of perennial wisdom often encountered in ancient Near Eastern as well as Hellenistic literatures and continuing into the Islamic era. In Islamic literature, one of the earliest expounders of the need for intellectuals to isolate themselves from the ignorant masses was the celebrated essayist Ibn al-Muqaffa' (d. circa 139/756). For a biblical parallel, see Proverbs 26:4.

290 A man said to Jesus, "Instruct me." Jesus said, "Take heed of where your bread comes from."

'Abd al-Wahhab al-Sha'rani (d. 973/1565), *al-Tabaqat al-Kubra*, 1:53 (Asin, p. 593, no. 209; Mansur, no. 246; Robson, p. 61).

Al-Sha'rani was the most celebrated Sufi thinker and historian of Sufism of his time. He was also a prolific author with very wide interests in the various Islamic sciences. This curious saying could be a reflection of the common Islamic injunction to ascertain the source of one's livelihood in order to avoid unlawful gain.

291 Jesus passed by a man making saddles who said as he prayed, "O God, if I knew where the ass You ride is, I would make him a saddle studded with jewels." Jesus shook him and said, "Woe to you! Does God Almighty have an ass?" God revealed to Jesus, "Leave the man alone, for he has glorified me as best he can."

'Abd al-Wahhab al-Sha'rani (d. 973/1565), *Lata'if al-Minan*, p. 51 (Asin, p. 593, no. 208; Mansur, no. 249; Robson, pp. 125–126). Cf. al-Damiri, *Hayat*, 1:229 (variant).

This story of Jesus and the man of simple faith resembles in form and spirit certain Gospel stories, as well as a number of Muhammadan Hadiths in which Muhammad smilingly indulges the simpleminded faithful.

292 Satan asked Jesus, "Can your God cause the world to be contained by an egg, in such a way that the world is not shrunk and the egg is not enlarged?" Jesus replied, "Woe to you! Incapacity cannot be attributed to

God. Who is more powerful than Him who can cause the world to become fine and delicate and the egg to grow great?"

Mulla Muhammad Baqir Majlisi (d. 1110/1698), *Bihar,* 4:142. Cf. Qa'im and Legenhausen, *Al-Tawhid,* 13/3, p. 25, no. 2.

Majlisi was a very influential Shi'i author, Hadith scholar, polymath, and public figure. For information on his life and works, see *EI* 2. This saying is supposedly a "devilish" theological conundrum having to do with God's capacity to effect miracles. One common Muslim view was that God was indeed capable of reversing natural custom but that the greatest of all his miracles was the Qur'an itself.

293 Jesus said, "The dinar is the disease of religion, and the scholar is the physician of religion. If you see the physician drawing the disease upon himself, beware of him and know that he is not fit to advise others."

Mulla Muhammad Baqir Majlisi (d. 1110/1698), *Bihar,* 14:319. Cf. Qa'im and Legenhausen, *Al-Tawhid,* 13/3, pp. 37–38, no. 50.

A saying similar to this one is found in Syriac literature; see Budge, *The Laughable Stories,* p. 76, no. 309.

294 Jesus said, "What does it profit a man if he sells his soul for all that is in the world, and then leaves all that he sold it for as an inheritance to someone else while he himself has ruined his soul? Blessed is he who saves his soul, preferring it to all that is in the world."

Mulla Muhammad Baqir Majlisi (d. 1110/1698), *Bihar*, 14:329. Cf. Qaʾim and Legenhausen, *Al-Tawhid*, 13/3, pp. 36, no. 47.

A reworking of Matthew 16:25–26.

295 Jesus stood up to preach to the Israelites. He said, "O Israelites, do not eat until you are hungry; and when you are hungry, eat but do not eat your fill, for if you eat your fill your necks will grow thick, your sides will grow fat, and you will forget your Lord."

Mulla Muhammad Baqir Majlisi (d. 1110/1698), *Bihar*, 66:337. Cf. Qaʾim and Legenhausen, *Al-Tawhid*, 13/3, p. 36, no. 45.

Another saying having to do with healthy diet and its connection with a pious life. See Sayings 152 and 266, above.

296 Jesus said, "There is no graver disease of the heart than cruelty, and there is nothing more unbearable to the soul than lack of hunger. These two act as bridles of [divine] banishment and abandonment."

Mulla Muhammad Baqir Majlisi (d. 1110/1698), *Bihar*, 66:337. Cf. Qaʾim and Legenhausen, *Al-Tawhid*, 13/3, p. 39, no. 54.

A complex saying whose meaning is not entirely clear. Jesus appears to be preaching against both hardness of heart and a luxurious lifestyle. By means of these two sins, God "reins in" the sinner, banishing him from His presence or else abandoning him to his sin.

297 Jesus sent forth two of his companions on an errand. One of them returned looking like a withered water-skin, while the other returned fleshy and fat. Jesus asked the first man, "What was it that reduced you to this state?" The man said, "Fear of God." He then asked the second man, "What was it that brought you to this state?" The man replied, "Trust in God."

Mulla Muhammad Baqir Majlisi (d. 1110/1698), *Bihar,* 70:400. Cf. Qa'im and Legenhausen, *Al-Tawhid,* 13/3, p. 34, no. 38.

Both fear of God and trust in him are desirable moral attributes, and the two disciples enact what are in effect complementary states of sincere faith, especially as taught in the Sufi ethic.

298 Jesus said, "If I have said it, You have known it, for it is You who say it in my image. You are the tongue I speak with, judging that You are united with my form and substance."

'Abd al-Ghani al-Nabulusi (d. 1143/1731), excerpted in Asin, p. 595 (no. 215), Mansur, no. 250, Robson, p. 93. The Arabic original could not be traced.

Al-Nabulusi, a widely traveled Palestinian mystic, was a major figure of early modern Sufi thought and wrote on a large range of subjects. The phrase "If I have said it, You have known it" is from Qur'an 5:116, uttered by Jesus to God, in the course of denying that he ever claimed divinity. The rest of the saying appears to be a Sufi paraphrase of the two principal Muslim epithets for Jesus: the Spirit of God and the Word of God.

299 Jesus said, "Woe to you, slaves of this world! What avails the blind man the broad sunlight which he cannot see? So, likewise, nothing avails the scholar of great learning if he does not act according to it. How many fruits there are, but not all are useful or edible! How many scholars there are, but not all make use of their learning! Be on your guard against false scholars, who wear woolen garments and bow their heads to the ground but glare up at you from under their eyebrows like wolves. Their words are at variance with their deeds. Who reaps grapes from thorn bushes and figs from colocynth? So, also, the words of a false scholar yield only falsehood. For the beast of burden, if not well tethered by its owner in the wilderness, makes for its land and kind. So, also, the learning which is not put into practice by its possessor leaves his heart, abandons him, and renders him useless. As a plant thrives only in water and soil, so, too, faith can thrive only in knowledge and deed. Woe to you, slaves of this world! Everything has a sign by which it is known and which testifies for or against it. Religion has three signs by which it is known: faith, knowledge, and deed."

Murtada al-Husayni al-Zabidi (d. 1205/1791), *Ithaf al-Sada al-Muttaqin*, 1:229–230 (Asin, p. 596, no. 216; Mansur, no. 251; Robson, p. 94). Cf. Abu Hayyan, *al-Imta'*, 2:123.

Al-Zabidi was a great Yemeni scholar, and the author of what is probably the most comprehensive dictionary of classical Arabic.

This is a long and composite saying made up of various elements but directed principally against scholars.

300 It is related that Satan appeared to Jesus decked out in pendants of diverse colors and kinds. Jesus asked, "What are these pendants?" "These are the lusts of mankind," Satan replied. "Have I anything to do with any of them?" Jesus asked. "Perhaps you ate your fill and we made you too sluggish to pray or mention God," Satan replied. "Is there anything else?" asked Jesus. "No," said Satan. "I vow before God never to fill my belly with food," said Jesus. "And I vow before God never again to advise a Muslim," Satan replied.

Murtada al-Husayni al-Zabidi (d. 1205/1791), *Ithaf al-Sada al-Muttaqin*, 7:445 (Asin, p. 574, no. 174 bis; Mansur, no. 253; Robson, pp. 76–77). Cf. al-Ghazali, *Minhaj*, p. 33 (Mansur, no. 196); and al-Suhrawardi, *'Awarif*, 3:102 (in both, John instead of Jesus).

See Sayings 152, 278, and 295, above.

301 Jesus said, "Children of Adam, beget what will die and build what will fall into ruin. In this way, your souls will perish and your homes will be ruined."

Murtada al-Husayni al-Zabidi (d. 1205/1791), *Ithaf al-Sada al-Muttaqin*, 8:85 and 10:223 (Asin, p. 597, no. 218; Mansur, no. 255).

See the comments on this saying by Asin, who finds that its opening phrase is identical to a line of verse by the ascetic poet Abu al-'Atahiya (d. 211/826).

302 Jesus was asked, "Why do you not build yourself a house?" He answered, "I build in the path of the flood."

Murtada al-Husayni al-Zabidi (d. 1205/1791), *Ithaf al-Sada al-Muttaqin*, 9:333 (Mansur, no. 259).

See Saying 110, above.

303 "How many people exhort others to remember God but themselves forget Him! How many people frighten others with God but themselves are insolent toward Him! How many people call others to God but themselves run away from Him! How many people recite the Book of God but themselves cast away its verses!"

Murtada al-Husayni al-Zabidi (d. 1205/1791), excerpted in Ghazali, *Ihya'*, 1:52, where this saying is attributed to the ascetic Ibn al-Sammak. I was unable to trace the attribution to Jesus.

Notes
Bibliography
Index to the Sayings
General Index

Notes

· · · · · · ·

In the formulation of dates—e.g., "fourth/tenth century"—the number preceding the slash indicates the date according to the Islamic calendar (A.H., or *anno hegirae*), while the number following the slash gives the date according to the Christian calendar (A.D., or *anno domini*).

1. For images of Jesus in modern Arabic and Islamic literature, see David Pinault, "Images of Christ in Arabic Literature," *Welt des Islams*, 27 (1987), 103–125; Anton Wessels, *Images of Jesus: How Jesus Is Perceived and Portrayed in Non-European Cultures* (London: SCM Press, 1990), pp. 43–56; Maurice Borrmans, *Jésus et les Musulmans d'aujourd'hui* (Paris: Desclée, 1996). For the survival of Jesus in modern Arabic Islamic lore, see, e.g., C. E. Padwick, "The Nabi 'Isa and the Skull," *The Muslim World*, 20 (1930), 56–62; and James Robson, "Stories of Jesus and Mary," *The Muslim World*, 40 (1950), 236–243. For an interesting example of the continuing relevance of Jesus to modern Muslim communities, see K. M. O'Connor, "The Islamic Jesus: Messiahhood and Human Divinity in African American Muslim Exegesis," *Journal of the American Academy of Religion*, 66, no. 3 (Fall 1998), 493–532. My thanks to Dr. G. L. Pattison of King's College, Cambridge, for this last reference.

2. For citations from the Muslim gospel in the eighteenth century, see Jeremiah Jones, *New and Full Method of Settling the Canonical Authority of the New Testament* (Oxford: J. Clark, 1798), as given in Donald Wismer, *The Islamic Jesus: An Annotated Bibliography of Sources in English and French* (New York: Garland, 1977), no. 379, pp. 141–142. For publication details of other important collections of the Muslim gospel, see Wismer, *The Islamic Jesus*, no. 441, p. 163 (Margoliouth); ibid., no. 79, p. 35 (Asin y Palacios); ibid., no. 550, p. 205 (Robson); and ibid., no. 301, pp. 112–113 (Hayek), the last-mentioned being of particular importance. The collection made by the Rev. Hanna Mansur, "Aqwal al-Sayyid al-Masih 'ind al-kuttab al-muslimin al-aqdamin" [The Sayings of Christ in Ancient Muslim writers], *Al-Masarra* (1976 *et seq.*), adds little to the Asin collec-

tion. Some ninety-six sayings of Jesus preserved in twelve classical Shiʿi works of literature, ethics, and Hadith were recently translated into English; see Mahdi Muntazir Qaʾim and Muhammad Legenhausen, "Jesus Christ Speaks through Shiʿi Traditions," *Al-Tawhid*, 13, no. 3 (Fall 1996), 21–40; and idem, "Jesus Christ in the Mirror of Shiʿi Narrations," *Al-Tawhid*, 13, no. 4 (Winter 1996), 45–56. The great majority of these sayings are derived from one source, Majlisi's *Bihar al-Anwar*. There is no commentary on the individual sayings, although there is a brief introduction to them. Most of these sayings are found in the present volume.

As early as 1910, Louis Cheikho declared: "One could write a whole volume on the sayings and actions of Jesus Christ as reported in Muslim authors." See Cheikho, "Quelques légendes islamiques apocryphes," *Mélanges de la Faculté Orientale, Université Saint-Joseph*, 4 (1910), 33–56.

3. Examples of such works include the traditions of Hammam ibn Munabbih and the ascetic collections of ʿAbdallah ibn al-Mubarak, Ahmad ibn Hanbal, Hannad ibn al-Sariyy, and Ibn Abiʾl Dunya. These are major authors from the second-third/eighth-ninth centuries.

4. The basic bibliographies in this field are Wismer, *The Islamic Jesus;* and Robert Caspar, "Bibliographie du dialogue islamo-chrétien," *Islamochristiana*, 1 (1975), 125–181, and 2 (1976), 187–249. There are also some useful items in the bibliography by Samir Khalil in *Islamochristiana*, 8 (1982), 10–12 (Khalil lists only Arabic texts). This journal has been a leading scholarly publication in the field of Muslim-Christian relations. Several items in the Wismer bibliography deal with one or more sayings of Jesus (see, e.g., the addenda to nos. 79 and 441), but there is no study of the corpus of sayings as a whole. See also E. Rudolph, *Dialogues islamo-chrétiens, 1950–1993* (Lausanne: Université de Lausanne, 1993).

5. The literature on pre-Islamic Arabian Christianity is fairly large. The modern starting point for any historical survey of this field is Irfan Shahid, *Rome and the Arabs* (Washington, D.C.: Dumbarton Oaks, 1984); idem, *Byzantium and the Arabs in the Fourth Century* (Washington, D.C.: Dumbarton Oaks, 1984); idem, *Byzantium and the Arabs in the Fifth Century* (Washington, D.C.: Dumbarton Oaks, 1989); and idem, *Byzantium and the Arabs in the Sixth Century* (Washington, D.C.: Dumbarton Oaks, 1995). Shahid's series will continue up to the seventh century A.D. Specifically on Jesus in the pre-Islamic Arabian context, see, e.g., F. V.

Winnett, "References to Jesus in Pre-Islamic Arabic Inscriptions," *The Muslim World*, 31 (1941), 341–353; G. Ryckmans, "La Mention de Jésus dans les inscriptions arabes préislamiques," *Analecta Bollandiana*, 67 (1949), 62–73; and Enno Littmann, "Jesus in a Pre-Islamic Arabic Inscription," *The Muslim World*, 40 (1950), 16–18. In pre-Islamic poetry, the best-known reference to Jesus is the poem by Umayya ibn Abi al-Salt; see his *Diwan*, ed. A. H. al-Satli (Damascus, 1974), pp. 484–487. This poem is cited in a work that dates to the fourth/tenth century, but there are serious doubts about its authenticity. For early Muslim attitudes to Judaism, see the convenient summary in Camilla Adang, *Muslim Writers on Judaism and the Hebrew Bible* (Leiden: Brill, 1996), ch. 1. This work also contains a valuable bibliography.

6. The opinions set forth in this paragraph may be found in such works as W. St. Clair Tisdall, *The Original Sources of the Qur'an* (London: SPCK, 1905); E. Sell and D. S. Margoliouth, "Christ in Mohammedan Literature," in James Hastings, ed., *Dictionary of Christ and the Gospels* (Edinburgh: T. and T. Clark, 1908), pp. 882–886; S. M. Zwemer, *The Moslem Christ* (Edinburgh: Oliphant, 1912); D. Sidersky, *Les Origines des légendes musulmanes dans le Coran et dans les vies des prophètes* (Paris: Geuthner, 1933), Thomas O'Shaughnessy, *The Koranic Concept of the Word of God* (Rome: Pontificio Istituto Biblico, 1940); Abraham Katsh, *Judaism in Islam: Biblical and Talmudic Backgrounds of the Koran and Its Commentaries* (New York: Bloch, 1954); W. M. Watt, "The Christianity Criticized in the Qur'an," *The Muslim World*, 57 (1967), 197–201; Olaf Schumann, *Der Christus der Muslime* (Gutersloh: Mohn, 1975); Kenneth Cragg, *Jesus and the Muslim* (London: Allen and Unwin, 1985); Jaroslav Pelikan, *Jesus through the Centuries* (New York: Harper Perennial Library, 1987), pp. 16–17.

7. For Nag Hammadi, see James M. Robinson, *The Nag Hammadi Library*, 3rd rev. ed. (Leiden: Brill, 1988); for Syriac, Coptic, and Ethiopic texts, see E. A. Wallis Budge, *Legends of Our Lady Mary the Perpetual Virgin and Her Mother Hanna* (London: Oxford University Press, 1933); and idem, *The Wit and Wisdom of the Christian Fathers of Egypt: The Syrian Version of the Apophthegmata Patrum of 'Anan Isho' of Beth 'Abhe* (London: Oxford University Press, 1934). See also Bentley Layton, *The Gnostic Scriptures* (New York: Doubleday, 1987); Benedicta Ward, *The Sayings*

of the Desert Fathers, rev. ed. (Oxford: Mowbray and Cistercian Publications, 1984); and Majella Franzmann, *Jesus in the Nag Hammadi Writings* (Edinburgh: T. and T. Clark, 1996).

8. The most authoritative of these collections is E. Hennecke, *New Testament Apocrypha* (London: Lutterworth, 1963–1964). It contains, in addition to the texts, valuable introductions and analyses by different scholars on the various strands of apocryphal literature. See also W. Schneemelcher, *New Testament Apocrypha*, English edition and translation by R. McL. Wilson (Cambridge: J. Clark, 1991–1992).

9. See, e.g., Claus Schedl, *Muhammad und Jesus* (Vienna: Herder, 1978), pp. 565–566.

10. One thinks of the work of scholars like Toshihiko Izutsu, Mohammed Arkoun, and Angelika Neuwirth.

11. For a thoughtful discussion of this issue in connection with the origins of Muslim jurisprudence, see Norman Calder, *Studies in Early Muslim Jurisprudence* (Oxford: Clarendon, 1993), ch. 8.

12. Apart from the diviners, it was well known to classical Islamic scholars that the poetry of, e.g., al-Nabigha al-Dhubyani or Umayya ibn Abi al-Salt was in most intimate relation with Qur'anic usage; see, e.g., Abu Zayd al-Qurashi (d. early fourth/tenth century), *Jamharat Ash'ar al-'Arab* (Beirut: Dar Bayrut, 1984), pp. 10–25.

13. There is an elegant discussion of this question in Frank Kermode, *The Genesis of Secrecy* (Cambridge, Mass.: Harvard University Press, 1979), p. 162, n. 20.

14. Thus, for example, despite the sensitive treatment of the Qur'anic Jesus in two fairly recent and influential studies—Geoffrey Parrinder, *Jesus in the Qur'an* (London: Faber, 1965); and Kenneth Cragg, *Jesus and the Muslim* (London: Allen and Unwin, 1985)—neither work adequately emphasizes the general prophetic context of the Qur'anic Jesus. There is a suggestive treatment of Qur'anic prophets in Fazlur Rahman, *Major Themes of the Qur'an* (Minneapolis: Bibliotheca Islamica, 1980). See also Helmut Gatje, *The Qur'an and Its Exegesis* (London: Routledge and Kegan Paul, 1976), esp. pp. 99–135.

15. One attempt to tackle these issues is O'Shaughnessy, *The Koranic Concept of the Word of God*. Unfortunately, it is marred by an anti-Islamic tone.

See also A. M. Charfi, "Christianity in the Qur'an Commentary of Tabari," *Islamochristiana*, 6 (1980), 105–148; and Schumann, *Der Christus der Muslime*, pp. 25–47. On early polemics regarding this concept, see D. J. Sahas, *John of Damascus on Islam* (Leiden: Brill, 1972), pp. 113ff.

16. As examples, see, e.g., Parrinder, *Jesus in the Qur'an*, pp. 22ff.; and G. Anawati, "'Isa," *Encyclopaedia of Islam*, new edition, ed. H. A. R. Gibb et al. (Leiden: Brill, 1960–).

17. For an authoritative classical Islamic discussion of the Crucifixion and the question of *shubbiha lahum*, see Tabari, *Tafsir*, 6:12–13. For early Muslim views as reflected in polemic, see Sahas, *John of Damascus*, pp. 78ff. For a fairly recent discussion, see Mahmoud Ayyoub, "Towards an Islamic Christology, 2: The Death of Jesus—Reality or Illusion?" *The Muslim World*, 70, no. 2 (1980), 91–121, which discusses the interpretation of this phrase in some classical and modern Qur'anic commentaries.

18. For other passages see Qur'an 6:101; 10:68; 17:111; 18:4; 19:88; 21:26; 39:4; and 72:3. The best-known of all is Sura 112. These sentiments are reflected in the earliest epigraphic references to Jesus in the Dome of the Rock in Jerusalem; see Max van Berchem, *Matériaux pour un Corpus inscriptionum arabicarum*, *12* (Cairo, 1927), pp. 228–257, esp. 230–231.

19. Especially such works as the Protevangelium of James; the Gospel of Pseudo-Matthew; the Gospel of Thomas; Budge, *Legends of Our Lady Mary;* and, in general, Hennecke, *New Testament Apocrypha*.

20. See the important discussion of the "death" of Jesus in Tabari, *Tafsir*, 3:202–205.

21. See Jane Dammen McAuliffe, *Quranic Christians: An Analysis of Classical and Modern Exegesis* (Cambridge: Cambridge University Press, 1991).

22. Hennecke, *New Testament Apocrypha*, 2:642. See also Mohammed Arkoun, "The Notion of Revelation: From Ahl al-Kitab to the Societies of the Book," *Welt des Islams*, 28 (1988), 62–89, for a corrective to the influence hunters. For other corrective views, see Heikki Raisanen, "The Portrait of Jesus in the Qur'an: Reflections of a Biblical Scholar," *The Muslim World*, 70, no. 2 (1980), 122–133; and Marilyn Waldman, "New Approaches to 'Biblical' Materials in the Qur'an," *The Muslim World*, 75, no. 1 (1985), 1–16.

23. The single most important classical text regarding the question of early Islamic scholarship is Al-Khatib al-Baghdadi (d. 463/1071), *Taqyid al-ʿIlm*, edited and with an important and largely neglected introduction by Yusuf al-ʿIshsh (Damascus, 1949). For some significant recent contributions to the debate on early Islam, see, e.g., John Wansbrough, *Qurʾanic Studies* (London: Oxford University Press, 1977); Patricia Crone and Michael Cook, *Hagarism: The Making of the Islamic World* (Cambridge: Cambridge University Press, 1977); Harald Motzki, "The *Musannaf* of ʿAbd al-Razzaq al-Sanʿani as a Source of Authentic *Ahadith* of the First Century A.H.," *Journal of Near Eastern Studies*, 50 (1991), 1–21; Albrecht Noth, *The Early Arabic Historical Tradition: A Source-Critical Study*, trans. Michael Bonner (Princeton: Darwin Press, 1994); Gregor Schoeler, "Writing and Publishing: On the Use and Function of Writing in the First Centuries of Islam," *Arabica*, 44 (1997), 423–435; Michael Cook, "The Opponents of the Writing of Tradition in Early Islam," *Arabica*, 44 (1997), 437–530; Wael B. Hallaq, *A History of Islamic Legal Theories* (Cambridge: Cambridge University Press, 1997), ch. 1. Many of these studies contain extensive bibliographies bearing on the theme of early Islamic scholarship and, by extension, on what we can or cannot know about "primitive Islam."

24. There is an unusual example of the absence of legal uniformity in a report said to date from about the year 720 A.D., when, it is claimed, jurists were sent to North Africa to confirm and establish the prohibition against wine drinking (Ibn ʿIdhari, *Al-Bayan al-Mughrib* [Leiden, 1948], 1:48). But there is a noticeable tendency among some students of early Islam to exaggerate the "primitivism" and confusion of early legal and administrative regulations. To balance this, one should consult the recent and important studies by Geoffrey Khan—for example, "The Pre-Islamic Background of Muslim Legal Formularies," *Aram*, 6 (1994), 193–224.

25. See the brief discussion of this question in Gerd-R. Puin, "Observations on Early Qurʾan Manuscripts in Sanʿaʾ," in Stefan Wild, ed., *The Qurʾan as Text* (Leiden: Brill, 1996), pp. 107–111. However, I understand that Puin will soon advance a new hypothesis regarding the evolution of the Qurʾanic text.

26. On divine Hadith *(hadith qudsi)*, see William A. Graham, *Divine Word and Prophetic Word in Early Islam* (The Hague: Mouton, 1977). On the transmission of Jewish and Christian traditions in the early Muslim envi-

ronment, see M. J. Kister, "*Haddithu ʿan Bani Israʾila wa la haraja:* A Study of an Early Tradition," in Kister, *Studies in Jahiliyya and Early Islam* (London: Variorum Reprints, 1980), which, among other things, criticizes the views expressed in W. M. Watt, "The Early Development of the Muslim Attitude to the Bible," *Transactions of the Glasgow University Oriental Society,* 16 (1957), 50–62; and J. Sadan, "Some Literary Problems concerning Judaism and Jewry in Medieval Arabic Sources," in M. Sharon, ed., *Studies in Honour of Professor David Ayalon* (Leiden: Brill, 1986), pp. 353–398, esp. pp. 370ff. On early debates about Jesus between Christians and Muslims, see Robert Hoyland, *Seeing Islam as Others Saw It: A Survey and Evaluation of Christian, Jewish, and Zoroastrian Writings on Early Islam* (Princeton, N.J.: Darwin Press, 1997), pp. 160–167, esp. p. 166.

27. See Cheikho, "Quelques légendes islamiques apocryphes."

28. The same charge of tampering with sacred texts had of course been leveled by the Christians against the Jews; see, e.g., Jaroslav Pelikan, *Jesus through the Centuries,* p. 26.

29. For examples of the progress of this scholarship, see Ignaz Goldziher, "Über Bibelcitate in Muhammedanischen Schriften," *Zeitschrift für die Alttestamentliche Wissenschaft,* 13 (1893), 315–321; Cheikho, "Quelques légendes islamiques apocryphes"; A. S. Tritton, "The Bible Text of Theodore Abu Qurra," *Journal of Theological Studies,* 34 (1933), 52–54; Alfred Guillaume, "The Version of the Gospels Used in Medina circa 700 A.D.," *Al-Andalus,* 15 (1950), 289–296; R. G. Khoury, "Quelques réflexions sur les citations de la Bible dans les premières générations islamiques du premier et du deuxième siècle de l'Hégire," *Bulletin d'Etudes Orientales,* 29 (1977), 269–278; and, most recently, Sidney H. Griffith, "The Gospel in Arabic: An Enquiry into Its Appearance in the First Abbasid Century," *Oriens Christianus,* 69 (1985), 126–167; and idem, "The Monks of Palestine and the Growth of Christian Literature in Arabic," *The Muslim World,* 78 (1988), 1–28. See also Camilla Adang, *Muslim Writers,* chs. 1 and 4; and Sadan, "Some Literary Problems concerning Judaism and Jewry."

30. See, e.g., Aziz al-Azmeh, *Muslim Kingship* (London: Tauris, 1997), ch. 4.

31. See T. Khalidi, "The Role of Jesus in Intra-Muslim Polemics of the First Two Islamic Centuries," in S. K. Samir and J. S. Nielsen, eds., *Christian*

Arabic Apologetics during the Abbasid Period, 750–1258 (Leiden: Brill, 1994), pp. 146–156 and notes 24 and 25; Khalil ʿAthamina, "Al-Qasas: Its Emergence, Religious Origin and Its Socio-Political Impact on Early Muslim Society," *Studia Islamica*, 76 (1992), 53–74; David Thomas, "The Miracles of Jesus in Early Islamic Polemics," *Journal of Semitic Studies*, 39 (1994), 221–243. On religious scholars and ascetics, there is much to learn from M. G. S. Hodgson, *The Venture of Islam* (Chicago: University of Chicago Press, 1974), vol. 1, pp. 359–409, esp. the reference to Jesus and the Sufis on p. 398.

32. See Arthur Jeffrey, "The Descent of Jesus in Muhammadan Eschatology," in S. E. Johnson, ed., *The Joy of Study: Papers on New Testament and Related Subjects Presented to Honor Frederick Clifton Grant* (New York: Macmillan, 1951), 107–126; W. Madelung, "Mahdi," *Encyclopaedia of Islam;* Al-Azmeh, *Muslim Kingship*, pp. 201–202; Fritz Meier, "Eine Auferstehung Mohammeds bei Suyuti," in *Bausteine II*, Beiruter Texte und Studien 53b (Istanbul, 1992), pp. 797–835.

33. See, e.g., Khalidi, "The Role of Jesus in Intra-Muslim Polemics"; and T. Nagel, "Kisas al-Anbiyaʾ," *Encyclopaedia of Islam.*

34. There is a good introduction to this literature in W. M. Thackston, *The Tales of the Prophets of al-Kisaʾi* (Boston: Twayne, 1978).

35. This prophetology is refined in Sufi writings; see, e.g., the discussion of the views of Ibn ʿArabi (d. 638/1240) in Caesar E. Farah, "The Prose Literature of Sufism," in M. J. L. Young et al., eds., *Religion, Learning and Science in the ʿAbbasid Period* (Cambridge: Cambridge University Press, 1990), pp. 72–74.

36. For examples of some of this editorial activity, see, e.g., R. G. Khoury, *Les Légendes prophétiques dans l'Islam* (Wiesbaden: Otto Harrassowitz, 1978), p. 27 (geographic identifications), p. 238 (prediction of Muhammad's coming), p. 240 (Qurʾanic phrases in prayers of prophets), p. 248 (parallels with Muhammad in the story of Isaiah).

37. On al-Kisaʾi, see Thackston, *The Tales of the Prophets of al-Kisaʾi.*

38. Abu Ishaq Ahmad al-Thaʿlabi, *Kitab Qisas al-Anbiyaʾ* (Cairo, 1306/1889). The style here does not derive, as Thackston assumes, "directly from Koranic commentary with the legendary material excerpted and arranged in chronological order" (*The Tales of the Prophets of al-Kisaʾi*, p. xvi). Rather, the idea of *majalis* which appears in the alternative title

of the work *('Ara'is al-Majalis)* is meant to evoke the Sufi *majalis al-dhikr*, sessions of prayers and devotional exercises, and the style and structure are reminiscent of Abu Hayyan al-Tawhidi, *Al-Imta' wa'l Mu'anasa*, a work which similarly combines Sufism with Adab.

39. See Hennecke, *New Testament Apocrypha*, 1:62ff.

40. Khalidi, "The Role of Jesus in Intra-Muslim Polemics."

41. For a general portrait of the city, see H. Djait, *Al-Kufa: Naissance de la ville islamique* (Paris: Maisonneuve, 1986); and Tarif Khalidi, *Arabic Historical Thought in the Classical Period* (Cambridge: Cambridge University Press, 1994), p. 50, n. 56.

42. As early as the ninth century, the Christian writer Stephen of Ramla commented that the teaching of Muhammad robs Jesus of his divine powers; see Hoyland, *Seeing Islam as Others Saw It*, p. 230. On Jesus and the "Hour," see Ibn al-Mubarak, *Zuhd*, p. 77; and Ibn Hanbal, *Zuhd*, p. 97. Eventually the Sunnites and Shi'ites were to differ as to whether the Mahdi, or Muslim Messiah, was higher in rank than Jesus (the Shi'ite view) or Jesus was higher than the Mahdi (the Sunnite view). In the summer of 1997, huge banners were raised in Beirut's largely Shi'ite southern suburbs on the occasion of the Mahdi's birthday—banners which "congratulated the expectant believers for the dawning of the light of salvation upon the appearance of the Mahdi and the Prophet Jesus son of Mary."

43. Matthew was arguably the Gospel most often referred to in the Arabic Islamic literary tradition as a whole; one indicator is provided in the index of references to the Gospels appended by M. Asin y Palacios to his collection, "Logia et agrapha domini Jesu apud moslemicos scriptores, asceticos praesertim, usitata," *Patrologia Orientalis*, 13 (1919), 335–431, and 19 (1926), 531–624. It may also be that as knowledge of the Gospels grew steadily in Muslim polemical circles after the ninth century A.D., the passage in Matthew 23:34, where Jesus speaks of sending "prophets and wise men and scribes; some you will slaughter and crucify, some you will scourge in your synagogues and hunt from town to town," was considered by Muslim apologists to be telling evidence for Muhammad's coming and tribulations—indeed, for his Hegira. But Parrinder (*Jesus in the Qur'an*, p. 95) argues that the Gospel of John is the one with the closest parallels to the Qur'an. See also Claus Schedl, "Die 114 Suren des Koran

und die 114 Logien Jesu im Thomas-Evangelium," *Der Islam*, 64, no. 2 (1987), 261–264. I should point out, however, that the Muslim gospel played no part in Christian-Muslim polemics. It is odd that the Christian apologists who could have quoted from this gospel in order to show that the Muslims had in their turn "perverted" the authentic sayings of Jesus did not in fact do so.

44. Ibn Hanbal, *Kitab al-Zuhd*, no. 319; and compare Saying 59 in this volume.

45. See Saying 51 in this volume.

46. See Saying 30 in this volume.

47. These attributions, so far as can be determined, will be indicated in the commentaries on each saying and story.

48. See Khalidi, "The Role of Jesus in Intra-Muslim Polemics."

49. On the Murji'a, see Khalil ʿAthamina, "The Early Murji'a: Some Notes," *Journal of Semitic Studies*, 35, no. 1 (1990), 109–130. ʿAthamina argues that the movement had both a quietist wing and an activist wing, although it is difficult to agree with his interpretation of the aims of the latter.

50. For these and other examples, see Khalidi, "The Role of Jesus in Intra-Muslim Polemics," n. 12.

51. For these and other examples, see ibid., n. 13.

52. For these and other references, see ibid., n. 17.

53. For these and other references, see ibid., n. 18.

54. The sayings are largely without *isnad*, making it impossible to trace their sources. These sayings were first studied by G. Lecomte, "Les Citations de l'Ancien et du Nouveau Testament dans l'oeuvre d'Ibn Qutayba," *Arabica*, 5 (1958), 34–46. See also André Ferré, "L'Historien al-Yaʿqubi et les évangiles," *Islamochristiana*, 3 (1977), 65–83; idem, "La Vie de Jésus d'après les Annales de Tabari," *Islamochristiana*, 5 (1979), 7–29.

55. The "Bridge" saying (see Ibn Qutayba, ʿ*Uyun al-Akhbar*, 2:268; also ʿ*Uyun*, 3:21) has been commented on in various sources, including Joachim Jeremias, *Unknown Sayings of Jesus*, 2nd ed. (London: SPCK, 1964), pp. 111–118; and Harald Sahlin, "Die Welt ist eine Brücke," *Zeitschrift für die Neutestamentliche Wissenschaft*, 47 (1956), 286–287.

Jeremias links it to the saying in Ghazali, "Be passers-by," and ultimately to the Gospel of Thomas. Sahlin, unaware that it is already found in Ibn Qutayba, traces it to the *Disciplina clericalis* of Petrus Alfonsi, who wrote ca. 1106 A.D..

56. On Ibn al-Muqaffaʿ, see M. Kurd ʿAli, ed., *Rasaʾil al-Bulagha*, 3rd ed. (Cairo, 1946), pp. 112–116, 146–172. On gnomological literature, see especially Dimitri Gutas, *Greek Wisdom Literature in Arabic Translation: A Study of the Graeco-Arabic Gnomologia* (New Haven, Conn.: American Oriental Society, 1975). See also the useful but less rigorous work by I. Alon, *Socrates in Mediaeval Arabic Literature* (Leiden: Brill, 1991).

57. Ibn Qutayba, *ʿUyun al-Akhbar* (Cairo, 1925–1930), 2:370; see also Saying 100 in this volume.

58. On Kufa's significance for Shiʿism, see E. Kohlberg, *Belief and Law in Imami Shiʿism* (London: Variorum Reprints, 1991), pp. xvi, 57–58, 65. For comparisons between the ascent of Jesus and the invisibility of the imams, see Nawbakhti, *Firaq al-Shiʿa* (Istanbul, 1931), p. 68. On the infant imam and the infant Jesus, see Nawbakhti, *Firaq*, p. 76. For other similarities, see Ibn Babuya al-Qummi, *ʿIlal al-Sharaʾiʿ* (Teheran, 1377/ 1957–1958), 1:196, 216; and Al-Shaykh al-Mufid, *Al-Ikhtisas* (Teheran, 1379/ 1959–1960), p. 56. For the Ismaʿilis, see Nawbakhti, *Firaq*, p. 63; and Note 63, below. See, further, M. Momen, *An Introduction to Shiʿi Islam* (New Haven, Conn.: Yale University Press, 1986), pp. 42–43, 52, 57; David Pinault, *The Shiʿites; Ritual and Popular Piety in a Muslim Community* (London: Tauris, 1992), p. 55; and Kohlberg, *Belief and Law*, pp. xvi, 59. For a collection of Jesus sayings in some classical Shiʿi works, see Mahdi Muntazir Qaʾim and Muhammad Legenhausen, "Jesus Christ Speaks through Shiʿi Traditions," *Al-Tawhid*, 13, no. 3 (Fall 1996), 21– 40; and idem, "Jesus Christ in the Mirror of Shiʿi Narrations," *Al-Tawhid*, 13, no. 4 (Winter 1996), 45–56.

59. See, e.g., Saying 100 in this volume; also Matthew 12:35.

60. Ibn Qutayba, *ʿUyun al-Akhbar*, 4:123; Ibn Babuya, *ʿIlal*, 2:184; see also Sayings 103 and 152 in this volume.

61. Ibn Qutayba, *ʿUyun*, 1:327; see also Saying 91 in this volume.

62. On this question, two studies should first be consulted: Louis Massignon, "L'Homme parfait en Islam et son originalité éschatologique," *Eranos-Jahrbuch*, 15 (1947), 287–314; and Hodgson, *The Venture of Islam*, vol. 1,

pp. 398–402. See also Louis Massignon, in Wismer, *The Islamic Jesus*, no. 448, for a possible connection between the wearing of wool *(suf)*, the origins of Sufism, and the imitation of Christ. The best study of Jesus in the Sufi tradition, with numerous quotations from the sources, is Annemarie Schimmel, *Jesus und Maria in der islamischen Mystik* (Munich: Kösel, 1996).

63. Some of the earliest and most astonishingly accurate translations from the Old and New Testaments are in Abu Hatim al-Razi (d. ca. 933 A.D.), *A'lam al-Nubuwwah* (Teheran, 1977). Abu Hatim was an Isma'ili missionary. See also Sulayman Murad, "A Twelfth-Century Biography of Jesus," *Islam and Christian-Muslim Relations*, 7, no. 1 (1996), 39–45.

64. Abu Hayyan al-Tawhidi, *Al-Basa'ir wa'l Dhakha'ir* (Tripoli, 1978), 7, paragraphs 243 and 489; see also Sayings 169 and 168 in this volume.

65. See A. d'Souza, "Jesus in Ibn 'Arabi's *Fusus al-Hikam*," *Islamochristiana*, 8 (1982), 185–200. See also Y. Marquet, "Les Ihwan al-Safa et le christianisme," *Islamochristiana*, 8 (1982), 129–158.

66. My colleague Basim Musallam suggested to me that Jesus occupies, in the Islamic tradition as a whole, a position not unlike that occupied by 'Ali in Sunni Islam: both Jesus and 'Ali were figures of towering spiritual stature, but both needed to be "rescued" from the excessive adoration of their followers. See also the prophetic Hadith to this effect in Baladhuri, *Ansab al-Ashraf*, 2:121.

67. The struggle with Satan is said by Peter Brown to have been formative of the mood of early Christianity; see Brown, *The World of Late Antiquity* (London: Thames and Hudson, 1978), pp. 53–56.

68. Ghazali, *Ihya' 'Ulum al-Din*, 3:28; see also Saying 119 in this volume. See also his extended comments on the "Bridge" saying (3:112) and on the "three diseases of wealth" (3:178). Ghazali seems to have singled out Jesus' sayings from among prophetic sayings for special commentary.

69. On Jesus and the pig, see Ibn Abi'l Dunya, *Kitab al-Samt*, p. 573; see also Saying 128 in this volume. On Muhammad and the icon in the Ka'ba, see Azraqi, *Akhbar Makka*, p. 111.

Bibliography of Arabic Sources

· · · · · · ·

Al-Abi, Abu Sa'd Mansur b. al-Husayn (d. 421/1030). *Nathr al-Durr.* Ed. Muhammad 'Ali Qarna et al. Cairo: al-Hay'a al-Misriyya al-'Amma, 1981–1991.

Al-Abshihi, Baha' al-Din Muhammad b. Ahmad (d. 892/1487). *Al-Mustatraf fi kulli Fannin Mustazraf.* Cairo: al-Matba'a al-'Amira al-'Uthmaniyya, A.H. 1306.

Abu al-Faraj al-Baghdadi, Qudama b. Ja'far (d. 337/948). *Kitab Naqd al-Nathr* [attributed]. Ed. Taha Husayn and 'Abd al-Hamid al-'Abbadi. Cairo: Dar al-Kutub al-Misriyya, 1933.

Abu Hayyan al-Tawhidi, 'Ali b. Muhammad al-Baghdadi (d. after 400/1010). *Risala fi al-Sadaqa wa al-Sadiq.* Istanbul: Matba'at al-Jawa'ib, A.H. 1301.

——— *Al-Imta' wa al-Mu'anasa.* Ed. Ahmad Amin and Ahmad al-Zayn. Cairo: Lajnat al-Ta'lif wa al-Tarjama wa al-Nashr, 1942.

——— *Al-Basa'ir wa al-Dhakha'ir.* Vols. 1–3, ed. Ibrahim al-Kaylani. Damascus: Maktabat Atlas, 1965–1977.

——— *Al-Basa'ir wa al-Dhakha'ir.* Vol. 7, ed. Wadad al-Qadi. Libya: al-Dar al-'Arabiyya li-l-Kitab, 1978.

Abu Nu'aym al-Isbahani, Ahmad b. 'Abdallah (d. 430/1038). *Hilyat al-Awliya' wa Tabaqat al-Asfiya'.* Cairo: Matba'at al-Sa'ada, 1932–1938.

Abu Rifa'a al-Fasawi, 'Umara b. Wathima al-Farisi (d. 289/902). *Les Légendes prophétiques dans l'Islam.* Ed. Raif G. Khuri. Wiesbaden: Harrassovitz, 1978.

Abu Talib al-Makki, Muhammad b. 'Ali (d. 386/996). *Qut al-Qulub fi Mu'amalat al-Mahbub.* Cairo: al-Matba'a al-Maymaniyya, A.H. 1310.

Al-'Amiri, Abu al-Hasan Muhammad b. Yusuf al-Naysaburi (d. 381/992). *Al-Sa'ada wa al-Is'ad.* Ed. Mujtaba Minowi. Wiesbaden: Franz Steiner, 1957–1958.

Al-Antaki, Dawud b. ʿUmar al-Darir (d. 1008/1599). *Tazyin al-Aswaq bi-Tafsil Ashwaq al-ʿUshshaq*. Ed. Muhammad al-Tanji. Beirut: ʿAlam al-Kutub, 1993.

Al-Baladhuri, Ahmad b. Yahya (d. 279/892) *Ansab al-Ashraf*. Vol.2, ed. M. B. al-Mahmudi. Beirut: Muʾassasat al-Aʿzami, 1974.

Al-Balawi, Abu al-Hajjaj Yusuf b. Muhammad (d. 604/1207). *Kitab Alif Baʾ*. Cairo: Jamʿiyyat al-Maʿarif, A.H. 1287.

Al-Damiri, Kamal al-Din Muhammad b. Musa (d. 808/1405). *Hayat al-Hayawan al-Kubra*. Cairo: al-Matbaʿa al-Maymaniyya, A.H. 1305.

Al-Ghazali, Abu Hamid Muhammad b. Muhammad (d. 505/1111). *Al-Tibr al-Masbuk fi Nasihat al-Muluk*. Cairo: Matbaʿat al-Adab wa al-Muʾayyad, A.H. 1317.

――― *Minhaj al-ʿAbidin*. Cairo: al-Matbaʿa al-Husayniyya, A.H. 1322.

――― *Ihyaʾ ʿUlum al-Din*. Cairo: Mustafa al-Babi al-Halabi, 1939.

――― *Ayyuha al-Walad*. Ed. ʿAli al-Qaradaghi. Beirut: Dar al-Bashaʾir al-Islamiyya, 1985.

――― *Mukashafat al-Qulub al-Muqarrib ila Hadrat ʿAllam al-Ghuyub*. Cairo: Matbaʿat Muhammad ʿAtif, n.d.

Al-Hakim al-Tirmidhi, Abu ʿAbdallah Muhammad b. ʿAli (d. 285/898). *Al-Salat wa Maqasidiha*. Ed. Husni Zaydan. Cairo: Dar al-Kitab al-ʿArabi, 1965.

Ibn ʿAbd al-Barr al-Qurtubi, Abu ʿUmar Yusuf (d. 463/1071). *Jamiʿ Bayan al-ʿIlm wa Fadlihi*. Medina: al-Maktaba al-ʿIlmiyya, n.d.

――― *Mukhtasar Jamiʿ Bayan al-ʿIlm wa Fadlihi*. Cairo: Matbaʿat al-Mawsuʿat, A.H. 1320.

――― *Bahjat al-Majalis*. Ed. M. M. al-Khawli. Cairo: Dar al-Katib al-ʿArabi, n.d.

Ibn ʿAbd al-Hakam, ʿAbd al-Rahman b. ʿAbdallah al-Misri (d. 257/870). *Futuh Misr wa Akhbaruha*. Ed. Charles Torrey. Leiden: E. J. Brill, 1920.

Ibn ʿAbd Rabbihi, Ahmad b. Muhammad al-Qurtubi (d. 328/940). *Al-ʿIqd al-Farid*. Cairo: Lajnat al-Taʾlif wa al-Tarjama wa al-Nashr, 1940–1953.

Ibn Abi al-Dunya, Abu Bakr ʿAbdallah b. Muhammad (d. 281/894). *Kitab al-Ashraf* Ed. Walid Qassab. Doha/Qatar: Dar al-Thaqafa, 1993.

———— *Al-Ikhwan.* Ed. Mustafa ʿAta. Beirut: Dar al-Kutub al-ʿIlmiyya, 1988.

———— *Kitab al-Samt wa Adab al-Lisan.* Ed. Najm Khalaf. Beirut: Dar al-Gharb al-Islami, 1986.

———— *Mawsuʿat Rasaʾil Ibn Abi al-Dunya.* Ed. Mustafa ʿAta. Beirut: Muʾassasat al-Kutub al-Thaqafiyya, 1993.

Ibn Abi al-Hadid, ʿAbd al-Hamid b. Hibatullah (d. 655/1257). *Sharh Nahj al-Balagha* Ed. M. A. F. Ibrahim. Cairo: ʿIsa al-Babi al-Halabi, 1959–1964.

Ibn ʿAqil, Abu al-Wafaʾ ʿAli al-Baghdadi (d. 513/1119). *Kitab al-Funun.* Ed. George Maqdisi. Beirut: Dar al-Mashriq, 1970.

Ibn ʿArabi, Abu ʿAbdallah Muhyi al-Din Muhammad b. ʿAli (d. 638/1240). *Al-Futuhat al-Makkiyya.* Cairo, A.H. 1305.

———— *Muhadarat al-Abrar wa Musamarat al-Akhyar fi al-Adabiyyat wa al-Nawadir wa al-Akhbar.* Cairo: Matbaʿat al-Saʿada, 1906.

Ibn ʿAsakir, Abu al-Qasim ʿAli b. al-Hasan (d. 571/1175). *Tarikh Madinat Dimashq.* Vol. 1, ed. Salah al-Din al-Munajjid. Damascus: al-Majmaʿ al-ʿIlmi al-ʿArabi, 1954.

———— *Sirat al-Sayyid al-Masih.* Ed. Sulayman Murad. ʿAmman: Dar al-Shuruq, 1996.

Ibn Babuya al-Qummi, Abu Jaʿfar Muhammad b. ʿAli (d. 381/991). *ʿIlal al-Sharaʾiʿ.* Ed. Fadlallah Tabatabaʾi. Tehran, A.H. 1377.

Ibn Hamdun, Abu al-Maʿali Muhammad b. al-Hasan (d. 562/1166). *Al-Tadhkira al-Hamduniyya.* Ed. Ihsan ʿAbbas. Beirut: Maʿhad al-Inmaʾ al-ʿArabi, 1983.

Ibn Hanbal, Abu ʿAbdallah Ahmad b. Muhammad al-Shaybani (d. 241/855). *Kitab al-Zuhd.* Ed. Muhammad Zaghlul. Beirut: Dar al-Kitab al-ʿArabi, 1988.

———— *Kitab al-Waraʿ.* Ed. Muhammad Zaghlul. Beirut: Dar al-Kitab al-ʿArabi, 1988.

Ibn al-Hanbali, Abu al-Faraj ʿAbd al-Rahman b. Najm (d. 634/1236). *Al-*

Istis'ad bi-man Laqaytuhu min Salihi al-'Ibad fi al-Bilad, in *Shadharat min Kutubin Mafquda,* ed. Ihsan 'Abbas. Beirut: Dar al-Gharb al-Islami, 1988. Pp. 175–205.

Ibn Hisham, 'Abd al-Malik (d. 218/833). *Kitab al-Tijan fi Muluk Himyar.* Ed. F. Krenkow. Hyderabad, India: Da'irat al-Ma'arif, 1928.

——— *Al-Sira al-Nabawiyya.* Ed. M. al-Saqqa et al. Cairo: Mustafa al-Babi al-Halabi, 1936.

Ibn al-Jawzi, Abu al-Faraj 'Abd al-Rahman b. 'Ali (d. 597/1201). *Al-Adhkiya'.* Ed. Usama al-Rifa'i. Damascus: Maktabat al-Ghazali, 1976.

——— *Dhamm al-Hawa.* Ed. Mustafa 'Abd al-Wahid. Cairo: Dar al-Kutub al-Haditha, 1962.

Ibn Maja, Muhammad b. Yazid (d. 274/887). *Al-Sunan.* Ed. M. F. 'Abd al-Baqi. Cairo: Dar Ihya' al-Kutub al-'Arabiyya, 1952.

Ibn al-Mubarak, 'Abdallah al-Marwazi (d. 181/797). *Kitab al-Zuhd wa al-Raqa'iq.* Ed. Habib al-Rahman al-A'zami. Beirut: Dar al-Kutub al-'Ilmiyya, n.d.

Ibn Munabbih, Hammam (d. 131/748). *Sahifat Hammam b. Munabbih.* Ed. Muhammad Hamidullah. Damascus: al-Majma' al-'Ilmi al-'Arabi, 1953.

Ibn Qudama al-Maqdisi, Abu Muhammad 'Abdallah b. Ahmad (d. 620/1223). *Kitab al-Tawwabin.* Ed. George Maqdisi. Damascus: al-Ma'had al-Faransi li-l-Dirasat al-'Arabiyya, 1961.

Ibn Qutayba, Abu Muhammad 'Abdallah b. Muslim (d. 271/884). *Kitab 'Uyun al-Akhbar.* Cairo: Dar al-Kutub al-Misriyya, 1925–1930.

Ibn al-Qutiyya, Abu Bakr Muhammad b. 'Umar al-Qurtubi (d. 367/977). *Tarikh Iftitah al-Andalus.* Ed. Ibrahim al-Abyari. Cairo: Dar al-Kitab al-Misri and Dar al-Kitab al-Lubnani, 1989.

Ibn Sa'd, Muhammad (d. 230/845). *Al-Tabaqat al-Kubra.* Beirut: Dar Sadir, n.d.

Ibn al-Salah, Abu 'Amr 'Uthman b. 'Abd al-Rahman (d. 643/1245). *Fatawa wa Masa'il Ibn al-Salah.* Ed. 'Abd al-Mu'ti Qal'aji. Beirut: Dar al-Ma'rifa, 1986.

Ibn al-Sariyy, Hannad (d. 243/857). *Kitab al-Zuhd*. Ed. ʿAbd al-Rahman al-Firyawaʾi. Kuwait: Dar al-Khulafaʾ li-l Kitab al-Islami, 1985.

Ibn Sida, Abu al-Hasan ʿAli b. Ismaʿil al-Andalusi (d. 458/1066). *Kitab al-Mukhassas*. Bulaq: al-Matbaʿa al-Kubra al-Amiriyya, A.H. 1316.

Ibn Wasil, Jamal al-Din Muhammad b. Salim (d. 697/1298). *Mufarrij al-Kurub fi Akhbar Bani Ayyub*. Ed. Jamal al-Din al-Shayyal. Cairo: Jamiʿat Fuʾad al-Awwal, 1953.

Ikhwan al-Safaʾ (d. fourth/tenth century). *Rasaʾil Ikhwan al-Safaʾ wa Khillan al-Wafaʾ*. Ed. Khayr al-Din al-Zirikli. Cairo: al-Matbaʿa al-ʿArabiyya, 1928.

Al-Jahiz, Abu ʿUthman ʿAmr b. Bahr (d. 255/868). *Al-Bayan wa al-Tabyin*. Ed. ʿAbd al-Salam Harun. Cairo: Matbaʿat Lajnat al-Taʾlif wa al-Tarjama wa al-Nashr, 1949.

――― *Kitab Kitman al-Sirr wa Hifẓ al-Lisan*, in *Rasaʾil al-Jahiẓ*. Ed. ʿAbd al-Salam Harun. Beirut: Dar al-Jil, 1991. Vol. 1, pp. 139–172.

――― *Al-Mahasin wa al-Addad*. Cairo: Matbaʿat al-Futuh, A.H. 1332.

Al-Kalabadhi, Abu Bakr Muhammad b. Ishaq (d. 380/990). *Al-Taʿarruf li-Madhhab Ahl al-Tasawwuf*. Ed. Arthur John Arberry. Cairo: Matbaʿat al-Saʿada, 1933.

Al-Kulayni, Abu Jaʿfar Muhammad b. Yaʿqub (d. 329/941). *Al-Usul min al-Kafi*. Ed. ʿAli Akbar al-Ghaffari. Beirut: Dar al-Adwaʾ, 1985.

Majlisi, Mulla Muhammad Baqir (d. 1110/1698). *Bihar al-Anwar*. Tehran: Dar al-Kutub al-Islamiyya, n.d. (1957?).

Al-Mawardi, Abu al-Hasan ʿAli b. Muhammad al-Basri (d. 450/1058). *Al-Ahkam al-Sultaniyya*. Cairo: Matbaʿat al-Watan, A.H. 1298.

――― *Adab al-Dunya wa al-Din*. Ed. Mustafa al-Saqqa. Cairo: Mustafa al-Babi al-Halabi, 1955.

Miskawayh, Abu ʿAli Ahmad b. Muhammad (d. 421/1030). *Al-Hikma al-Khalida*. Ed. ʿAbd al-Rahman Badawi. Cairo: Maktabat al-Nahda al-Misriyya, 1952.

Al-Mubarrad, Abu al-ʿAbbas Muhammad b. Yazid (d. 285/898). *Al-Fadil*. Ed. ʿAbd al-ʿAziz al-Maymani. Cairo: Dar al-Kutub al-Misriyya, 1956.

———— *Al-Kamil*. Ed. M. Abu'l Fadl Ibrahim and A. Shahata. Cairo: Dar Nahdat Misr, n.d. (1970?).

Al-Mubashshir b. Fatik, Abu'l Wafa' (wrote 445/1053). *Mukhtar al-Hikam wa Mahasin al-Kalim*. Ed. ʿAbd al-Rahman Badawi. Beirut: Al-Muʾassasa al-ʿArabiyya liʾl Dirasat waʾl Nashr, 1980.

Muslim b. al-Hajjaj (d. 261/875) *Sahih Muslim*. Beirut: Dar al-Maʿrifa, 1972.

Al-Qurashi, Abu Zayd Muhammad b. Abiʾl Khattab (d. circa 171/787). *Jamharat Ashʿar al-ʿArab*. Beirut: Dar Beirut, 1984.

Al-Qushayri, Abu al-Qasim (d. 465/1073). *Al-Risala al-Qushayriyya fi ʿIlm al-Tasawwuf*. Cairo: Mustafa al-Babi al-Halabi, A.H. 1318 (A.D. 1900).

Al-Raghib al-Isfahani, Abu al-Qasim al-Husayn b. Muhammad (d. early fifth/early eleventh century). *Muhadarat al-Udabaʾ*. Beirut: Maktabat al-Hayat, n.d.

Al-Samarqandi, Abu al-Layth Nasr b. Muhammad (d. 373/983). *Tanbih al-Ghafilin*. Cairo: al-Matbaʿa al-Yusufiyya, n.d.

Al-Shaʿrani, ʿAbd al-Wahhab b. Ahmad al-Misri (d. 973/1565). *Al-Tabaqat al-Kubra*. Cairo, 1286.

———— *Lataʾif al-Minan wa al-Akhlaq*. Cairo: Dar al-Tibaʿa, A.H. 1288.

Sibt Ibn al-Jawzi, Shams al-Din Yusuf b. Quzughli (d. 654/1256). *Mirʾat al-Zaman*. Hyderabad, India: Daʾirat al-Maʿarif al-ʿUthmaniyya, n.d.

Al-Suhrawardi, Shihab al-Din ʿUmar (d. 632/1234). *ʿAwarif al-Maʿarif*, in the margins of Ghazali, *Ihyaʾ ʿUlum al-Din*. Cairo: Al-Matbaʿa al-Maymaniyya, A.H. 1306.

Al-Tabari, Muhammad b. Jarir (d. 310/923) *Tafsir al-Qurʾan*. Cairo: Al-Matbaʿa al-Maymaniyya, 1903.

Al-Turtushi, Muhammad b. al-Walid b. Abi Randaqa (d. 520/1126). *Siraj al-Muluk*. Ed. J. al-Bayati. London: Riyad al-Rayyis, 1990.

Al-Waqidi, Muhammad b. ʿUmar (d. 207/823). *Al-Maghazi*. Ed. J. Marsden Jones. London: Oxford University Press, 1966.

Warram b. Abi Firas, Abu al-Husayn (d. 606/1208). *Majmuʿat Warram; Tanbih al-Khawatir wa Nuzhat al-Nawazir*. Ed. Muhammad Akhundi. Tehran, Dar al-Kutub al-Sultaniyya, n.d.

Al-Zabidi, Muhammad Murtada b. Muhammad al-Husayni (d. 1205/1791). *Ithaf al-Sada al-Muttaqin bi-Sharh Asrar Ihya' 'Ulum al-Din.* Cairo: al-Matba'a al-Maymaniyya, A.H. 1311.

Al-Zamakhshari, Mahmud b. 'Umar (d. 538/1144). *Rabi' al-Abrar.* Ed. Salim al-Nu'aymi. Baghdad: Matba'at al-'Ani, n.d.

Al-Zubayr b. Bakkar (d. 256/870) *Jamharat Nasab Quraysh.* Vol. 1. Ed. M. M. Shakir. Cairo, 1962.

Index to the Sayings

·······

Numerals refer to the numbers of the sayings.

General Index

•••••••

Al-Abi, Abu Saʿd (as source), 151–152

Abraham, 8, 11, 26, 28

Al-Abshihi, Bahaʾ al-Din (as source), 211

Abu Hayyan al-Tawhidi (as source), 144–147

Abu Nuʿaym al-Isbahani, 42; (as source), 152–160

Abu Rifaʿa al-Fasawi (as source), 126–127

Abu Talib al-Makki, 42; (as source), 138–141

Adab: defined, 3; and Tales of the Prophets, 28; and Muslim gospel, 38; and sayings, 54, 59, 63, 64, 76, 77, 84, 95, 98, 104, 122, 144, 149, 152, 153, 188, 209, 211

Al-ʿAmiri, Abu al-Hasan (as source), 138

Apocrypha, 7, 8–9, 17, 19. *See also* Bible; New Testament

Arabia, 6, 7, 22, 23

Arabic, 20–21

Asin y Palacios, Miguel, 4, 5, 30, 93, 122, 123, 165, 173, 176

Al-Balawi, Abu al-Hajjaj (as source), 196–198

Bible, 11; and Jesus, 3, 5, 12; and Muslim gospel, 3, 33–34, 40; as source, 4; canonical, 9; and

Qurʾan, 9, 16, 19–20; and Islam, 19–20, 33–34; Arabic, 21; and maxims, 21; Second Coming, 25; and Ibn Qutayba, 38; and Sufism, 41

Budge, E. A. Wallis, 116–117, 150, 152, 168, 213

Byzantium, 6, 7, 23

Christians/Christianity: and Muslims, 5; and Islam, 5, 7, 8, 19–22, 29–30, 45; and Arabia, 6; and apocrypha, 7, 8–9, 17, 19; and Muhammad, 7, 20–21; and Nag Hammadi texts, 8; Eastern, 8, 9, 19, 25; and Qurʾan, 9, 13, 15, 16, 19; and Jesus, 12; and Jews, 17; and Hadith, 24; converts from, 30; and ascetics, 32; Near Eastern, 40; and Shiʿism, 40

Companion, 24, 26, 30

Al-Damiri, Kamal al-Din (as source), 208–211

David, 8, 11, 26, 27

Docetism, 12

Evangel, 19, 20. *See also* Bible

Al-Ghazali, Abu Hamid, 42; (as source), 164–187

God: and Jesus, 4, 11, 12, 13, 14, 15,

Other books in the *Convergences* series: